Justice Performed

Also available from Bloomsbury Methuen Drama

Brecht On Theatre (3rd ed)
Bertolt Brecht
ISBN 978 1 408 14545 6

Brecht on Performance
Messingkauf and Modelbooks
Bertolt Brecht
ISBN 978 1 408 15455 7

Dramaturgy in the Making:
A User's Guide for Theatre Practitioners
Katalin Trencsényi
ISBN 978 1 408 15565 3

New Dramaturgy: International Perspectives on Theory and Practice
Edited by Katalin Trencsényi and Bernadette Cochrane
ISBN 978 1 408 17708 2

Performance Studies in Motion:
International Perspectives and Practices in the Twenty-First Century
Edited by Atay Citron, Sharon Aronson-Lehavi and David Zerbib
ISBN 978 1 408 18407 3

Replay: Classic Modern Drama Reimagined
Toby Zinman
ISBN 978 1 408 18269 7

Theatre and Adaptation
Return, Rewrite, Repeat
Edited by Margherita Laera
ISBN 978 1 408 18472 1

Theatre in the Expanded Field:
Seven Approaches to Performance
Alan Read
ISBN 978 1 408 18495 0

Justice Performed: Courtroom TV Shows and The Theaters of Popular Law

Sarah Kozinn

Bloomsbury Methuen Drama
An imprint of Bloomsbury Publishing Plc

B L O O M S B U R Y
LONDON • NEW DELHI • NEW YORK • SYDNEY

Bloomsbury Methuen Drama
An imprint of Bloomsbury Publishing Plc

50 Bedford Square	1385 Broadway
London	New York
WC1B 3DP	NY 10018
UK	USA

www.bloomsbury.com

BLOOMSBURY, METHUEN DRAMA and the Diana logo are trademarks of
Bloomsbury Publishing Plc

First published 2015

© Sarah Kozinn, 2015

Sarah Kozinn has asserted her right under the Copyright, Designs and Patents Act, 1988, to be identified as author of this work.

All rights reserved. No part of this publication may be reproduced or transmitted in any form or by any means, electronic or mechanical, including photocopying, recording, or any information storage or retrieval system, without prior permission in writing from the publishers.

No responsibility for loss caused to any individual or organization acting on or refraining from action as a result of the material in this publication can be accepted by Bloomsbury or the author.

British Library Cataloguing-in-Publication Data
A catalogue record for this book is available from the British Library.

ISBN: HB: 978-1-4725-3234-3
PB: 978-1-4725-2784-4
ePDF: 978-1-4725-3383-8
ePub: 978-1-4725-2600-7

Library of Congress Cataloging-in-Publication Data
A catalog record for this book is available from the Library of Congress

Typeset by Deanta Global Publishing Services, Chennai, India

Contents

List of Illustrations	vi
Acknowledgments and Attributions	vii
Preface: A Long Day in "Court"	xi
Introduction: "Judge Judy did not prepare me for this"	1
1 Becoming the People's Judges: Staging Reality Courtroom TV Law	19
2 The Law/Theater Continuum: Performing Real Disputes on Courtroom Stages	69
3 The Compassionate Courtroom	111
4 Rehearsing Citizenship: Exercises in Tough Justice	143
5 The Judiciary's "Lonely Splendor": Courtroom TV and the Battle for Ideological Influence	173
Appendix	197
Notes	207
Bibliography	233
Author Biography	255
Index	257

List of Illustrations

Figure 1	Judge Karen set, author's photo	94
Figure 2	Judge Karen set, author's photo	94
Figure 3	Judge Judy set, author's photo	95
Figure 4	Judge Judy set, author's photo	95
Figure 5	Judge Judy set, author's photo	96
Figure 6	The People's Court set, author's photo	97
Figure 7	The People's Court set, author's photo	97
Figure 8	Judge David Young set, author's photo	98

Acknowledgments and Attributions

The seed for this project was planted 8 years ago during a conversation with Dr Richard Schechner. After conducting extensive research on high school mock trials and theatrical trials staged during the Russian Revolution, I wanted to take my work in a new direction. Over a quick coffee he mentioned that I might be interested in looking into reality courtroom television. This "look" turned into a 7-year investigation of the genre. Dr Schechner's insight into this project and his unwavering encouragement have been invaluable. I continue to be inspired by the force of his thinking and his generous spirit. I am truly grateful that he is not only an advisor, but also a dear friend. This project would not have been possible without the guidance of Dr Karen Shimakawa and Dr Ann Pellegrini. Dr Shimakawa fanned my interest in law and performance and motivated me to think more holistically about the role of television justice. My conversations with Dr Pellegrini always awakened me to new angles of analysis and reminded me how to find joy in rigorous scholarship. Dr Ted Ziter and Richard Sherwin gave me extraordinarily helpful notes that have profoundly influenced my revisions, and Richard Sherwin's research on law and popular culture has been a guiding light for my project.

I want to extend my appreciation to the TV judges who took the time out from their busy schedules to speak to me. Their passion for their jobs kept me motivated throughout this process. I would also like to acknowledge the programs' producers and production staff who showed me around set, answered my questions, and always worked tirelessly to keep the shows running smoothly. And thank you to all the background actors who patiently played the underappreciated role of the audience and kept me company between takes.

I would like to extend my gratitude to the Performance Studies department at New York University, the administrative staff, faculty, and my colleagues. What I learned from the talented, driven, and curious scholars and artists who made the sixth floor their home is immeasurable. I revised this project during my Mellon Postdoctoral Fellowship in the Theater Department at Occidental College, and I am thankful for the support of my colleagues and students. I would also like to thank Dr Carol Martin, Caroline Winter, Tim Sullivan, Dr Debra Levine, Amy Wolf, Kate Purdy, Sarah Hirshan, Josh Matthews, Dr Sean Simon, Jennifer Tuft, Dr Benjamin Wise, Bradley Richie, David Iserson, Jordan Belfi, Allis Iserson, the Dr Kozinns and all my friends, family, and colleagues who have patiently listened to me talk on and on about reality courtroom TV.

Last, but definitely not least, thank you, Sasha.

Attributions

(In order of appearance)

60 Minutes. "Law and Disorder." *60 Minutes* Digital Video. CBS News. October 24, 1993. http://www.cbsnews.com/videos/law-and-disorder-50130205/.

Judge Mills Lane. Intro. WPIX Channel 11. New York, New York. 1999.

Swift Justice With Nancy Grace. Intro. WNYW-FOX 5. New York, New York. 2010.

Street Stories. "Memphis Judge Allows Victims to Even Score With Criminals" CBS. September 24, 1992.

Nightline. "Judge Joe Brown." *Nightline.* ABC. April 3, 1997.

Judge Joe Brown. Intro. WNYW-TV Channel 5. New York, New York. 2009.

Judge Mathis. Intro. WPIX Channel 11. New York, New York. 2009.

Family Court with Judge Penny. Intro. WWOR-TV Channel 9. New York, New York. 2009.

"Sex on the bench." *Cristina's Court* Promotional Advertisement. WWOR-TV Channel 9. New York, New York. 2008. (accessed July 26, 2014) https://www.youtube.com/watch?v=r6HtSltnl0k

Judge Maria Lopez. Intro. WPIX Channel 11. New York, New York. 2006.

NBC News Transcripts. "Miami Judge Sentences Two Pilots Drunk on Job." July 22, 2005.

Judge David Young. Intro. WWOR-TV Channel 9. New York, New York. March 3, 2008.

"Kiana vs. Deon Tillery." *Divorce Court.* WWOR Channel 9. New York, New York. June 12, 2008.

"Greg vs. Eric Matyjasik." *Family Court With Judge Penny.* KTTV Channel 11. Los Angeles, CA. January 28, 2009.

"The Alonzo Mourning Intervention: Part One." *Judge Hatchett.* WNYW-TV Channel 5. New York, New York. July 1, 2009.

"The Alonzo Mourning Intervention: Part Two." *Judge Hatchett.* WNYW-TV Channel 5. New York, New York. July 3, 2009.

"Bad Night at Woodforest: Part One." *Cristina's Court.* WWOR-TV Channel 9. New York, New York. November 10, 2008.

"Bad Night at Woodforest: Part Two." *Cristina's Court.* WWOR-TV Channel 9. New York, New York. November 11, 2008.

"Eggleton v. Murphy." *Judge Joe Brown.* WNYW-TV Channel 5. New York, New York. October 29, 2009.

"Ellison v. Williams." *Judge Joe Brown.* WNYW-TV Channel 5. New York, New York. October 22, 2009.

"Dixon v. Dixon." *Judge Joe Brown.* WNYW-TV Channel 5. New York, New York. September 14, 2012.

"Jones v. Jeffries." *Judge Joe Brown.* WNYW-TV Channel 5. New York, New York. May 7, 2013.

"Allen v. Reid." *Judge Joe Brown.* WNYW-TV Channel 5. New York, New York. January 13, 2009.

"Ross v. Ross." *Judge Judy.* WCBS-TV Channel 2. New York, New York. May 26, 2008.

Preface: A Long Day in "Court"

It has been a long day in court. The next case was supposed to start 15 minutes ago, but the judge is still on recess. Some people in the gallery lay back against the hard benches to catch a quick nap before the next case begins. Others seem restless, frustrated by the wait. Five more minutes pass before the bailiff enters. We jolt upright, coming to attention as he takes his place in the center of the courtroom. He looks to the rear doors and waves his hand, gesturing for the litigants to enter. One by one they open the door and walk down the aisle, moving purposefully to their respective podiums. The plaintiff takes the right podium, and the defendant the left one. Once positioned the bailiff bellows, "All rise," and we stand.

After the rustling of clothes and bags settle, I hear the sharp clack of heels on a hardwood floor echoing down the hallway outside. The door on the front left side of the courtroom swings open and the judge, a beautiful and well-styled middle-aged African American woman, bursts through it. Her long, black robe billows behind her as if she was floating, not walking, to her bench. The bailiff follows, case file in hand, and announces, "Rodriguez versus Allen," before passing the file up to the judge now perched behind her raised bench. "You may be seated," she says assuredly, and we sit. Though it appears that I am in court, I am not. But I am also not *not* in court. I am sitting in the studio audience of a taping of *Judge Hatchett* at Metropolis Studios in New York City.

Judge Hatchett (2000–8) was a reality courtroom TV show, a half-hour syndicated and unscripted daytime program that staged binding arbitrations as if they were small claims trials. The genre goes by other names as well. Legal scholars and professionals refer to the programs as "syndi-courts," television industry professionals call them "court shows" or "court TV," and the Emmy Awards Committee puts them in the category of "Legal/Courtroom programs." To distinguish the subjects of this book from dramatizations, scripted programs, and the former Court TV channel, I refer to the genre as reality courtroom TV.

The genre's origins date back to 1981 when Ralph Edwards and Stu Billett produced *The People's Court*, the program that made famous former Los Angeles County Superior Court judge, Judge Joseph A. Wapner. Since then dozens of copycat productions have colonized airtime on local channels across the country due both to their popularity and their relatively low production costs. Most reality court shows cost half as much to produce as a talk show.[1] Costs are held down when the same production company produces multiple programs; research and recruitment can be done for several shows at once. Sony Pictures President of Distribution John Weiser: "The costs are controlled, repeatability is high, and the genre has longevity."[2] Therefore, even if a particular show does not have high ratings, the production companies lose substantially less money than if they had invested in another type of half-hour non-syndicated program. (On the other extreme, Judge Judith Sheindlin (aka "Judge Judy") earns 47 million dollars a year.[3] Other celebrity judges earn less, but still significant sums.) Regardless, the reality courtroom TV costs are relatively low, and this has made them not only very profitable, but also a draw to producers looking for inexpensive content that pulls in advertising dollars.

While some countries have created their own versions of reality courtroom TV, like Canada's French language *L'Arbitre* starring tough-talking celebrity divorce attorney, Ms Anne-France Goldwater, *Judge Judy* has international distribution. There are also Spanish language courtroom TV shows like *El Tribunal de Pueblo*, *La Corte de Familia* and *Verdicto Final* that air on Univision and Telemundo. (Judge Cristina Perez of *Cristina's Court* started on *La Corte de Familia* and *El Tribunal de Pueblo* before making the move onto English language reality courtroom TV.) While the phenomenon once was uniquely American, the popularity and mass appeal of these shows have attracted international audiences and productions abroad.

The programs' ubiquity does more than overwhelm television lineups. Their prevalence has also made them a recognizable and popular form of entertainment that participates in the construction of what we know and expect from the justice system. Even with this awareness, I was surprised to encounter my own disappointment when I was faced with the "real thing." In March 2010, after 2 days of jury selection, I was chosen to sit on the jury of a personal injury case being litigated in the Kings County Supreme Court in Brooklyn, New York. When the lawyers finished their selection, they sent me to a clerk in the outside hallway. I stood in front of an open service window as the young man behind it asked me to raise my right hand. Three other jurors stood next to me, and together we recited our promise to perform our duty. The collective ritual of being sworn in translated me from an ordinary New Yorker and into a jurist. After that moment I was at the mercy of the Court's scheduling, and for 3 weeks I listened to the expert witnesses, took notes on the evidence and patiently waited in the stuffy juror room several floors above the din of Jay Street. The process was far from quick, and, at times, less than entertaining. The judge rarely chimed in, and most of the times when he did, it was to offer us instructions that he read from an official-looking blue binder. The judge was, by no means, the central player in the case. The experience was completely different from what I had been watching on TV.

Introduction: "Judge Judy did not prepare me for this"

In 1998, the United States Supreme Court heard the case the *National Endowment for the Arts v. Finley*. The case centered on four performance artists: Holly Hughes, Karen Finley, Tim Miller and John Fleck who were nicknamed the "NEA Four." These artists took the National Endowment for the Arts (NEA) to court when their applications for "grants-in-aid" were denied. The NEA reasoned that their work did not comply with "general standards of decency and respect for the diverse beliefs and values of the American public."[1] From the artists' perspective it seemed that the NEA's decision was not only a grant denial, but also a determination that their works did not represent American values. The NEA Four filed a suit against the NEA, charging that their applications were rejected for political reasons. After winning the first case in 1993, The NEA Four appealed the legality of the NEA's "decency clause." In 1998, after 6 years of appeals, the United States Supreme Court ruled with the NEA.

When interviewed in 1999 by *New York Times* reporter Alvin Klein, Holly Hughes told him that she would have rather had the case heard by "Judge Koch" than the Supreme Court Justices. "Judge Koch" was not only the (allegedly closeted gay) former mayor of New York City, but also, at the time, the presiding jurist on the reality courtroom TV show, *The People's Court*. Hughes then remarked, "Judge Judy did not prepare me for this."[2] The years The NEA Four spent battling their case in court bared no resemblance to Judge Judy's rapid and surefire process. However, Hughes's sarcasm may have been doing more than indicating the obvious. Her aside poignantly marked how these programs inform viewer expectations and may produce the resulting disappointment when the real thing does not meet them. Furthermore, it spotlighted her preference for the theatrical courtroom over the Supreme Court of the United States, a partiality that suggested the kind of justice Hughes wanted and expected had a better chance of being served on *Judge Judy's* and *The People's Court's* soundstages than in a court of law. Hughes's comments raise several questions: Why did she feel she could plead her case better and have a more successful outcome in a theatrical space? And would she have wanted *Judge Judy* justice before there was a "Judge Judy"? Do courtroom TV shows produce these yearnings? Or do they satisfy preexisting ones?

Like millions of Americans who have never set foot inside an actual courtroom, their first introductions to the legal process might well be through cultural representations of trials in plays, films, books and television shows.[3] So, it is probable that a program like *Judge Judy* could constitute a substantial part of someone's knowledge of the legal process. As Philip Z. Kimball wrote, "Visually, Judge Judy's courtroom looks very much like one might imagine a New York State courtroom to appear if they had never actually been inside one."[4] Furthermore, unlike Judge Judy and Judge Koch, the nine United States Supreme Court Justices are, for the most part, unrecognizable to the average person walking down the street. This may be because Supreme Court hearings are heard, but not seen. Cameras are forbidden inside the Supreme Court. The absence of the Justices' visual representation during hearings could be read as a way to sustain (or generate) the public's faith in the Court's objectivity by obscuring the impact of the subject on legal decisions and the effects of cameras on the Justices' decision making. Reality courtroom TV judges do the opposite. They annunciate and market their race, ethnicity, class, gender and sexual orientation. They want to be seen not as objective arbiters, but as people whose experiences shape their decisions. The judges' visibility and individuality is crucial to their programs' survival. And while the programs may be claiming to do little more than entertain and educate audiences in simple life lessons, the genre's diverse benches also perform a critique of judicial objectivity. This may seem like too large a claim to make about a genre often disregarded as trash television, but my analysis has less to do with the programs' stated objectives and more to do with how these performances interrupt, compliment, or intervene in actual legal process and the public's perception of it. I am interested in how the programs' theatricality substantiates judicial ideals that cannot be actualized anywhere else but on a stage.

Reality courtroom TV programs all follow the same basic formulaic structure. Every one of them features a charismatic former judge or lawyer who arbitrates disputes between neighbors, family members, spouses, or partners on a courtroom set. Arbitrations are legally recognized alternatives to litigation that take place outside of the court. In arbitration, the two parties involved in the dispute agree to adhere to the binding decision made by a neutral third-party, which on reality courtroom TV is the person playing the role of the judge. Reality courtroom TV takes this alternative dispute method and makes it look like small claims litigation, staging it on a set that resembles a courtroom and with participants cast in courtroom roles such as the judge, bailiff, reporter, gallery member, plaintiff, and defendant. Unlike in other arbitrations where the losing party is responsible for paying the award (the amount of money owed), on reality courtroom TV the production companies pay. But that is not the only financial incentive: the parties (called the "plaintiffs" and "defendants" instead of the more commonly used "claimants" and "respondents" in arbitration) receive appearance fees, hotel rooms, and transportation to cities like New York, Los Angeles, Chicago, and Houston. The reoccurring star actors, the judges, bailiffs, and courtroom reporters, are compensated according to SAG-AFTRA union rules.

Despite the programs' theatrical elements, the decisions are legally enforceable. Before going on set the litigants sign contracts binding them to the judge's decision. Within the theatrical context of these courtrooms, taking place on a stage with a production staff and directed by a creative team, the ramifications of the judge's decisions extend beyond the given circumstances of this fictional space. They provide a legal service in addition to entertainment. This crossing over from the realm of entertainment into legal practice precariously situates these programs in the contested intersection between law and its pop cultural representation. In this "both" and "between" space these media products are vulnerable not only to misinterpretation—viewers mistaking them for accurate representations of legal process—but also, as Hughes's above comments illustrated, to setting viewer expectations for what goes on in state and federal courts.

But reality courtroom TV shows are far from representative of the bureaucratic law at work in actual courts. Instead, TV judges render decisions quickly and efficiently, using everyday vernacular to translate legalese into simplified terms. Fairness is not measured only by adherence to legal procedure and precedence, but to judge-specific morals and standards, and these differ from program to program. Each show targets and tries to appeal to a particular viewing audience, and therefore, reality court shows actualize local, community-based, popular performances of the kind of legal practice made defunct by the centralization of courts at the end of the eighteenth century. The disparate versions of justice enacted speak to the changing needs of a pluralistic, multicultural, and individualistic society, and therefore reality courtroom TV ends up illuminating a significant challenge to legal and political practice: What happens to law and politics when the center no longer holds and there is no longer a belief in political and legal neutrality?

To answer these questions I analyze reality courtroom TV from multiple angles. As a viewer I consider reality courtroom TV shows as teaching plays and interrogate their pedagogical resonances. I examine the performance strategies each judge uses to best deliver his or her lesson, and I study how these performances simplify complex issues, making reality courtroom TV justice always remediable. Using my experience as a studio audience member, I look at the programs dramaturgically and study how they are produced and directed. From this internal position I scrutinize the seams of production and analyze what happens before, during, and after the show.

Using a performance studies methodology widens my interrogative lens to encompass an assessment of how the judges and legal professionals behaved in actual courtrooms before becoming stars of their own TV shows. I look at how producers helped translate the judges' performances on their state and federal benches into marketable television brands and how the judges' prior legal experiences inflect their performances of the judge role. Accumulatively, my analysis regards the performativity of reality courtroom TV as consequential and as performing a varied and decentralized rendering of justice by and for people who feel most excluded (and were historically barred) from legal protections and equal access to courts and counsel.

Reproducing small claims

Reality courtroom TV mimics the process of the most informal courts in the country: small claims courts. In small claims courts civil disputes over damages under a certain state-set amount go to the small claims sections when arbitration and mediation are either not viable options or do not work. Small claims courts are a relatively new part of the United States' court system, and the first small claims court was not established until 1913 in Cleveland, Ohio. The emergence of small claims courts lightened the dockets of overburdened state courts by taking on disputes between private individuals where the damages were under a certain amount determined by each state, thus leaving the federal and state courts time to hear the more complicated cases.[5]

Unlike federal courts, each state decides the rules of its small claims courts such as determining a method for serving the defendant, the jurisdictional limit (amount for which the plaintiff can sue), if the litigants can hire counsel, methods of appeal, and the ways the awards are collected. Most states set their jurisdictional limits between $2,500 and $12,000, though Tennessee's cap is $25,000.[6] Cases with awards exceeding this amount are outside the small claims courts' jurisdiction. The kinds of disputes that can be brought to small claims tend to be as follows: debts, repayment of loans, failure to provide agreed upon services, breach or cancelation of contracts, minor personal injuries, breach of warranty, property damages, evictions, and return of property.

Issues that cannot be brought to small claims courts are criminal matters, class-action lawsuits, disputes of traffic violations, divorces, bankruptcy filings, name changes, guardianship requests, and lawsuits against a state or federal government or agency.[7]

Most small claims trials are held inside courthouses, have judges or lawyers adjudicating the cases, and are decided in under an hour. Small claims trials are adversarial, and the plaintiff and defendant must each show up with evidence defending their position. Defendants who do not show up to court most often receive a default judgment for the full amount sought by the plaintiff and court costs. But winning a small claims case does not guarantee payment of the award because the court does not participate in the collection process. If the defendant refuses to pay, it is the plaintiff's responsibility to take further actions such as issuing a court order to garnish the defendant's wages or bank accounts. If the defendant is judgment-proof, meaning they have no money, then there is no way for the plaintiff to collect his or her award.

Because small claims courts only handle cases of limited import, its process produces a unique kind of drama that differs from the drama that arises in civil and criminal trials. Criminal trials involve the violation of state and federal law, putting the individual in dispute with the state. In these cases the stakes are high. Like in the story of *Oedipus,* when stakes are high and the passions are high the situation is rife for tragedy. Civil law deals with the violation of contracts and unfulfilled obligations. These kinds of cases can have high stakes without the passionate drive. Small claims are disputes between individuals. These kinds of cases tend to have low stakes and high passions. This relationship tends to lead to comedy and farce. When stakes are low and the passions are low there is no reason to come to court. These are the kinds of claims that can get settled outside the system.

Reality courtroom TV disputes have low stakes with high passions, and the productions take advantage of this dynamic and the drama that ensues. The main actors (the TV judges, bailiffs, and reporters) feed the small claims' drama by probing into the litigants' private lives and encouraging them to reveal personal details that are often ancillary to the monetary dispute. While in an actual trial judges are constrained by Federal Rules of Evidence that require all admissible evidence to be probative and relevant to the case, TV judges are free to reveal extraneous and provocative information in order to "spice up" what would otherwise be boring disputes over violated contracts, unpaid debts, and minor injuries.[8] In the words of Judge Arthur P. McNulty, "I dare say that the presentation of the average actual courtroom case would be dull as ditch water to the average listener."[9] By invigorating petty arguments with the pomp of a trial, the scandal of a talk show and the reward of a game show, the television small claims court becomes much more entertaining.

Reality courtroom TV invites a theatrics of law barred in state and federal courts. This becomes evident when looking at the pre-TV performances of several reality courtroom TV judges who were disbarred or asked to recuse themselves from cases because of professional conduct violations, which I discuss at length in the following chapter. The judges' creative sentencing, untraditional methods, and outrageous courtroom behavior exhibited an excess of theatricality unsuitable for the state and federal benches, but perfect for television. This leads to one of the most exigent questions about this genre: How do these shows realize part of law's performative function: that of providing a participatory spectacle the public can recognize as justice?

Legal scholar Bernard Hibbitts wrote: "In performance, people can manifest their allegiance to and respect for law. They can at the same time enjoy its application in the community. This enjoyment can stem from several sources: physical participation, communal involvement, the engagement of the senses by argument or ritual, or the general association of performed law with the restoration of order."[10] Hibbitts acknowledged the playful quality that comes from the improvisational performance of law and how this can lead to loyalty to it. To apply Hibbitts' contention to the performance of reality courtroom TV law assumes that participants in TV legal process may develop fidelity not to the kind of process enacted in state and federal courts, but to those taking place on courtroom stages. This devotion may be part of what draws and keeps viewers tuned in to formulaic scenes of discipline, ridicule, compassion and mercy day after day.

Appearances of justice

Small claims courts are the most accessible courts in the country. With low filing costs, the price of bringing a claim to court is not as prohibitive as civil lawsuits or criminal ones. But, as mentioned above, the kinds of cases brought to small claims relate primarily to interpersonal disputes and therefore have little or no impact on policy. Susan E. Lawrence argued that litigation is an "activity that promotes the citizenry's control over the formulation and implementation of public policy."[11] In other words, those who have access to litigation have a hand in public policy, and those without access, do not. In her study of poor litigants and how economic inequalities put a strain on maintaining counsel, Lawrence reasoned that "A measure of the extent of democracy in a nation must include access to the courts among its list of political rights."[12] While growing trends in tort reform legislation have made it more difficult for the average person with a complaint against a company to have their case heard in court because of financial, political, or contractual reasons, televisual representations of individuals with ease of access to courts is pervasive—especially on reality courtroom TV. On reality courtroom TV it appears as if everyone has equal access to the television courtroom. In fact, the more dire one's financial straits are the more likely it is to see him or her on reality courtroom TV. (We rarely see the educated and rich litigant in reality courtroom TV courtrooms.) Not only that, many of the programs' star judges share similar socioeconomic, racial, or ethnic backgrounds as their litigants. So the guests on reality courtroom TV not only appear to have access to TV court, but they also get to have their cases heard by judges who appear to relate to them.

Images of law and legal process, whether actual images or ones presented in films, on stages, or in television shows, work in tandem to construct our perceptions of law and justice. Jean Baudrillard reasoned that the world we live in is a product of a media-saturated existence where the real and the simulation become indistinguishable. It is a world based on images that are based on images, a copy or fabricated version of reality where media contributes to the construction of what we know: "Simulation is no longer that of a territory, a referential being, or a substance. It is the generation by models of a real without origin or reality: a hyperreal."[13] Following this logic, it is conceivable that the lines of perception that discriminate between entertainment and actual legal process are permeable, and that images from actual trials and from fictional ones may work collectively to formulate our conceptions of law. (How many of us when we visualize a criminal trial conjure up scenes from *Perry Mason* (1957–66) or *Law and Order* (1990–2010) or even that memorable scene in *A Few Good Men* (1992) when Jack Nicholson's character, Colonel Jessup, exploded on the stand during his cross-examination, "You can't handle the truth!"? Do we also visualize scenes from the 1995 O. J. Simpson trial when Johnny Cochran famously defended Simpson by rhyming, "If it doesn't fit, you must acquit"?) These scenes and images, regardless of whether or not they document a real event, become muddled together into a palimpsest-like understanding of law that layers real on top of fiction on top of real on top of fiction.

It should come as no surprise that media representations of law color our perceptions of the legal process. However, this leads us to ask how much of justice depends on appearances? In his book *When Law Goes Pop: The Vanishing Line Between Law and Popular Culture*, Richard Sherwin wrote extensively about what happens to law when it becomes "dominated by image and perception."[14] Using the findings of psychologist Richard Gerrig and the Italian linguist and novelist Umberto Eco, Sherwin argued that the veracity of the image has no bearing on its affective power. This is why a fictional movie like *Jaws* (1975) could make viewers afraid of and avoid the ocean. In other words when images look real, they can feel real and therefore have a resounding impact on people's perceptions of reality. The realm of law is no exception.[15]

Sherwin also looked at how the United States Supreme Court has been complicit in moving law into the realm of the "hyperreal." In the 1965 Supreme Court case *Estes v. Texas*, a case that dealt first hand with the appearances of justice, or more specifically, cameras in courtrooms, Sherwin recounted how Chief Justice Earl Warren misused photographs taken of the *Estes* pretrial hearing, citing them as evidence in his concurring decision as if they were from the actual trial. He deliberately misrepresented these images in order to support his position that cameras in courtrooms created a circus-like and chaotic atmosphere. (The images from the pretrial hearing showed cameras, lights, and wires spread throughout the courtroom. However, during the trial the wires were hidden.) Warren's opinion deliberately "overshadow[ed]" their unreality" in order to implant an idea about television's negative impact on the courtroom.[16]

Sixteen years later, in the 1981 Supreme Court case *Chandler v. Florida*, a case that reopened the debate about the constitutionality of cameras in courtrooms, the tides had shifted. Amidst a political landscape of general skepticism about the scrupulousness of government and judicial power (a skepticism that Sherwin attributed to events such as the Watergate scandal, the Vietnam counter-culture movement and the publishing of *The Brethren*, a book that detailed the United States Supreme Court under Chief Justice Burger) Chief Justice Burger defended the presence of cameras by writing about their utility. He averred that televising trials allowed the public inside the courtroom, an entry he hoped would bolster the Court's image. Justice Burger was a proponent of a judicial process that "satisf[ies] the appearance of justice."[17] He had faith that the legal process's inherent theatricality could convey to the public an effectual justice system. Appearances of justice, he believed, could restore and sustain public faith in the justice system in the same way that appearances have challenged the public's confidence in it. Chief Justice Burger anticipated the ways that TV could work for law, yet, as Sherwin pointed out, he did not foresee the extent in which the law would become fodder for TV.[18]

Chief Justice Burger's majority opinion was written in 1981, the same year that retired California Supreme Court Judge, Judge Wapner, took a seat in what would become one of the most famous courtrooms in the United States: the courtroom set of the still-running daytime television show *The People's Court*. *The People's Court* producers, Stu Billet and Ralph Edwards, and Chief Justice Burger all recognized the use-value of appearances. Burger saw how cameras could work for the court, and Billett and Edwards predicted viewers' desire to see the court working.

From the courtroom drama to reality courtroom TV

The People's Court depended on audience interest in watching non-actors argue over real problems while appealing to audiences who wanted to see a picture of a proficient legal proceeding presided over by a wise and fair judge. This was unlike any other courtroom show that had been on television, but it was far from being the first TV courtroom. Prior to *The People's Court*, there was the genre of courtroom dramas. Their heyday was in the late 1940s through the early 1960s, and these courtroom-centric shows were reenactments of real trials or scripted trials performed in a fictional setting by trained actors and, on some shows, legal professionals. They differed from other legal programs because the entire drama centered on the scripted trial. With a few exceptions these TV shows were either reenactments of real trials or fictional trials created by each programs' writing staff (see appendix for the full list).

In the decades between the courtroom dramas and the debut of *The People's Court*, the culture of television changed, and this transition coincided with the advent of reality TV. In 1973 PBS broadcast *An American Family*, a 12-part series that many consider the first reality TV show (see Jersley 2002; Andrejevich 2004; Murray and Ouellette 2009). *An American Family* presented the Loud family, a middle-class, white family from Santa Barbara, California. Producer Craig Gilbert promoted the series as a documentary experiment conducted to understand the changing face of the American family. To do so, a camera crew closely followed the family in intimate and public settings for 7 months. Millions watched, and the Louds became America's first reality TV stars.[19]

In the time since the Louds made television history, reality TV programs have become abundant, occupying time slots on major networks and cable stations and dominating the programming on Lifetime, MTV, the History Channel, Vh1, the Food Network, and BRAVO. Networks value the shows because of their relatively low production costs and popularity, and during the Writers Guild (WGA) strike in 2007–8 using nonunion talent and writers to create new low-cost reality programs became even more appealing.[20] As dramas waned, reality TV waxed. Reality TV and competition reality TV programming consistently stay within the top ten highest ratings on cable network TV and prime broadcast network TV.[21] Programs like *Judge Judy*, *Judge Joe Brown*, and *The People's Court* capitalized on the genre's popularity by employing the entertaining appeal of the trial drama and meshing it with reality TV strategies.

While the burgeoning of courtroom programs in the late 1940s and 1950s followed in the wake of the media frenzy surrounding the 1935 case against Bruno Hauptmann for kidnapping Charles and Anne Lindbergh's baby, it may come as no surprise that reality courtroom TV surged after the major media trials of the 1990s. These trials were in effect "show trials," exposing and enacting underlying societal tensions in a legal venue. Trials and hearings broadcast on television, such as the Clarence Thomas Confirmation Hearings (1991), the Rodney King Trial (1992), The Menendez Brothers Trial (1993), and the O. J. Simpson trial (1995) attracted millions of viewers (see Hariman 1993).[22] Viewer responses to these trials demonstrated to producers the willingness of audiences to watch courtroom proceedings on television. But now that viewers had been exposed to the workings of actual courts, productions responded by trying to present representations with more verisimilitude.

With that, legal TV programming surged and the popularity of reality courtroom TV grew.

While TV's representations of trials may have had to appear more authentic to gratify knowledgeable audiences, reality courtroom TV proceedings elaborated on the small claims process to fulfill popular expectations of justice. Reality courtroom TV attends more to affect—the experience and feeling of justice—than the accuracy of its portrayal. This is because legal process sometimes (if not often) leads to a misalignment between the execution of law and a public experience of justice. In other words, sometimes law and popular justice do not line up. Take the 2013 Trayvon Martin case. On February 26, 2012, in the gated Twin Lakes community in Sanford, Florida, an off-duty and armed neighborhood watch volunteer, 28-year-old George Zimmerman, shot and killed 17-year-old Trayvon Martin in what he claimed was self-defense. Zimmerman's acquittal spurred protests across the country. For many, the court's decision seemed to sanction the presumed criminality of black men and authorize acting on those prejudices without repercussion. When asked about the case, Chicago resident Velma Henderson told the *New York Times*, "I'm heartbroken, but it didn't surprise me.... The system is screwed. It's a racist system, and it's not designed for African-Americans."[23] The ways in which communities across the country emotionally responded to the verdict had less to do with the specifics of Florida state law or whether the lawyers followed correct procedure and more to do with how they were experiencing the fairness of the justice system on the whole. It did not matter that the jury decided that Zimmerman acted within the protections of Florida's Self-Defense Law. For many, the case and what it represented begged for a kind of justice that the law could not deliver. As Florida defense lawyer Michael Band said, "Trials, for better or worse, are not morality plays."[24]

While actual trials are not morality plays and cannot privilege the satisfaction of the public's emotional desires or promise a cathartic ending, reality courtroom TV proceedings do. They offer emotion-based decisions that operate according to different standards of logic than actual legal process, standards that within the world of each drama guarantee that the right thing always happens in the end—at least according to each judge. In this way, reality courtroom TV's devotion to affect aligns its objectives not with justice as fair process, but with popular justice as the feeling that the right thing happened in the end. Reality courtroom TV cultivates an experience of justice that tries to reflect the common will and deep-seated beliefs of its star jurist and his or her viewers while projecting ideals of good and evil unbound to a constitutional or governmental text. This difference points to some of the questions in this book: How do these alternatives to small claims trials illustrate theater's potential to fulfill needs unmet in and by state and federal courts, and how is judge TV's theatricality intrinsic to the experience of justice it produces? As a mode of performance that stages civic instruction, models good and bad citizenship and preaches social responsibility, how do the judges' lessons perpetuate certain ideological biases about race and gender performance? How do the judges' subjective decision-making processes critique law's posture of neutrality for an audience largely composed of women from underserved and underrepresented communities?

TV's landscape is constantly in flux, and since I began this study many shows have come and gone. Because of these shifts, I focus my analysis primarily on programs airing on network stations (non-cable broadcasts) from 2007 to 2012. In Chapter 1, I situate reality courtroom TV as a mode of performance for modeling citizenship and social instruction by judges with varying aims and pedagogical objectives determined by their race, ethnicity, sexual orientation, and gender. I discuss the political resonances of TV judges' diverse performances of legal process and how these culturally specific arbitrations restage a model for a populist court system. Furthermore, I compare the way the judges behaved on their state and federal benches to their performances on their programs in order to understand how producers and directors helped transition the judges from civil servants into sellable and recognizable brands.

In Chapter 2, "The Law/Theater Continuum: Performing Real Disputes on Courtroom Stages," I consider reality courtroom TV a social drama and a legal and theatrical performance and study the potentialities of its mixed representation. I explicate the aesthetic nature of the programs and think through the performances of non-actors and what Allan Kaprow called "lifelike art." I focus on the seams of production and use my experience on set to detail the simple and complex acting strategies the participants use. In the following chapter, "The Compassionate Courtroom," I study TV judges who strategically employ a therapeutic ethos by attributing intrapsychic distress as the cause of conflict. I look at how employing compassion structures the television courtroom's power dynamic, situating the judge as the giver of compassion and the defendant the receiver, which also reorients the adversarial relationship between litigants to one between judge and litigants. To further elucidate the techniques of compassionate judge TV justice, I do a close reading of three cases from three different programs. All three cases illustrate how certain judge TV programs fashion themselves as sites of redress and rehabilitation, but these attempts also reveal the limits of the reality courtroom TV framework, which demand that the judges skirt over complex personal and social issues in order to resolve problems within the 30-minute (or less) segments.

Chapter 4, "Rehearsing Citizenship: Exercises In Tough Justice," concentrates on judges who use comedic performance strategies punitively. These judges use humor to draw litigants into recognizable stereotypes in order to hold them up as examples of failed citizenship and to plug them into instructive narratives the judges claim will solve broader social dilemmas. I engage Sigmund Freud's analysis of the joke and how it structures power relationships in social groups. To illustrate this strategy, I use several scenes from *Judge Joe Brown's* series of cases titled "Bad Boys" and "Bad Girls." The series featured litigants that producers deemed in desperate need of Judge Brown's signature man and woman training.

In Chapter 5, "The Judiciary's 'Lonely Splendor': Courtroom TV and the Battle for Ideological Influence," I position the reader within a larger discourse about the relationship between law and its representation. I use the 2010 case *Kahn v. New York Department of Housing* to exemplify the complicated effects of reality courtroom TV on actual courts and how sitting judges and legal professionals respond to the genre's influence. I also unpack moments when legal professionals and theorists have tried to regulate reality courtroom TV, fearing that these programs' jury-free courts presided over by all-knowing judges would lower the courts' esteem and misinform potential jurors about how the legal system operates. I also discuss the future trajectory of the drama as more shows go off the air and scripted formats take their place.

Looking at these programs through a performance lens opens the possibility to examine them as what Jill Dolan termed "utopian performatives." Building off of Marxist philosophers Ernst Bloch's and Herbert Marcuse's assertion that art can impart an "alternative world" through the "communication of an alternative experience," Dolan wrote that utopian performatives "spring from a complex alchemy of form and content, context and location, which take shape in moments of utopia as doings, as process, as never finished gestures toward a potentially better future."[25] Though Dolan considered performance's ephemerality one of its key attributes, I do not think this precludes locating the utopian performative in the theater of reality courtroom TV.[26] This is not to erase what distinguishes theater from television, but to suggest that viewers and the participants may also experience the melancholic dance between what could be and what is not when watching the judges' personally inflected performances of law that point, sometimes directly, to the blatant absences in actual courts—even when the communion between audience and players is mediated by a television or computer screen. In other words, reality courtroom TV's diverse benches, subjective decisions, and pedagogical aims may satisfy a desire for justice unmet in actual courts. In the programs actualization of binding decisions, they not only direct viewers toward an imaginary future, but also stage it then and there.

While the above postulation stakes an optimistic claim on the work of reality courtroom TV, the instruction TV judges offer has been critiqued because their lessons tend to mimic a neoliberal agenda of self-responsibility that transposes state obligations onto the individual.

In her study of reality TV, Anna McCarthy wrote: "In short, to see reality television as merely trivial entertainment is to avoid recognizing the degree to which the genre is preoccupied with the government of the self, and how, in that capacity, it demarcates a zone for the production of everyday discourses of citizenship."[27] This is indeed part of the reality courtroom TV process and certain judges use litigants to model good and failed citizenship. Their proffered counsel frequently extends into the micro-management of the litigants' everyday lives, and the programs' performance strategies make these instructions entertaining.

As a performance studies scholar my analytical approach differs from the media studies and legal studies scholars who have published work on reality courtroom TV. I pay specific attention to the productions' performance strategies, their moments of theatricality, and I also examine the seams of production. I look not only at what is there, but what happens in the gaps—in the moments when the cameras stop rolling and the performers break character. I include the stage action and what happens outside the purview of the camera lens. My hope is that by peering into the fissures I may discover new aspects of this genre. I also recognize that like the genre itself, this book crosses boundaries. Although theater scholars' privileged site is the live event, I use a performance and theater lens to analyze live and recorded performances. This is not to discount the importance of the vital communion between subjects on stage and in the audience, but to think through how exploring reality courtroom dramas with theater and performance theory reveal something about the subject that otherwise would go unseen. Subject wise, my work encroaches on the fields of media studies and visual culture, and with this in mind I understand that I am walking a delicate line between fields, between subject sites and between performance modes. I do this with the anticipation that this crossing has resulted in the production of new insights about a subject that can only come from leaving one's home turf.

1

Becoming the People's Judges: Staging Reality Courtroom TV Law

The picture of judicial plurality painted by the ethnically and racially diverse reality courtroom TV judges misrepresents the demography of judges sitting on state and federal benches.[1] As of this writing most federal court judges are white men.[2] While the majority of legal professionals are white, reality courtroom TV judges and their personally inflected performances cultivate an alternative drama of American jurisprudence. They demand of their audiences (and their participants) the suspension of disbelief that legal process tends to privilege some while disadvantaging others. This is not because these programs present a single type of magistrate who judges all equivalently, but because instead they hire a diverse range of judges to appeal to particular audiences. Not everyone is treated the same in reality TV courtrooms, and this is part of their attraction.

The performances taking place on reality courtroom TV stages are indicative of how in the age of postcritical race theory and postcritical legal studies fragmentation reigns. Reality courtroom TV's judges brazenly assert their biases and unabashedly celebrate how their ethnic and racial experiences shape their opinions. Yet on their courtroom stages, they perform their versions of law as if they were universal. As such, these programs illustrate how the political and the legal are personal, racial, gendered, and classist even while each constituent community imagines itself as universal. In other words, each judge's partiality reflects how impossible any universal ideal is. But unlike in actual courts, all audiences have to do to feel represented, to experience being part of this imaginary whole, is to change the channel.

Reality courtroom TV did not start off this way. For 12 years Judge Joseph Wapner, a white Los Angeles Superior Court judge, was the face of the first and only reality courtroom TV program. After a remarkably successful first run, viewership waned in the early 1990s, and by 1993 the program was canceled due to poor ratings. *The People's Court's* flailing numbers may have had something to do with a temperament change in US audiences, a shift that correlated with the sudden attention given to a different California courtroom. On March 5, 1992, in the predominately white neighborhood of Simi Valley, California, less than 50 miles from the studio where *The People's Court* was taped, the Rodney King trial began.

The case centered on an event that occurred 1 year earlier. On March 3, 1991, four Los Angeles police officers brutally beat Rodney King, a black California resident on parole for robbery, after King led them on a high-speed car chase. The incident made national headlines when bystander George Holliday, a resident in a building nearby where King was beaten, captured the assault on videotape. Holliday brought the footage to KTLA, a Los Angeles television station that aired the tape; the video quickly went viral. The graphic images of the officers assaulting King with force far beyond what the situation necessitated became a symbol of the systemic mistreatment of blacks by people in positions of authority and, in particular, by the LAPD. Footage of the nearly 2-month-long trial aired on Court TV to millions of viewers who watched the defendants plead their case in front of a white judge and to a jury with no black members. To many people's surprise, on April 29, 1992, the jury acquitted three of the four policemen (Stacey Koon, Timothy Wind, and Theodore Briseno). In response to a verdict that seemed to further confirm that the justice system only worked for some, African American, Hispanic, and Korean communities across Los Angeles erupted in riots that lasted for 6 days.

It was in this climate that *The People's Court* went off the air. It was as if the footage of King's attack repeatedly played across the country bludgeoned the illusion that the white judge, the paternalistic, grandpa-like figure, could still represent fairness and equity. The impartial and just arbitrator could no longer look like Judge Wapner. The canceling of the first run of *The People's Court* marked a new beginning for the reality courtroom TV judge. As I will discuss throughout this chapter, the judges who came on air in the late 1990s looked nothing like Wapner, and their styles were far from traditional. TV's new judges were outspoken, brash, and were presented far differently than the way depictions of the judge character in popular culture tended to be. These judges broke with a custom of representing judges as what E. M. Forster described as monochromatic, frequently "constructed around a single idea or quality."[3]

Throughout the twentieth century, readers and viewers rarely saw the always-white male, stoic figure anywhere but in the fiction's courtroom where he did little to forward the plot or add details to the narrative. David Ray Papke confirmed Forster's assertion when he wrote that early incarnations of pop culture's judges were one-dimensional:

> When developing judicial characters, writers, actors, and producers rarely developed them fully. The judge himself—and traditionally the judge was always male—showed little emotion or passion. We learned little about his motivation and goals, his personal history and politics. The judge lacked individualizing detail and was also static, that is, he did not develop or change in the course of the film, short story, or television show. The judicial character was like a table top or a linoleum floor. He was flatter than flat.[4]

Flat judges serve a purpose. Through their monochromatic illustrations, authors can project the formalist belief that autonomous legal thought, a theoretical logic unhampered by social determination, can exist. As Ian Haney Lopez wrote, "One of the defining elements of law is its universal aspiration, its will to apply equally in all cases and across all situations."[5] Illustrations of flat judges aspire to this universal, and they essentially resist an instrumentalist critique of jurisprudence—a critique that perceives legal practice as an exercise by a dominant group to maintain social power relations. Therefore, the portrayal of flat judges reflects not only the social position of the author and his or her experiences or desires for the law, but also of the model readers'. This optimistic stance suggests, perhaps, that the belief in the possibility of neutrality is sustained until one's experiences dictate otherwise. For white, heterosexual, middle-class, or rich Americans, fair treatment may feel like the norm, so thinking about how race, class, ethnicity, or sexuality bares on legal outcomes may not have ever been an issue. As Barbara Flagg put it, "The most striking characteristic of whites' consciousness of whiteness is that most of the time we don't have any. . . . [W]hites' social dominance allows us to relegate our own racial specificity to the realm of the subconscious. Whiteness is the racial norm."[6] People of color do not have the same liberty to ignore race, as it is most often those on the margins who have experienced law's unequal application.

Reality courtroom TV's new judges spoke to this inequity because they too came from the borders. Over the past 15 years, pop culture's judges, and reality courtroom TV's judges in particular, have become rounder. The rounding of cultural representations of judges evidences a seismic shift in popular perceptions of law. It is one that recognizes the impossibility of objectivity in jurisprudence and welcomes readers who often reside outside the dominant sector. This development parallels the emergence of "other Americans" as full-fledged participants in society. It is not that racism or classism has vanished, but that the claims of the "others" are much more visible. Pop culture has both led and followed this tendency to experience a more diverse society.

Becoming Judge Judy

For the 4 years following *The People's Court*'s cancelation, no other reality courtroom TV shows took its place. During this period, however, viewer interest in courtroom proceedings was being stoked by the media frenzy surrounding the O. J. Simpson murder trial. The criminal trial was held in Los Angeles, California from November 2, 1994, until the verdict on October 3, 1995. It became one of the most watched media events in history.[7] The culmination of sex, celebrity, and race drew enormous public interest. Certain trials, as Prina Lahav described, have something about them that "creates a fascination with the law, and crowns them (temporarily) with the title 'trial of the century.'"[8] The Simpson trial fell into the category: "Such trials have several features in common. First, they generally represent a problem of justice that polarizes society, fracturing its consensus and radicalizing perceived differences and disagreements."[9] In the wake of Rodney King, seeing another black man on trial dredged up memories of King's first verdict handed down in Simi Valley. But instead of being a victim of police brutality, this time the defendant was facing charges for allegedly murdering his white wife.

Devon Carbado wrote: "[W]hen a Black man is on trial for a crime, in particular an alleged crime against a white person, the Black community often sees first and foremost his status as racial victim."[10] The defense's cross-examination of Los Angeles Police Officer Mark Fuhrman (the officer accused of planting the bloody glove at the crime scene) about his prior use of racist epithets further reinforced this perception. But unlike the King trial, this time the jury was predominately black, a detail that gave hope that the perceived injustices of King's trial might not be repeated in Simpson's. But race was not the only concern on the table. The plight of Nicole Brown Simpson became associated with the abuse women in violent relationships sustain day after day and the lack of protection available to them. Brown's murder was held up as another example of how few defenses are afforded to women in abusive relationships. The Simpson trial, like the King trial, raised questions about who is entitled to justice.

The presence of television cameras in the courtroom and the daily broadcasting of the proceedings flamed the dramatic nature of these hot button issues. Media's presence meant that the counsel, the witnesses, and the defendant were not only playing to those in the courtroom, but also to the millions of viewers in their homes across the globe. Their performances and the reporters', scholars', and journalists' interpretation of them became, as Richard Sherwin wrote, "absorbed into the vernacular of society."[11] The viewer passions enflamed by the case's subject matter contributed to the reimagining and to the rebirth of reality courtroom TV. The shift in how Americans viewed the law manifested itself in a new image of the TV judge.

The first two judges to colonize this new territory were Judge Judith Sheindlin and Judge Joe Brown. Judge Judy is a petite, tough talking, white, Jewish woman with a New York accent and a fervent dislike of victimhood, and her program, *Judge Judy*, continues to be a stalwart ratings leader. It is not only syndicated across the United States, but also internationally. The next new show to debut was *Judge Joe Brown* starring Los Angeles born Joe Brown, a rotund, mustachioed, black man with a penchant for lugubrious soliloquies on gender and responsibility. *Judge Joe Brown* ended its run in 2013 after 14 successful years, and Brown is currently running for District Attorney in Shelby County Tennessee—a race that may be impacted by his recent stint in jail for contempt of court.[12] Considering the issues raised in the Simpson trial and the divisiveness of viewers' responses to them, it may come as no surprise that the first two new programs hired jurists who were embodied representatives of both sides of that case: a white woman and a black man.

Brown's and Sheindlin's success spearheaded copycat productions of many more reality courtroom TV shows, each trying to find a charismatic star judge who could cater to previously untapped viewing communities. Since the first run of *The People's Court* there have been dozens of others, but only *Judge Judy* (1996), *The People's Court* (1997 [2nd version][13]), *Judge Joe Brown* (1998), *Judge Mathis* (1999), *Judge Hatchett* (2000), and *Divorce Court* (1999 [3rd version]) have lasted more than a handful of seasons (see Appendix). Finding the right judge is an alchemic process. As Richard Huff wrote: "Seems anyone who's ever been around a legal textbook these days wants to be the new 'Judge Judy.' Many try. Most fail."[14]

If all reality courtroom TV producers are looking for the next Judge Judy, how do they find her? Joe Scotti, president of Pearson Television, said, "You go through the entire court system in every major market, getting background on individual judges and you put the word out to every agent in the world, and eventually you narrow it down to a few good prospects and one is the clear winner."[15] Andy Friendly, president of first-run programming at King World Productions, said, "Personality is the entire game in court shows...."[16] When I asked Cristina Perez, the former star of *Cristina's Court* and presiding judge on the scripted program *Justice for All with Judge Cristina Perez*, what it takes to be a reality courtroom TV judge, she told me the key was having a charismatic personality: ". . . I think a key element for a television court show host is to have a personality and ability to naturally think 'outside of the box.' One that can be funny, one that can exaggerate, give a scolding or a kind word when needed."[17]

Scouring courtrooms across the country is one method producers use to find star judges, but how do they find judges with the star power of Judge Judy? Better yet, how did producers find Judge Judy?

Judge Judith Sheindlin's big break came after she appeared on *60 Minutes* on CBS on October 24, 1993, although she had already made a name for herself in the New York Family Court circuit. Her uninhibited personality on the bench earned her a write up in the *LA Times* in 1993 in which Josh Getlin called her "tart, tough-talking and hopelessly blunt."[18] But it was the *60 Minutes* episode that skyrocketed her to national fame. When I asked Sheindlin why she thought she was chosen to be the star of her own show she told me:

> I think the reason I was approached by the two gals was that they were looking for work. [She laughs.] They had just been relieved of their duties after twelve years on *The People's Court* and they were looking for a new gig. They saw me on *60 minutes* and gave me a call. That's what happened.[19]

The two "gals" Sheindlin mentioned are Kaye Switzer and Sandi Spreckman, cocreators of *Judge Judy*. They had worked on *The People's Court* until it was canceled in 1993. They phoned Sheindlin after they saw the *60 Minutes* interview and asked if she would be interested in doing what she did in her Family Court on national television. Sheindlin, thinking nothing would actually happen, said yes.

Watching the CBS segment it becomes immediately apparent what drew producers to Sheindlin. The episode began with Morley Safer, the CBS 60 Minutes' correspondent who profiled Sheindlin, introducing the judge. He sat in a cushioned chair in front of a backdrop featuring an enlarged and towering photo of Judge Sheindlin who was not yet known by her celebrity moniker, "Judge Judy." In the photo Sheindlin's head, peering out from above her lace collar, is tilted downward. She looks above her eyeglass frames, and her finger points upward, as if chastising God. Her mouth is opened slightly, frozen midway into what looks like the beginning of a growl. After describing the kinds of truants, criminals, lawyers, and social workers who came through New York's family court, Safer said: "And you'll find presiding there Judith Sheindlin. Judge Judith Sheindlin. And if you find her a little bit shrill, a little bit testy, she'd be pleased."[20]

The episode cut to inside Sheindlin's Family Court. Sheindlin looked intensely at a lawyer standing off camera. The shot was tight on the judge, capturing only her face and upper torso. She dominated the frame. A montage of short clips followed. Judge Sheindlin pointed her finger and lowered her head: "Unless he's in a hospital he needs to be in school. Clear?!" The shot cut to another close-up: "This is not a game, counselor!" It cut to another close-up: "This witness may not have a very good memory, but I have a very good memory, sir!" The shot cut again: "Well, what do you want me to give him, a testimonial dinner?" Sheindlin's eyes rolled while Safer's voice-over described her: "She's a five foot two package of attitude, with a capital 'A'. . . . To Sheindlin justice must not only be done and seen to be done, it must be seen to be done *fast*."

The segment cut to Sheindlin holding her watch while she ordered the lawyer to make her claim quickly. When the lawyer tried to make an objection Judge Sheindlin berated her in a patronizing tone, ordering her to sit down and be quiet. The counselor sat, and then turned and mouthed something to her neighbor. The *60 Minutes*' camera caught the moment, and it was replayed in slow motion. In quarter time, the counselor's lips clenched and then flared into what was unmistakably the word "bitch." Safer said over the image, "Mrs Levy had only one more thing to say. Just read her lips. If you missed it, it rhymes with 'witch.'"

The segment cut back to Sheindlin in the interview with Safer. She was more soft-spoken now, out of her judge's robes, and confessing that she worried about reappointment, yet she also knew the value of being hard-nosed and hardworking: "You can put families back together again. You can find the right place for a kid who's in trouble. You can make the difference in the life of a family." This introduction to Sheindlin's softer side led viewers into the next segment, filmed on the terrace of Sheindlin's Manhattan apartment while she prepared dinner with her five children. In a narration over clips of Sheindlin hugging her family, Safer told the audience that Sheindlin kept "a unique code of justice at home." The cameras cut to Adam, her son, sitting at the dinner table. He looked to camera and said: "There's the Court of Appeals and there's even the Appellate Division. But there is no appeals here. It's Judy's Law." Even at home, Sheindlin exuded what would become her trademark personality.

What may be surprising is how closely Judge Judy's television performance approximates the one she gave on the Brooklyn bench. She did not change much to become a star. The characteristics that made her stand out in Family Court were the ones the *Judge Judy* producers marketed and turned into her particular brand. Even Sheindlin perceives what she does on television as similar to what she did in Brooklyn. When I asked Sheindlin if her television performance is different from how she heard cases in her family courtroom, she told me: "I think that when I was sitting judge in the Family Court I may have had to restrain myself a little bit more than I do now [laughs] with my frustration with people. But what I do here is, very often, as theatrical, if you want to use the word 'theatrical', as what I did in the courtroom."[21] Perhaps more surprising is the way Morley Safer's narration predicted *Judge Judy* catchphrases, slogans that would not be conceived until 3 years later. Safer said, "She's a five foot two package of attitude, with a capital 'A'. . . . To Sheindlin justice must not only be done and seen to be done, it must be seen to be done *fast*." One of *Judge Judy's* most enduring catchphrases is: "Justice served at lightning speed."[22] But Safer was not alone in his witty descriptors. Even her son forecast a potential slogan: "There is no appeals here. It's 'Judy's law.'" Safer and Sheindlin's son exemplified how ready-made Judge Judith Sheindlin was for television. Spreckman and Switzer did not have to manufacture a charismatic judge because they already found one. They merely built on the brand Sheindlin had already established.

Sheindlin's style was a significant departure from Judge Wapner's. Viewers knew *The People's Court* Judge Wapner as the avuncular and compassionate judge. In his autobiography he wrote: "The law is for any conflict where human beings need another sensitive human being to hear the facts and mete out fairness."[23] Sheindlin's philosophy, on the other hand, embraced the idea that life is unfair and that the law too often fails to adequately punish laziness and irresponsibility. Unlike Wapner, Sheindlin was less interested in presenting herself as gentle, understanding, and kindhearted. Instead, she focused on teaching self-responsibility, a quality she saw crippled by the welfare system. Her disdain for the inefficiency of public programs became part of her brand, and she developed this sentiment while in New York. During her tenure on the Brooklyn bench she began to see reliance on government assistance as "infantal[izing] an entire population" and became more vocal about its detrimental effects. She adopted the mantra: "People, not government, create opportunity."[24] In her 1996 book *Don't Pee on My Leg and Tell Me It's Raining* she railed against the pervasiveness of victimhood and saw her courtroom as a tool to combat it: "If my court were a classroom, I would call it Responsibility 1-A. Most of the people passing through—lawyers and bureaucrats as well as defendants—would get failing marks. But they would all get straight A's in Victimology."[25]

The *Judge Judy* brand is intricately tied to her political stance on public programs and what she sees as the ineptitude of the welfare bureaucracy. By moving onto television, Sheindlin got what she wished for, a job outside the bureaucratic disaster zone of the criminal justice system and onto a bully pulpit bench where her message about its inadequacy would be broadcast into homes across the country. This move not only set her free from the actual constraints of courtroom behavior that restrict a judge's performance, but it also fulfilled her wish for transparency. For telling it as it is—according to her own lights, of course. She has been teaching these lessons episode after episode, and this is one of the reasons *Judge Judy* is so successful: She stays on message. Viewers know what they're going to get, so they tune into the program with certain expectations that Sheindlin most often meets.

Producers help Sheindlin deliver her message by looking for cases that will showcase her beliefs. One of *Judge Judy's* former producers, Jenny Hope, told me that producers have to recognize what kind of cases the judges are good at and bring only these types of cases onto the program:

> What makes a successful courtroom show is really sticking to your format and figuring out what your judge gravitates towards. Whatever your judge flourishes in whether it's because of the kind of cases they were gravitating towards in their practice or in their courtroom before they came onto the show or in their personal life or issues that they're passionate about then you will see that play out through the cases that they hear. And there are some cases that some judges do particularly well with.[26]

This holds true for all the long-running programs. It also means that the message that Sheindlin was passionate about delivering while serving as a judge continues to be spread—but this time to a much larger audience.

The gavel bangers

Judge Judy was the first to establish the no nonsense, tough love brand of reality courtroom TV justice. Her passionate and consistent style made it easy for producers to market her. As more and more reality courtroom TV shows came on air, producers tried to emulate *Judge Judy*'s success by finding new and unique ways to brand their star judges. In their efforts to target specific viewing populations, the judge's brand frequently exaggerates personal details about his or her history, background, and in particular, race and ethnicity. Although producers try to come up with distinctive angles for each judge, certain trends emerge, and these similarities in performance styles and marketing strategies have a lot to do with how producers employ stereotypes of race, gender, sexual orientation, and ethnicity.

When it comes to the white judges who have presided over reality television courtrooms since Judge Wapner, the programs enunciate their star's legal and professional pasts, almost always casting former prosecutors and judges known for tough sentencing. *Swift Justice with Nancy Grace*'s star, Nancy Grace, who I will discuss in more detail below, was a criminal prosecutor; her successor, Jackie Glass, was a Nevada judge who was known for her tough and expeditious sentencing, which provoked the ire of the American Civil Liberties Union.[27] *Texas Justice*'s judge, Larry J. Doherty, was, and still is, a Texas prosecutor; *Judge Mills Lane*'s star judge, Judge Mills Lane, was a District Attorney in Nevada; Jeanine Pirro of *Judge Jeanine Pirro* was a former New York prosecutor and judge. These judges' styles and politics seem to have evolved out of their dislike of the perceived failures of the legal system to sufficiently punish and handle criminals, and many of them took it upon themselves to address these inadequacies in their books, in their courtrooms, on their programs and in interviews. Like the flat judges of yore, these judges rarely, if ever, publically addressed systemic inequities or questioned the fairness of law, but instead situated themselves as enforcers of it.

When it came to debuting new white male TV judges, the programs tended to illustrate them through clichéd tropes of white masculinity such as the cowboy, police officer and the soldier. Although *Texas Justice* went off the air before the time of this study, the show flaunted the masculine traits of its white male star. In a publicity photo for the program, Doherty, or "Judge Larry Joe" as he was referred to on the show, was poised like John Wayne in a production still and adorned with a black cowboy hat that matched his robe.[28] In the center left of the frame, Judge Larry Joe gripped the head of his gavel, pointing the stem at the viewer as if it were a gun. The metaphor was blatant: The law is his weapon, and it is drawn and ready to fire. Just like the Texas Department of Transportation told drivers, "Don't Mess with Texas," Larry Joe's illusory holdup cautioned viewers to not mess with Texas Justice. Larry Joe's white cowboy judge persona evoked frontier justice, law and order. One can imagine how differently the image would be read if instead of Larry Joe Doherty, a black judge stood in his place.

Even before Judge Larry Joe drew his gavel, Judge Mills Lane had a short stint on air as the toughest white male judge on TV. *Judge Mills Lane,* which debuted August 17, 1998, was the first reality courtroom TV program after *The People's Court* to cast a white male judge. At that time the only other white, male judge on air was former mayor Ed Koch who starred on the second run of *The People's Court*, which began its run on September 8, 1997. *The People's Court* producers did not change the format of the show for Koch, and in fact the show continued in the same vein as before its cancelation. *Judge Mills Lane,* however, had a very different tone. Lane was pitched as the hyperbolic incarnation of the white all-American man, and he had the career history to support the description. Lane was a former professional heavyweight boxing referee who famously started matches by belting, "Let's get it on." He was also a member of the Marine Corps, a former Chief Deputy Sheriff of Investigative Services at the Washoe County Sherriff's Office (1979), a District Attorney (1982), and a District judge in Nevada (1990). When Lane was elected to district court judge in 1991, an article in the LA Times described Lane as "a fast-talking, tough-talking former Marine."[29] His reputation and style preceded his program and was vastly different from the other white male TV judges. In comparison with Koch, a suspected homosexual and a wrinkled, balding, round-headed statesman with a New York brogue, Lane looked like a gladiator. With his shaved head and serious expression, he appeared as if he could handle the roughest and toughest. He exuded an unshakeable confidence and surety. He told Larry King in 2000, "I'm not necessarily final because I'm right, I'm right because I'm final."[30]

Lane's tough brand was driven home in his program's intro. It started with three gavel bangs like hits on a drum queuing a military march. The words "Judge", "Mills", and "Lane" came into frame, one by one, each entrance punctuated by the sound of a gavel banging. An additional sound effect was added so that each hit echoed with the clanking of a jail cell door. The effect invited audiences to imagine the virtual prison to which he would send lawbreakers. Then the intro cut to a triple split screen. Lane stood in front of the pillars of a courthouse dressed in his judicial robes, his arms crossed and his gaze fixed outward. Horns played in the musical mix, introducing the baritone narrator who growled, "He grew up in the country, and in the corps." The shot cut to a sepia colored photo of Lane in uniform. In it he stood upright, holding his hat in his left hand. Once again his name ran across the bottom of the screen in large letters as the frame above split into two. The left frame showed a lawyerly Lane, talking on the phone in what appeared to be his office while the right frame hosted a video of him walking between the pillars of the courthouse like a guard on duty. The credits cut to a picture of a newspaper article that read: "This fight bites," a reference to the famous 1997 Mike Tyson-Evander Holyfield heavyweight boxing match that Lane refereed during which Tyson bit off part of Holyfield's ear. The clipping showed Tyson and Lane in the ring. Lane, much smaller than the heavyweight champs, separated the towering figures. The voice-over narrated that Lane was "A fighter and a family man." The intro then cut to framed pictures of Lane hugging two children, presumably his own. The opening ended with a shot of the sun peeking through the pillars of the courthouse followed by a close-up of a gavel banging. The narrator declaimed, "America's Judge."

Like with *Texas Justice*, the intro begs the question, "Which America?" Lane was born in Georgia to a wealthy southern family. His friend, John Becker, told *LA Times* reporter Earl Gustkey that, "Mills Lane's family here [in Savannah] is our equivalent of the Rockefellers. He grew up on a plantation that covers thousands of acres. His grandfather, Mills

Lane I, started the Citizens and Southern Bank, which is our equivalent to the Bank of America. He had neighbors like Bernard Baruch and Barbara Hutton."[31] Becker's description of Lane's advantaged early life on a plantation figured him as not only the son of privilege, but also the son of a particular kind of white, southern privilege. His appearance reinforced this assessment. Lane's baldhead and militaristic demeanor conjured up images of skinheads and other white power movements. This is not at all to suggest that Lane was racist or that he forwarded such an agenda, but rather that in reading Mills Lane, certain qualities evoke particular ideas about white hegemony. The branding of his program emphasized Lane's link to historical models of power, continuing the legacy of the white judge.

Also from Georgia, Nancy Grace became the star of her reality courtroom TV show, *Swift Justice with Nancy Grace*, in 2011. Like with Lane and Doherty, Grace was also positioned as a crime-fighter. A vociferous southerner with a helmet of blonde hair, Grace began her legal career as a criminal prosecutor, an occupation she became interested in after the murder of her first husband, Keith Griffin. As a lawyer in Georgia, Grace was accused several times of prosecutorial misconduct. In 2005, the US Court of Appeals for the Eleventh Circuit noted that Grace "played 'fast and loose' with her ethical duties for failing to turn over exculpatory evidence in a murder case. *Stephens v. Hall*, 407 F.3d 1195, 1206 (11th Cir. 2005)."[32] In the 1994 case *Bell v. State*, Grace's behavior was so egregious that the Georgia Supreme Court gave the defendant a mistrial, writing: "By referring to such extraneous and prejudicially inflammatory material in her closing argument, the prosecutor exceeded the wide latitude of closing argument, to the detriment of the accused and to the detriment of the fair administration of justice."[33]

Outside of her legal profession, Grace is notorious for rallying against criminal defenders and their clients. As a legal commentator she has used her position to assign guilt before the trial proceedings even began. In his analysis of Grace's legal philosophy, University of Georgia Law Professor Donald E. Wilkes Jr wrote: "Grace demonizes persons charged with crime. She ascribes to criminal defendants the same qualities the Nazis ascribed to the Jews: they are vicious, dangerous, clever, cunning, sly, and diabolically evil."[34] In her book *Objection!: How High-priced Defense Attorneys, Celebrity Defendants, and a 24/7 Media Have Hijacked Our Criminal Justice System*, Grace bragged that she "quickly gained a reputation for being unreasonable when negotiating pleas and vicious at trial. I didn't care. The battle was all that mattered."[35] Grace's Kafkaesque "guilty until proven guilty" approach as both a lawyer and a television anchor seems to be compensation for what she deems are the failures of a legal system that too often lets criminals go free.

Grace brought this firebrand approach to her work as a legal commentator first on her talk show with Johnny Cochran, *Cochran & Grace* (1997), and then on her CNN and HLN show *Nancy Grace* (2005). As an anchor on these programs, Grace instigated several controversies because of her on-air bullying. In a 2006 interview, Grace accused the mother of a missing 2-year-old of being responsible for his disappearance. After the interview, the mother, Melinda Duckett, committed suicide. Her family attributed her death to the stress caused by Grace's interview and the ensuing media attention. Grace also made headlines for her witch hunt of the three Duke lacrosse players who in 2006 were accused of gang raping Crystal Gail Mangum at a house party. Before and during the trial Grace berated the players, charging them with a crime without attending to all the details of the case. When the court found the three players innocent, Grace had a substitute reporter come on her show to discuss the verdict.

Drawn to her controversial personality and the attention she attracted, producers cast Grace in *Swift Justice with Nancy Grace*. (After 1 year Grace was replaced with Nevada District Court judge Jackie Glass, the judge who presided over the 2008 O. J. Simpson robbery case.) Known for making snap judgments, the name "Swift Justice" was well suited for Grace's signature style. But beyond the name, *Swift Justice* carved its own niche by replacing the courtroom with what resembled a newsroom. *Swift Justice* worked from the TV news model, not from a courtroom one. Instead of sitting behind a bench Grace stood behind a semicircular podium. This orientation let her freely move around the space. She did not wear a robe either. Instead, she dressed in business-casual outfits more akin to what she wears as a commentator. In this news anchor/legal commentator/judge position, Grace arbitrated cases between her guest litigants stationed behind two podiums facing Grace's central platform. She used Skype and on set monitors to telecast witnesses and experts. In this multimedia courtroom Grace decided her cases.

Swift Justice's opening had the tough task of introducing this new reality courtroom model, and it did so by using animated sweeping, flying shots through tall buildings. Courtroom visual references were minimal, suggesting that Grace's preferred court was that of public opinion. Fast-paced synthetic string instruments and tinker bell sounds underscored the opening while the camera continued to rush through this computer-generated modern cityscape. A female narrator began: "For ten years she was America's toughest and most successful prosecutor." Three glamor shots of Grace, all taken in the same black suit, lined up next to each other, divided only by one shot of a courthouse's exterior. The narrator continued over the pictures: "Now she has her own court, and she is the judge." The camera soared into a still picture of Grace in action, which unfroze to play a scene during which Grace warned the litigants that she would find out the truth. The opening ended with the camera rushing down another city street until it dead ended into a tall glass building that opened like horizontal window blinds, switching their folds to reveal a giant billboard that said, "Swift Justice with Nancy Grace."

Like Sheindlin, Grace also came to the television bench with a clearly articulated stance on the problems with the American legal system. While Sheindlin expressed frustration with the ineptitude of the welfare system and how it was an obstacle to the work she did in her Brooklyn court, Grace made it crystal clear in her book and as an anchor that despite the Sixth Amendment of the US Constitution, criminal defendants need to be dealt with more severely. As the rest of this chapter illustrates, most TV judges have problems with the legal system that they seek to rectify in their performances on their courtroom sets. Sheindlin and Grace share the position that the legal and welfare systems are routine obstacles to their work. To them, the people who came into their actual courtrooms too frequently got away with their misdeeds, their abuses of the welfare system, their irresponsibility, or in Grace's case, criminal behavior. Their shows' styles situate them as additional and supplementary policing forces. Their meritocratic philosophies seem to ignore or diminish the existing social, political, and economic arrangements that advantage some people over others. This position is one of the main differentiators between the judges on TV who identify—or are identified—as white, and those who do not.

The "Village Chieftain"

While programs with white judges tend to pitch their stars as law enforcers, producers routinely brand black judges as working through the law. African American TV judges like Judge Karen, Judge Hatchett, Judge Lynn Toler, Judge Joe Brown, and Judge Mathis—all former actual judges—were known in their districts for their creative sentencing, for trying to find alternatives to jail sentences, and for addressing the systemic inequalities faced by minorities in their communities. The first judge to establish this trend was Judge Joe Brown.

Judge Joe Brown was a prosecutor in Memphis before being appointed judge of the Shelby County State Criminal Courts, Division Nine in Tennessee in 1990. Brown began attracting media attention early on in his judicial career because of his creative sentencing, such as allowing burglary victims to go into the burglars' homes and take whatever they wanted. Brown reasoned that these methods punished criminals without burdening the already overcrowded jails.[36] Brown described his sentencing in a 1991 interview in The Advertiser: "It's do-as-you-would-be-done-by, a television-for-a-television, and you should see their faces drop when I pass sentence ... I issue guidelines of what they can take, according to what was taken from them; jewelry, television sets, radios and even, depending on the value, their cars."[37] In 1992, Mark Curriden of the Atlanta Journal and Constitution interviewed Andrew Sonner, the chairmen of the Criminal Justice Committee of the American Bar Association, who detailed why lawyers and the media criticize creative sentencing measures: "Everyone wants alternative sentencing, but when a judge actually attempts it, they are criticized by lawyers, the media and the public for being soft on crime or being a publicity-seeking rebel."[38]

Whether or not getting publicity was Brown's intention, CBS took notice and profiled him on an episode of *Street Stories* hosted by Ed Bradley that aired on September 24, 1992. The segment had a religiously themed title, "An Eye for an Eye." Bradley introduced Brown as a judge who helps victims "even the score."[39] The segment cut to footage of Judge Brown, two police officers, and the victim of a burglary, Alice Alexander, walking onto the porch of a house. Darnell Roberts opened the door and Brown said, "Don't panic. I'm Judge Joe Brown. How you doing?" The officers told Roberts they were from the Sheriff's office. The cameras followed as Roberts let the officers, Brown, and Alexander enter the house. Alexander walked through Roberts's living room and looked at his belongings while a voice-over narrated:

> It's a new idea in justice here in Memphis, a new idea as old as the Bible. It's an eye for an eye, a tooth for a tooth, or, as Miss Alexander hopes, an appliance for an appliance.... Judge Brown calls this "reverse theft."... If it seems an unusual form of justice, consider this: The Shelby County Jail, which serves all of Memphis, was built in 1981, designed to hold 1,200 prisoners. Today the jail population is almost double that.[40]

The segment cut to inside the packed Shelby County Jail. The cameras followed Mr Terry Legett, a jailer, while he walked through the corridors. He told the cameras that by putting men in jails, "We're not solving the problem, we're managing it." Then the segment cut to Judge Brown as he walked into his Memphis courthouse. Brown's voice-over avowed that "I'm doing a different kind of thing. I'm using the court for social engineering, to prevent crime by going after the root causes, to correct what was not done through the family, church—if that's your thing—and the schools." Brown's adamancy about using the court for "social engineering" demonstrated how he saw himself performing corrective measures to compensate for the failures of the family, religious institutions and schools.

The segment then cut to an interview with Memphis Judge Neal Small. Small told Roth that he thought Brown's sentencing was ineffective, and that if the jails were overcrowded Tennessee should build more jails. Brown responded to his critic, condemning the racial disparity in American incarceration rates:

> 96.7 percent of the people that are locked up are African-Americans, and I have a very direct interest in that.... I'm playing village chieftain. Village chieftain is supposed to protect the village, help those who need help, correct those who need correction and weed out those that you can't do anything with.... Got a whole lot of people can't go any further down, but there's potential to bring them up. Let's bring them up before the potential evaporates. Maybe if we make it work here, we can take it elsewhere.

Brown's speech acknowledged his personal investment in addressing the incongruity in rates of incarceration for black men. As civil rights lawyer and law professor Michelle Alexander postulated, it is not just that these men are going to prison, but it is also that upon release they are still denied numerous rights of citizenship afforded to nonfelons: "Once you're labeled a felon, the old forms of discrimination—employment discrimination, housing discrimination, denial of the right to vote, denial of educational opportunity, denial of food stamps and other public benefits, and exclusion from jury service—are suddenly legal."[41] Alexander argued that the imprisonment of black men has created a racial caste in America that reproduces the one under Jim Crow: "We have not ended racial caste in America; we have merely redesigned it."[42] In her book, The New Jim Crow, she offered the harrowing statistic that in 2011, more black Americans were in jail, in prison, on probation and on parole than were enslaved in 1850.[43] Brown's self-assignment as the chieftain of the Memphis black community helped defendants circumvent jail sentences and avoid the disenfranchisement that comes with a felony charge.

While the CBS broadcast put Brown on the map, it was not until 1994 that Brown became a nightly news subject. That year James Earl Ray, the man who plead guilty to the 1968 assassination of Martin Luther King, Jr, submitted a request to the Ninth Division Court to test the 0.30-06 Remington rifle Ray claimed was planted to frame him. By routine rotation assignment Judge Brown got the case. This was the eighth time Ray had petitioned the court, and although several conspiracy theories surrounded King's assassination putting Ray's guilt in question, no court would open its doors to Ray's pleas. But in 1994, while still serving a 99-year sentence, Ray's health declined because of a liver ailment, and for the first time the King family joined in support of Ray's petition. On February 20, 1997, Coretta Scott King appeared before Judge Joe Brown. She asked him to test the rifle and "bring some sense of closure to the pain we have endured. . . . Even if no new light is shed on the facts . . . at least we and the nation can have the satisfaction of knowing that justice has run its course in this tragedy."[44]

The case ran anything but smoothly. In April 1997, prosecutors asked the Court of Criminal Appeals and local Criminal Court administrative Judge Chris Craft to review the way Brown was handling the case, but the appeals court did not take action.[45] On August 6, 1997, Criminal Court Judge John P. Colton Jr made a commercial appeal requesting that all files be removed from Judge Brown's possession because, according to the plea, ". . . Brown has made a 'shambles' of the Ray files by holding them haphazardly in his office . . ."[46] University of Memphis law professor Mike Roberts, hired as a special master to review Brown's oversight of the Ray case, filed a report along with Colton's. Roberts's report raised issues over whether Brown had jurisdiction to hear the Ray case and questioned his handling of evidence. A few days later prosecutors moved that Brown recuse himself, but Brown did not act for months. On January 16, 1998, Brown denied the motion that he step down, and ordered new tests on the rifle. Prosecutors went back to the appeals court, which in February halted any more tests.

On March 6, 1998, the Court of Criminal Appeals of Tennessee reviewed Shelby County Criminal Court's denial of Judge Joe Brown's recusal. The three-judge panel of Judge Paul G. Summers, Judge David G. Hayes, and Judge Joe G. Riley ruled in favor of removing Brown from the case and denied Brown's request for oral argument. Unlike in the earlier petitions noting Brown's mishandling of evidence, the judges based their decision on the extralegal leniencies Brown was taking with the case. In their opinion the judges found several examples of "the trial court's engaging in a fact-finding mission in violation of Tennessee Superior Court R. 10, Canon 3B(2), its appearance of bias, and its improper interjection of political matters into the proceedings in violation of Tennessee Superior Court R. 10, Canon 2B."[47]

To support their decision the court cited statements Brown made in a January 15, 1998, broadcast of the case on *Prime Time Justice* on Court TV where he characterized the court's role as "fact finding." On the program he criticized the state as being "singularly opposed to vigorously proceeding to ascertain the true facts of this case," and responding to the state's objection, "We're trying to get the facts . . . I'm not going to allow the vicissitudes of somebody's artful cross-examination to keep me as a trier of fact from getting to the bottom of this. Overruled."[48] The court used the same broadcast as evidence of Brown's bias. In an interview on *Prime Time Justice* Brown told reporters: "A lot of the shenanigans that you have observed have simply been due to local politics and power plays going on around and about the criminal courthouse and specifically involving a political action committee that is operating in the attorney general's office."[49] The appeals hearing listed several other appearances as evidence of partiality. In another interview Brown told reporters that the case is "of great historical interest to this country" and that "When a great man who tried to promote harmony, peace and freedom is assassinated, then the circumstances of that assassination are of paramount importance to the historical record and the moral and psychological nature of the nation. The public needs to be reassured that no stones are left unturned."⁵⁰ In a press interview Brown told reporters that he expected a "sneak attack from Republicans" and "went out of town intentionally just to see what they would do. They want to take me off this case because I'm vigorously trying to get to the bottom of it." He then went on to say, "[I]n the scheme of things how would it look historically for a black judge to be taken off this case with what it means to the black folks in this country and throughout the whole world and all fair minded people?"⁵¹ The list goes on. While Brown made a name for himself because of his personal investment in his untraditional punitive measures, in the Ray case, his similar expression of what the case meant to him and black Americans was used as evidence of his inability to fairly hear the case, eventually forcing him to step down from arbitrating it.

All the press surrounding the case caught the attention of *Nightline*, an ABC news national broadcast hosted by Ted Koppel. On April 3, 1997, in the midst of the Ray trial and prior to his recusal, *Nightline* profiled Judge Joe Brown. The segment opened with Brown in his Shelby County courtroom, yelling at a litigant: "I'm gonna kick your natural ass if you [word omitted] up in here, do you understand? . . . You [word omitted] damn little gutless little girl fool."⁵² Ted Koppel reacted to the clip: "A foul mouth, a lousy temper and he carries a gun. Joe Brown is a man on a mission. . . . Oh, did I mention it's Judge Joe Brown and he is a criminal court judge in Memphis who has his own way of running a courtroom?" *Nightline* painted a pricklier picture of Brown than *Street Stories* did in 1992. In the 5 years after *Street Stories* Brown's style hardened while he spent more and more time in the spotlight— evidenced by countless interviews, radio and TV appearances, and featured segments.

The scenes taped in Brown's Memphis courtroom also evinced how Judge Joe Brown justice was established on his Tennessee bench. An excerpt from a trial used in the segment revealed the signature way in which Brown leveled with his litigants by code switching, adopting various forms of speech and behavior depending on the situation, a performance strategy I discuss in greater detail in Chapter 4. In the clip, Brown spoke to a defendant accused of selling cocaine, asking him why he would bring the drug into his neighborhood. Dave Marash, an ABC correspondent, voiced-over footage of the courtroom: "The key to Joe Brown's communication is credibility. His convicts know he knows where they've been and where they're headed." The segment cut to Marash's interview with Brown. Brown told Marash that his method is to speak to "young brothers" and to listen to them: "Talk to a young brother. I stop every now and then and I chat with some of the young folk." Brown then did an impression of what the "young folk" said back to him, ventriloquizing a young black drug dealer: "You know, I just got to get my thing together, man. You know, they ain't got no gig out there for me, man. . . . [T]hat's why I'm moving these stones, man. I need that change, man, some finance."

Brown then dropped the character, switching roles to respond as himself to the dealer he impersonated:

> You just messed your thing up. That's why you ain't got any economy in your community, in my community. Check reality. The slave masters understood a very important thing. They said if you do what you should do to make these folks slaves, you don't have to worry about it anymore, they will make better slaves out of themselves than you ever could.

Brown linked the bad decisions of black youth to fulfilling a trajectory of subjugation and subservience established by slave masters. The connection makes black youth complicit in their own "enslavement," which in Brown's contemporary analogy is a cycle of imprisonment, drug addiction, and joblessness. Marash described Brown's sermonizing as credible to convicts because "[Brown] knows where they've been and where they're headed." Although Brown did not grow up in Memphis, had no prison record, and was raised by married parents who worked as teachers, Brown presented himself as being able to relate to his litigants because he too is black and grew up in a tough, black neighborhood. The bio on the Judge Joe Brown official website even stressed this: "If you saw the movie 'Boyz 'n the Hood' that was the way I grew up."[53] From this internal position, he asserted himself as understanding and being able to improve the social condition of Memphis's black community.

Then Marash summarized Brown's perspective on the root causes of problems in the black community: "Today's drive by, let 'em die violence, he says, is spawned by the ghettoes female dominated households." Brown enumerated his lessons in protecting womanhood and promoting manhood as a means to safeguard the black community, which would become one of the most prominent messages dispensed on his TV show. The segment cut to Brown in the interview: "That's what these young bucks are doing out there in the neighborhood. They've been seeing mama too often. They haven't seen a grown man and don't understand what being a man's about. They had nobody train them." Brown mourned the lack of man training, a type of pedagogical instruction he offered in his courtroom and, eventually, on his program.

Like in his *Street Stories* segment, this episode also filmed Brown inside the Shelby County Penal Farm, a prison on the periphery of Memphis. This time Brown spoke with prisoners: "They don't want you to get out and they don't want you to get a job. They want you to stay right here." Though Brown did not explicitly say who "they" were, his address to the predominately black prisoners implicitly suggested that the obstacle to black male success is the white Establishment and various apparatuses of the state. As a judge, Brown was a part of the Establishment. Yet, as a black judge, he located himself on its periphery. He could be in both worlds, and as such, paint the us/them dichotomy to develop in the prisoners a productively antagonistic stance. By crafting "they" as an enemy, Brown challenged the men to see positive behavior and life choices as a weapon in the war against a system that does not want black men to succeed.

The *Nightline* segment confirmed Brown as a judge who developed alternative punitive strategies because of the legal system's inherent biases against African-Americans. Koppel closed the segment: "Judge Brown is operating on the undeniable premise that justice in America has not been blind, that African-Americans frequently receive shabby treatment in our courts. What he does to remedy that situation in his free time on the streets and in the jails is both his business and commendable."

Brown's numerous newspaper interviews and TV appearances, along with the 1998 Court of Appeals records, read like evidence of someone who used his judgeship beyond the purview of the law because he did not believe the legal process, as it stood, could adequately address problems in the black community. His statements reflected a lack of faith in the penal system, the belief that there was prejudice on the side of the state, and the need for him to use his judicial seat to enact social change. The qualities that put Judge Brown in violation of his judicial obligations in the eyes of the Tennessee Appeals Court—his biasness, his fact-finding mission, and his politics—were exactly what attracted the producers of *Judge Joe Brown*.

Brown's persona was already clearly developed, his mission for promoting manhood established, and his ability to entertain was already verified by the time Larry Lyttle, president of Big Ticket Television, and Executive Producer Peter Brennan saw the *Nightline* segment, which was the reason they approached Brown for his own show. Lyttle told Kate Fitzgerald, a reporter for Electronic Media, that when he saw the *Nightline* segment: "[Brown] jolted me awake.... He had a wonderful quality, a fervor and an evangelical zeal that reflected his real integrity and his intentions."[54] Like with Judith Sheindlin, all producers had to do was market the brand. But Lyttle, who already had one "tough talking" judge, needed to differentiate Brown from Sheindlin. Lyttle hired Scott Friedland, president of the entertainment ad agency, Friedland Jacobs Communications, to put together a sales tape of Brown to sell the show to television stations. (Friedland also worked on *Judge Judy's* launch.) Big Ticket wanted to present Brown as "more compassionate" in dealing with people: "Friedland's sales tape showed a warm personality. There's Brown sitting at home in casual clothes talking about life growing up in South-Central Los Angeles walking in Memphis neighborhoods to check up on the people he prosecuted philosophizing on the right things people should do."[55] Lyttle asked Friedland to amend the tape, adding a segment from *Nightline* where Brown berated a defendant. Lyttle said he wanted to add "fire and ice." The tape appealed to station executives across the country, and by January 22, 1998, Big Ticket had sold the show to 60 percent of the market. Judge Joe Brown debuted September 14, 1998.

It's Joe time

The marketing strategies used to attract viewers to Brown's brand of justice condensed the interesting and unique aspects of his performance on the Memphis bench into a few catch phrases and postures that were encapsulated in the show's intro. *Judge Joe Brown*'s credits began with a female announcer saying, "All rise for Judge Joe Brown." A musical beat orchestrated by a record scratch, like a sample from a hip-hop song, played along with it. The word "Joe" flew into frame in bright red letters as Brown, in a Hitchcockian silhouette, walked across the screen carrying his gavel. The voice-over continued as the clip cut to him on his bench where he told the audience, "I'm protecting womanhood and promoting manhood." The cameras cut to a shot of Brown making a dour face, his mustache edges turned downward. The credits ended on a picture of the judge's bench with the judicial seal in the center. The American flag stood prominently in the left side of the frame, and the words "IN GOD WE TRUST" were visible at the top of the bench. A shadow of Brown's arm holding a gavel extended across the right side of the frame, poised to swing down and interrupt the static image of justice. The moving shadow of his arm stood in stark contrast with the red hue of the bench. The gavel slammed down center frame, completely obstructing the image of the bench, emitting a bright yellow glow. The glow expanded, obscuring the gavel, which swelled into a sun-like orb. Its radiant presence seemed to be a stand-in for Brown; Judge Joe Brown was the center of his courtroom's solar system.

The credits helped celebrate the brand Brown had been establishing since he took the Shelby County Criminal Court seat in 1990, echoing statements Brown had been making for 10 years about "protecting womanhood" and "promoting manhood." His southern drawl and his serious tone, his sarcasm and his wit, and even his mustache were just like the way they were on his Memphis bench. Like with Sheindlin, Big Ticket did not have to manufacture a star or coach Brown how to behave for the cameras, Brown had already been doing it for years.

The b(l)ack story: The courtroom of second chances

Judge Joe Brown kick started a rush of hiring black TV judges, many of whom imparted similar performance strategies of empathy and commiseration. Take Judge Greg Mathis. As a teenager in the mid-1970s, Greg Mathis was a leader in Errol Flynn's notorious Detroit street gang, a high school dropout, and at 17 years old did time as a juvenile tried as an adult in Michigan's Wayne County Jail. Mathis told National Public Radio's Tavis Smiley that he had been arrested four times, convicted once, and given probation. He even went to adult jail, an experience that was his "wake-up call."[56] Mathis connected his personal narrative to the "many brothers" who also get "wake-up" calls, but differentiated himself by the way he answered it. He spoke to that moment of "wake-up" as a time of possibility necessary to change somebody's life course. This led to his enrollment in Eastern Michigan University, and after graduating in 1983, Mathis moved to Detroit and began working for City Council President Clyde Cleveland.

Mathis enrolled at the University of Detroit Law School where he took night classes. He graduated and passed the State's Bar exam in 1987 on his second try, but the State Bar authorities questioned Mathis's eligibility because of his arrest record. They moved to prohibit him from becoming a lawyer. Mathis described this experience with the State Bar to Smiley:

> And so I was very confused by that, until I just one day understood that, quite frankly, this society isn't too particular about letting everybody through the door, particularly those of us who have had a background

that is less than flattering, if you will. But I didn't give up, and that's what I like to teach these brothers and tell these brothers when I'm speaking in the prisons and the juvenile detention centers.[57]

Like Judge Joe Brown, Mathis also spoke to the media about "they" as an obstacle to his success. "They" tried to prevent Mathis from getting licensed to practice law. "They" exposed his juvenile record to the media when he ran for judge. But Mathis took the State Bar to court and won, and despite "their" attempts to keep him off the bench, in 1995 he was elected Superior Court judge for Michigan's 36th District, becoming the youngest judge in the state's history at 35 years old.

Mathis's achievements drew press attention. During *Both Sides with Jesse Jackson*, a CNN broadcast airing October 29, 1995, Jesse Jackson spoke with Mathis about the need for black men to better their communities. Mathis told Jackson that he saw his job as motivating young people to have faith in themselves and encouraging them to succeed by reminding them, "that their forefathers and ancestors were kings and queens and founders of civilization, because first they must believe in themselves before they can believe they fit in and before they believe they're capable of success." Mathis stated that young black men and women feel unwanted by "white America", which makes them "retreat to a culture of self-destruction and ... crime and violence." Mathis said he aimed to combat that by instilling a sense of hope and by mobilizing black youth: "If we stick together like we did at the march, we can compete and we can win."[58] Delivered 7 years prior to his radio interview with Tavis Smiley, Mathis's message was the same: black youth feel unwanted and unfairly positioned. The system's injustices provoke black youth to stop trying. However, by example, Mathis proved that a black man, even one with a record, can achieve a position of power.

Mathis's success story also caught the attention of playwright Ron Milner. Milner, the author of the Broadway plays *What the Wine-Sellers Buy* (1974) and *Checkmates* (1988), latched onto Mathis's story and wrote a gospel musical with Mathis based on his life called *Inner City Miracle* (1997). The play opened in Detroit in 1997. Mathis would later use this title for his memoir, *Inner City Miracle*, published in 2002 by One World/Ballentine Books and cowritten with Blair S. Walker.

By the time Mathis had been on the bench for 4 years, he had already made a name for himself as a compassionate jurist, an activist in the black community, and a model of black success. At that time, Telepictures and Warner Brothers producers were on the lookout for another syndi-court judge, especially after the success of *Judge Judy* and *Judge Joe Brown*, so they flew Mathis to Los Angeles. After his visit, Telepictures Productions signed Mathis. *Judge Mathis* debuted on September 29, 1999. Mathis told *The Detroit News* that when he was a judge in Detroit, he "used his own story to try to influence those who came before him to straighten out their lives."[59] He justified his move to TV as a way to bring this message to more people: "[When I was a judge in Detroit] I had a commitment to changing lives. I thought I could influence (people) with my own brand of justice. I think I was able to influence 15 to 20 people a week—a handful of lives. . . . Now my inspirational justice might do the same thing for many more people in the living rooms of America."[60] He expressed deep empathy with his litigants and desire to connect with them, telling *Jet* magazine in 1999 that he had "lived their lives."[61]

When *Judge Mathis* aired in 1999, he was in the reality courtroom TV line up with *Judge Mills Lane*, *Judge Judy*, *Judge Joe Brown*, and Judge Koch of *The People's Court*. He was the only other black male judge on TV, and his "take responsibility" style was different from Brown's and Sheindlin's. Judge Mathis emerged on the TV judge market as the "inspirational judge." By empathizing with his litigants, Mathis invested in them the same expectation of success he had for himself. Herein lies the root of his inspirational message: On Mathis's show he promises the success he experienced is accessible to anyone and everyone regardless of race or economic position. The American dream is just a life change away. As Judge Mathis told Larry King: "I want to help uplift young people and parents dealing with troubled young people all around the country to let them know and inspire them to know that they too can overcome life's challenges."[62]

Judge Mathis took the objectives he had on the 36th Circuit Court's bench and translated them into his particular brand, which was helped by Mathis's age and good looks. At 38 years old, Judge Mathis was the youngest TV judge on television. Scott Carlin, the executive vice president of Warner Brothers Domestic Television Distribution, told Greg Spring that Mathis's youth was part of his draw. The program was designed to attract younger viewers: "We think there is a real opportunity to 'young down' court shows."[63] Judge Mathis also appealed to female viewers: "The studio-audience members, mostly African American women, eat it up. It's a passion they feel. So much so that the audience coordinator tells the giggling spectators before the taping that it's OK to smile, 'but no blowing kisses. And if you want his number, you're on your own.'"[64] Judge Mathis was the first attractive TV judge under 40 years old, and this helped entice advertisers who wanted to reach young, female viewers.

Although Mathis made audience members swoon, producers focused their marketing on his motivating message. They employed ecclesiastical visual references that figured into both the set design and in the program's intro to suggest the spiritual value of Mathis's message as well as figuring the audience as members' of his virtual congregation. The 2009 opening credits of *Judge Mathis* began with shots of Mathis dressed in a suit, standing behind a podium, addressing an audience that was not visible in the frame. A woman sat in the foreground, watching in rapt attention. The back of her head filled the right edge of the frame while Mathis spoke. The camera panned left tracking the judge and showing the elegance of the space decorated with a chandelier and floor to ceiling windows hedged in by long champagne-colored curtains. Mathis told the congregation about his life on the streets as the opening cut to a grainy flashback of a young black boy walking alone on an empty city sidewalk. The memory starkly contrasted the opulence of the previous space as he recounted his multiple arrests. The scene cut to a young black man in prison, then a close-up of a young black man being handcuffed, and then back to the elegant room where Mathis said: "I went from jail to judge in fifteen years." The camera showed Mathis studying in a judge's chambers and then cut to Mathis walking through an office, putting on his robes with focused purpose, not even stopping to adjust the fabric. "And that's when I began to make a difference, giving back through public service. I believed in myself." The credits cut to Mathis smiling and talking with a group of black youth. Then the cameras cut to inside the *Judge Mathis* courtroom where two white litigants cried and hugged each other in the foreground while Mathis applauded, perched above them on his bench. Behind him, stained glass windows cast a ministerial air over the intro: "I believe in every single person who comes into this courtroom. I know people can change. Obstacles can be overcome and great success can be achieved. Because in my courtroom it's been happening for ten years." Mathis entered the courtroom, turned around, and crossed his arms. He smiled as the "Judge Mathis 10th Season" logo filled the screen. This intro figured Mathis as an inspirational example who gives the second chances that most other courts and authority figures do not.

Judge Penny Brown Reynolds, who I will discuss in more detail in Chapter 3, was also a TV judge who liked to spread motivating messages and had a troubled past. After graduating from Georgia State University in 1991, Reynolds attended Georgia State University College of Law and graduated in 1994. Reynolds became Georgia Governor Ray Barnes executive counsel in 1999. In the summer of 2000, Governor Barnes bypassed the nominating process and appointed Reynolds judge in Fulton County. While serving on the state bench Reynolds graduated first in her class from the Interdenominational Theological Center in Atlanta, Georgia in 2008. She is an ordained minister and currently serves as Associate Pastor of the Midway Missionary Baptist Church in College Park, Georgia.

In 2007, Judge Penny Brown Reynolds caught producers' eyes when she made a guest appearance on *Dr. Phil* as an expert on postnuptial agreements. She wore a simply tailored, dark navy suit and a light coat of bright pink lipstick. She sat in the front row while Dr Phil spoke with the guests, Bobby and Darlene, about their impending divorce. Bobby wanted Darlene to sign a contract waving her rights to Bobby's money.

Dr Phil turned the issue over to Reynolds who in addition to her legal advice, added personal guidance to the mix: "Is this a marriage or a business transaction? You're keeping score on everything! Marriage is about sacrifice, not about keeping score about how many purses she has or how many horses you bought!"[65] *Family Court* executive producer Stephanie Drachkovitch saw the episode and thought Reynolds "just popped off the screen" and "took over the whole show."[66] Producers from 44 Blue Productions contacted Reynolds to offer her the role, but she waited until graduating from seminary school before accepting. Reynolds resigned from the bench in 2008 in a letter to then Georgia Governor Sonny Perdue telling him, "God has called me to a higher place."[67]

The marketing for *Family Court with Judge Penny* capitalized on the warmth and kindness that Reynolds exudes. Like *Judge Mathis*, the intro also featured her rags to riches story. It began with a synthetic horn-heavy musical score peppered with lightly crashing symbols as Judge Penny filled the frame in a three quarter shot with her bench in the background. She looked slightly off camera and said, "Families in crisis. I know exactly what they're facing." The word "CRISIS" flew into the bottom center of the frame. The cameras cut to Judge Penny's profile as she continued to speak: "I have been there. From a life of hardship." The opening cut to a picture of Judge Penny as a child, held in her mother's arms, with the word "HARDSHIP" written underneath. The cameras cut back to Judge Penny in the courtroom, looking sternly off camera and shaking her pointer finger for emphasis: "I was able to build a lifetime of experience. Now after years of serving on the bench . . ." The cameras cut to a straight shot of her, looking intensely into camera as she banged her gavel. "I use the law to fight for families." Reynolds narrated over shots of litigants hugging each other: "It's not only about verdicts. It's about solutions." Another photo of litigants hugging appeared, and the word "SOLUTIONS" filled the bottom half of the frame. The opening cut back to Judge Penny's profile as she said, "It's about the passion and the mercy that justice requires." The cameras cut to a close-up of Judge Penny looking directly into camera: "I'm justice Penny Brown Reynolds, and in my court family comes first." The music swelled as the *Family Court* logo flew into frame letter by letter. A soft bell sound-effect swept the graphics out of frame revealing the inside of the *Family Court* courtroom.

The biography on her website, "Judge Penny.com", went into even more detail about her difficult upbringing, describing being raised by a poor single mother who was "abused and marginalized."[68] The bio also remarked that living through these hardships was what made Reynolds the compassionate judge she became. Like *Judge Mathis*'s brand, *Family Court with Judge Penny*'s marketing also claimed that her ability to empathize with "families in crisis" made her a better and fairer judge. With a lighter touch than many of the other judges, she self-identified as a "cross between straight-talking Judge Greg Mathis and life-affirming Oprah Winfrey."[69] Like Mathis, she was a model of success, and the show's intro based her credibility more on her past than her extensive legal and volunteer experience. (She started The Judge Penny Reynolds Foundation, Inc, served on the Executive Board of the NAACP, and was president of the Georgia Chapter of the International Women's Forum.) It also used implicit religious references such as the invocation of "mercy." In interviews Reynolds was more assertive about making the connection between her faith and her job: "All I see is God, what God has done for me. I stand before you as God's representative."[70] Judge Penny's merciful justice intricately tied together her upbringing, her race, and her religion.

"I know you"

Judge Mathis, Judge Joe Brown, and Judge Penny Brown Reynolds, like Judge Judy, propagated a message of self-responsibility, but these judges used their personal stories to narrate a system of inequality that puts people of color on an uneven playing field. As members of the black community who struggled to overcome a multitude of obstacles, their stories served as examples of how to succeed against the odds. And these stories helped producers target and draw black audiences. Since the 1970s, viewer trends have revealed that black viewers prefer to watch black characters and storylines that reflect the black experience.[71] The same goes for reality courtroom TV. My analysis of over 10 years of viewer data evidenced that black judges attracted higher percentages of black viewers, and white judges attracted the smallest.[72]

While attracting wider viewership might have been the producers' strategy for hiring black judges, the presence of these judges and their alternative stories and performance methods enact a counter-narrative about American law. This does not rely only on visual presentation—the judge's look—but also on how the judges perform race and with whom they sympathize on their courtroom stages. It is also inscribed in their language and how they speak to the litigants. In his sociological analysis of the juridical field, Pierre Bourdieu wrote that juridical language distinguishes itself from everyday language. The legal professional uses formal language, passive and impersonal constructions, expressions of the factual, and the reliance on "fixed formulas" without individual variation: "[I]t bears all the marks of rhetoric of impersonality and of neutrality."[73] Bourdieu wrote that the linguistic procedures of juridical language produce the "neutralization effect" and the "universalization effect." The neutralization effect marks the "impersonality of normative utterances" and establishes the speaker "as universal subject at once impartial and objective."[74] Simply put, the neutralization effect tries to erase any appearance of bias by positioning the speaker as a general representative, not as a subjective individual. Similarly, the legal professional's adoption of legal language and "fixed formulations" produces a "universalization effect", the purpose of which is to make nonlegal professionals experience law through universal principals and not through personal opinion or "individual variation." The use of legal language does not guarantee impartiality, but it gives the appearance of it.

In the late 1970s and early 1980s, legal scholars and professionals of color unsatisfied with the way law was taught and theorized carved out a space for a new path of inquiry. What emerged became known as critical race theory, a political and academic movement that queried law's role in the construction of race and its maintenance of racial subjugation. Critical race theorists brought race consciousness into legal discourse and scholarship (see Krenshaw 1995; Lawrence III 1995; Bell 1995; Delgado 1995). Cornel West wrote: "Critical Race Theorists have, for the first time, examined the entire edifice of contemporary legal thought and doctrine from the viewpoint of law's role in the construction and maintenance of social domination and subordination."[75] An active participant in the movement, Patricia Williams wrote about the impossible aspirations of legal writing:

> Law and legal writing aspire to formalized, color-blind, liberal ideals. Neutrality is the standard for assuring these ideals; yet the adherence to it is often determined by reference to an aesthetic of uniformity, in which difference is simply omitted. For example, when segregation was eradicated from the American lexicon, its omission led many to actually believe that racism therefore no longer existed. Race-neutrality in law has become the presumed antidote for race bias in real life.[76]

Williams wrote that neutrality in legal writing asserts the nonexistence of race biasness, an omission that leads many to presume that racism is also no longer present. Williams's reasoning and her treatment of personal narrative in legal texts work against this omission. She perceived her technique as inclusive as opposed to the "exclusive" disciplinary property of law: "Another advantage is that this sort of analytic technique can serve to describe a community of context for those social actors whose traditional legal status has been the isolation of oxymoron, of oddity, of outsider."[77]

The exclusionary techniques of legal logic go beyond language. Bourdieu analyzed the juridical field's ritual processes. He wrote that legal authority depends on ritual acts (such as giving a formal opinion or reading from legal texts) that symbolize the jurist's sublimation of personal opinion to the "will of the law or the legislature."[78] The technical mastery of these rituals of sublimation separates legal professionals from laymen, who, as Bourdieu distinguished, make decisions with "the simple counsels of common sense," the "non-specialists' sense of fairness," and their "view of the case."[79]

Reality Courtroom TV has flipped this logic, giving symbolic legal authority to jurists who make decisions like laymen—based on personal opinions and a subjective sense of fairness. Instead of deferring to the formalism of legal sublimation, reality courtroom TV judges resist a system of practice that puts their opinions and conceptions of fairness second to any institutionalized belief system. Their performances are refusals of shared core values. They abide by the resisting practices of critical race theorists by representatively denying the existence of a "universal" subject, especially because for centuries American law imagined that universal subject as white and male. Making the connection between reality courtroom TV and critical race theory may seem slighting to a field that has so vociferously and effectively challenged legal practice. However, these TV judges' roots are in actual courts where they cultivated their performances. The TV product evidences, in a more showy way, how these judges were already resisting law's neutralizing effect in their state courtrooms. Furthermore, by continuing their resistance on stage, they demonstrate what scholar Joshua Chambers-Letson described as the possibility of embodied performances to free "the raced subject from the structural conditions that produce racial injustice and the negation of freedom while allowing the minoritarian subject to negotiate, acknowledge, and display the material effects that the history of racism continues to affect in and on the body."[80]

Justice served spicy

While many of the black TV judges' inspirational messages are tied to their race and rough upbringings, the Latino/a TV judges' programs tend to underscore and celebrate the immigrant story and the judge's physical appearance or feisty personality. On almost every reality courtroom TV show that has starred a Latino/a judge, the judge is lauded for having come to the United States and achieved the "American Dream" while holding on to their home-country traditions. Their ethnicity flavors their behavior in the courtroom, and that flavor, as their programs' marketing sells it, is spicy.

One could presume that Judge Alex Ferrer had his sights set on becoming a celebrity when he hired talent agent, Miami Lawyer Arnold Preston in 2002, 3 years prior to getting cast on his own show. Liz Balmaseda wrote in 2007: "If you ever had the occasion to sit in Judge Alex Ferrer's courtroom while he was on the Miami-Dade Circuit bench, commanding the place with authority, panache and a judicious amount of humor, you might have seen it all coming."[81] Like Mathis, Judge Alex Ferrer was both young and attractive, qualities not lost on his program's marketing team. Billboards and advertisements for his show called him "Tall, Dark and Judgmental," and when his program premiered Krys Longan wrote, "[E]ven though this jurist has more than two decades of experience, he could moonlight as a male model."[82] His official show website could not escape bragging about his good looks. After a summary of his history, "Judge Alex and his family escaped from Fidel Castro's Communist regime to America when he was one year old", the blurb added that he was "recently featured in People Magazine's 'Sexiest Men Alive' issue."[83] Although Mathis's show runner gleefully reported that women swooned in his audience, his appearance was never a conspicuous part of the show's marketing. In Judge Alex's case, it was. And this is one of the ways Latino/a judges have been packaged and sold to the viewing public.

Never a sitting judge in a state or federal courtroom, Cristina Perez began presiding over Spanish television courtrooms in 1998 with her lead role on *La Corte del Pueblo* on Telemundo. She made the move to English television in 2006 with *Cristina's Court* (2006–9), and the show won a Daytime Emmy in 2008 and 2009. Perez is a kind, smart, and attractive legal professional, author, and TV and radio personality, and although stylistically her *Cristina's Court* performance inclined toward compassion and understanding (as I will discuss in Chapter 3), producers did not always shy away from focusing the show's marketing on her good looks.

After her 2008 Daytime Emmy win, her producers launched a new ad campaign, to celebrate.[84] The spot opened on a dimly lit and glamorously designed hallway. Perez walked into frame with her back to camera and stepped past a dog asleep on a plush dog bed. The dog woke up, looking at the judge as she passed. The shot returned to Perez, lingering on her back as she strutted down the hallway in a gold satin robe that silhouetted her body. Her coiffed long blonde hair bounced seductively behind her as if she was in a shampoo commercial. Soft instrumental music underscored the baritone announcement, "Every season something new comes into fashion." Perez stopped in front of a set of large black doors. The camera panned down to Perez's hands as she opened the doors revealing . . . a closet instead of a courtroom. Black robe after black robe hung on the rack. Below was a shelf that displayed an endless supply of black high heel pumps. The voice-over continued: "And once it's in style, everybody wants it." The camera moved to a close-up of Perez's right eye, professionally smudged with charcoal liner, more fitting for a night out on the town than a day on the bench. From this angle Perez becomes the object that everyone wants, and her eye, staring seductively, fans our desires. "But it's not something that looks good on everyone," the male voice cooed, "because it's really about the woman who wears it." Perez started to undress, deftly slipping off one of the black robes and replacing it with another one. The camera caught bits of her skin as the fabric cascaded down her long leg lifted by a pair of high heels. Then the camera rose up her body and hovered at her clavicle. Her robe, slightly opened, revealed her skin as her hands entered frame to clasp on a gold necklace. The pendant dangled neatly below her collarbone. She drew her other hand up to flip her blonde hair behind her shoulder. "This fall there is one accessory no other television judge will have." Perez opened what looked like a lingerie drawer and pulled out, not a negligee, but her Emmy award. She held the gold statue in her hands while an inexplicable gust of wind blew her hair back as if she was standing on a beach. She smiled into camera, and for the first time we see her in her entirety instead of body part by body part. The voice-over finished: "Check out the hot new season of the Daytime Emmy Winner *Cristina's Court*."

This promo's emphasis was a departure from her program's other advertising campaigns that demonstrated her professional side and TV courtroom demeanor, and it sent a message to viewers that Perez would trumpet after her show went off the air: It is possible to be smart, successful and sexy. The same year her show ended, Perez published her second advice book—*It's All About the Woman Who Wears It: 10 Laws for Being Smart, Successful, and Sexy Too* (2010)—and started a radio career as a guest on Playboy Radio's program "Afternoon Advice" in their "Sex in the News" segment.[85]

Judge Maria Lopez was also a product of "sexy Latina" marketing. Lopez began her career as a civil rights attorney and was appointed to the Massachusetts Suffolk Superior Court in 1993. She married Stephen Mindich, a Boston media mogul who published the Boston Phoenix. In 2000, Lopez faced media scrutiny after she sentenced a 22-year-old transsexual man, Charles "Ebony" Horton, to a year of home detention and 5 years' probation instead of sending him to jail after he plead guilty to kidnaping 12-year-old Ramon Suarez and performing simulated sex acts with him.[86] In addition to the negative media attention, the Commission of Judicial Conduct Review filed formal charges against Lopez on May 7, 2002 for her treatment of Assistant District Attorney, Ms Leora Joseph, and District Attorney David Deacon during the plea hearing on September 6, 2000. The Commission raised issue with Lopez telling Ms Joseph she "belonged in the suburbs."[87] During the Commission hearing Judge Lopez clarified: "What I meant by that is that she really you know—she wouldn't be able to understand an Ebony Horton; that if she understood—if her life experience was a little broader, if she was a little more sophisticated about people who are marginalized in our society and had a little more compassion about it, she would understand better."[88] Lopez articulated how a lawyer's subject position could influence the fairness of a case's outcome, and in this case Lopez believed that the assistant DA's background was an obstacle to giving a just trial to Ebony Horton. Lopez preached the underlying philosophy of reality courtroom TV: Popular justice is best executed by judges who understand and can empathize with their litigants' life experiences.

In addition to thinking Ms Joseph was unfit for the job of an urban prosecutor because of her ignorance of "marginalized" people, Judge Lopez also disliked the state prosecutor's, David Deacon's, use of the media. She criticized the DA's press release for sensationalizing the case, finding that it "sought to turn the court proceedings into a circus."[89] However, the commission focused on a moment toward the end of the September 6, 2000, plea hearing to justify their claims of improper conduct. After Judge Lopez had administered the sentence and ceded the floor to the defendant's counsel, Mr Deacon refused to sit down. In response to his refusal, Judge Lopez yelled at Mr Deacon.

During the hearing she apologized for her outburst: "I was probably—allowed my emotions to get the better of me in that situation... I should have been able to exercise more control in the circumstances."[90] Rather than continue with the review of her judicial conduct, Judge Maria Lopez resigned from the bench on May 19, 2003, but she was not unemployed for long. Her media presence caught the eye of Sony Television Productions who invited her to star in a new reality courtroom TV program. Like with Judge Joe Brown, the qualities that got Lopez in trouble with the Commission on Judicial Conduct—her tempestuousness, her passion, and her emotional investment—were recognized as the qualities that make for a good TV judge.

Judge Maria Lopez debuted in 2005, and producers reshaped the hotheadedness that got Lopez in trouble in her actual courtroom into a sexy and feisty brand of TV justice. One poster for her show posed Lopez in a close-up with her face tilted downward as she gave the camera a "come hither" look. Next to her the caption read: "Justice will be served spicy." This double meaning of spicy, as both alluring and argumentative, was also repeated on her website. At the bottom of the front page of the program's site, Lopez sat cross-legged with her bare knee exposed. Below her was the caption, "Judge Maria Lopez turns up the heat in the courtroom." This was continued in the program's intro credits, which began with a full-body shot of her leaning against a railing inside a courthouse. Her robe was open and she wore a short skirt. Each hand held onto the railing behind her, pushing her chest forward as if she was offering herself to the viewer. In her deep, gravelly voice, Lopez purred the narration: "There is only one person who decides the truth here. I do." As the intro continued, her tone became more firm and commanding, but maintained her signature low growl. The opening cut to a clip from a previously aired case showing Lopez leaning over her judge's bench as she told an unruly off screen litigant, "Take that bone to another dog." The words "dog" and "bone" rang seductively. Then, the intro shifted tone to acknowledge her Cuban heritage. Standing in front of a picture of herself as a girl she said: "I came here as a little girl from Cuba. Want to talk about the American dream? I am the American dream." She walked into the center of the courthouse, crossed her arms, and looked into the camera stationed above her. She glared up into the lens with a determined expression. Her show's logo flew into the right of frame as the music crescendoed.

Judge Marilyn Milian is another judge of Cuban descent and the first woman to preside over *The People's Court*, replacing Judge Judy Sheindlin's husband, Jerry Sheindlin, in 2001. To market their new female judge, one of the program's earlier intros plugged not only her adjudication style, but also her appearance. The male voice-over in the *People's Court* intro announced, "Everybody is talking about the honorable Marilyn Milian, the hottest judge on television." Judge Milian smiled and waved her hair back and forth as the show's graphics cut across the frame. Underneath there were pictures of her family, establishing her as a mother and wife. These photos alluded to her softer side and the prototypical qualities that come from those familial roles.

When Warner Brothers cast Milian in 2001, they were ahead of the curve in hiring a Latina judge. By 2005, a wave of Latino/a judges hit the market; however, David Scott, the executive producer of *The People's*

Court, said they did not cast Milian because she was Latina: "After 16 years of older men as 'People's Court' judges, we were just looking for somebody different.... That Marilyn Milian is a Latina was not a factor.... We just liked the variety of emotions she projected, from compassion to anger. The anger surges when she thinks a complainant is lying."[91] Scott did not call her "spicy" or "hot," but the attribute he liked best was her "surging anger"—an emotional parallel to the "hotness" her intro advertised.

With growing Hispanic and Latino/a populations in the United States and few TV role models, production companies looked to tap this new market by casting Latino/a judges. However, their marketing strategies played up stereotypes of the "hot" and "spicy" Latina, stereotypes most recognizably embodied by Hollywood icons like Carmen Miranda, Dolores del Rio, and Lupe Velez—stars who projected, "not only exotic, inviting, and flamboyant sexuality, but also a particular social class derived from a perceived ethnicity."[92] The "spicy" Latina stereotype translated on to reality courtroom TV as sexy and temperamental judges, and in their programs' marketing these stereotypes occasionally overshadowed the judges' professional attributes.

There's only one queen in this courtroom

Gerette Allegra-Samiian, former vice president of programming at Sony Pictures Television, discovered Judge David Young, a three-term Miami-Dade County Circuit Court Judge elected in 2000, by watching the 2005 America West Flight 556 case *Florida v. Cloyd & Hughes* on Court TV, the case in which two America West pilots were accused of flying drunk. She found Young to be compassionate and wise, "like your favorite uncle."[93] In an evening news segment, NBC aired footage of the trial introducing Young as the judge who gave the pilots a strict behavioral lesson along with their sentence. Inside the courtroom Young told the defendants, "What you did was absolutely wrong, outrageous and horrendous." NBC reporter Mark Potter reported that "Former America West pilot Thomas Cloyd and co-pilot Christopher Hughes faced the wrath of Judge David Young, who gave them stiff sentences and a harsh rebuke."[94] The trial footage demonstrated Young's proclivity for moralizing and lecturing, veering away from the sentencing to make sure the pilots understood their transgression. Young scolded them like a school teacher: "What was not deserved, sir, were those members who were flying on your aircraft having pilots who were drunk.... You understand that?" He waited for their reply, making sure his point was made.

Young's behavior during the pretrial hearings was consistent with what was shown on Court TV. He used the same sarcasm, wit, and, at times, firmness when revoking the pilots' passports. He told the defendants' counsel, "There is no bar from them getting a crop duster and flying anywhere they want to."[95] Elaborating his decision with a dramatic reference to the pilots escaping on a crop duster was one way he entertained the courtroom. On a different note, he executed a stricter verdict when Christopher Hughes's wife asked the judge to release her husband before the July 20, 2005 sentencing for the sake of their children. Young responded: "He thought more about what he was doing that night than about his two children.... There's no sufficient cause to release them."[96] Young justified keeping the pilots in custody by calling into question Hughes's character, asserting that the night he got drunk with his copilot he was not thinking about his children. Young implied that going home would have no impact on the welfare of his kids because Hughes did not demonstrate the qualities of a good father when he flew drunk. The transcripts and footage from the case and the pretrial hearings exhibited how entertaining and stern Young could be, but in the crowded reality courtroom TV landscape producers needed to find a new niche for Young.

In addition to his charisma, charm, and his professional record, Judge David Young is also an openly gay man. This was a first for TV judges, so when branding their new star, producers tied the show to an aesthetic sensibility and vocabulary associated with gay male culture. Before *Judge David Young* premiered on September 10, 2007 a *PR Newswire* article described the new judge as being known for his "fierce intelligence and occasional bursts into show tunes."[97] Voice-overs between segments announced, "Judge David is compassionate. Judge David is fierce."[98] The repetition of Young's "fierceness" across advertising and media platforms alluded to a kind of performance of queerness that whether or not Young exhibited, revealed Young's sexual identity without coming right out and saying it. It turned his sexuality into a demonstration in line with popular cultural representations of the "gay man." *Judge David Young*, as the show's catchphrase broadcast, was "justice with a snap."

As discussed throughout the chapter, most of the judges exaggerated their personalities on their TV benches, amplifying tendencies they exhibited in their actual courtrooms for their TV audiences. Unlike Sheindlin, Brown, or Mathis, Young did not have a specific political agenda he continued to espouse on his TV bench. Instead, he had a style that producers could sell. Judge David Young's television performance played up the campiness of his judge character. According to Lydia Martin's 2007 article in *Tribune Business News*: "[Young] has always been known for his perky judicial style. But in fifteen years on the bench he never gayed it up as much as he's gaying it up for *Judge David Young*." The article went on to describe one of the first cases on the program between three gay musicians and their manager: "Young, bespectacled and conservative (you would even call him a tad dowdy, but he'd probably hold it against you forever), feared the guys were getting out of hand. But why shout something trite like, "Order in the court!" when instead you can hit 'em with, 'There is only one queen in this courtroom, and it's not you!'"[99] In addition to his asides about his sexuality, such as joking with the audience about his bailiff, Tawya, "If I were straight, I'd marry her," Young livened up dry cases with funny puns, references to musicals, and the occasional song. These were behaviors that he obviously did not perform in his Miami courtroom.[100]

Young told the gay pop culture site *After Elton* he considered his camp performance strategic, shaking off criticism that he was performing a detrimental gay stereotype. He said that his detractors should watch the show:

> When they watch the show, they're not going to see a Jack McFarland. They're going to see someone with almost fifteen years of experience, someone who knows the law, someone who's no nonsense, someone who's compassionate, someone who's thoughtful. And if something comes along and I can be a little campy to make a point, to get it through somebody's head, to make a difference in their lives, I'm gonna do it.[101]

Young rationalized his occasional camp performance as calculated, accentuating the positive effects of using humor to teach valuable lessons, and this became part of the concept behind the intro for *Judge David Young*.

The intro to *Judge David Young* began with a close-up of the judge speaking to someone just off camera, his bench in the background, and an electronic and upbeat instrumental lead-in. Over the music Young said, "I've dedicated my life to justice." From this point on the opening effects became more elaborate. Stills from past cases were frozen and flattened to look like cutout photographs standing in relief from the background. The two-dimensional images rotated sideways to reveal their flatness, as if they were pictures composing a scrapbook of Young's courtroom. In the scene, Young pled to the off screen litigants to be more accepting: "I know a bigot when I see one. You have to open your heart to embrace people who are different than you." The opening cut back to Young's three quarter shot in front of the bench: "I'm passionate about the law." The word "Compelling" flew in underneath his image. The opening cut back to a flat image of Young singing, "It's wrong, it's wrong, it's wrong," then cut to litigants, also cutouts, laughing with a laugh track. Young continued: "Did I say it's wrong?" The opening cut back to Young's direct address to camera: "You'll never, *ever* see a judge run a courtroom the way I do." The word "Original" flew in underneath his image, cuing the next scene. Back in the two-dimensional courtroom, Young, leaning back in his leather chair, shook his head side to side and said, "Denial is not a river in Egypt. It does not flow through this courtrooooooooooooooooom." Young sang the end of the word "courtroom," letting it draw out while he raised his arm across his body and snapped. The opening ended with the cameras moving in for a tight shot. In a close-up Young winked directly into camera. A glowing orb grew from the center of the screen filling the frame in complete whiteness and then cross-faded to reveal the inside of the courtroom as the music swelled and then tapered out.

Young's wink, a gesture used to indicate that something is a joke or a secret and sometimes used as a welcoming nod, was the final impression given to the audience. It cued the audience that justice with a wink, like justice with a snap, may not be staid or solemn. Young's wink seemed to promise a funnier judge than the others on TV, and the intro's and advertisements' allusions to gay stereotypes suggested a particular kind of camp humor. Currently, camp images of gay men are some of the few acceptable images for public consumption, and this has been helped by TV programs like *Will & Grace, Community* and *Rupaul's Drag Race*, to name merely a few.[102] However, camp's origins are rooted in its rebellious and provocative nature. Susan Sontag famously wrote that camp was perception in "quotation marks": "It's not a lamp, but a 'lamp'; not a woman, but a 'woman'. To perceive camp in objects and persons is to understand Being-as-Playing-a-Role. It is the farthest extension, in sensibility, of the metaphor of life as theater."[103] Young's campy performance was not the subversive queer aesthetic about which Sontag was writing. Young camped camp—playing the role of a campy judge in order to bring levity to arbitration hearings and stake his claim in the daytime TV lineup. The difference has to do with its usage as a commodity or a political act. Elizabeth Whitney: "Queer identity is acceptable as a product, as a performance that offers partial entry into the world of an 'other,' as long as this performance remains under the unpredictable jurisdiction of heteronormativity."[104] Young used his brand of camp to appeal to a largely heterosexual viewing audience. It was managed and fun, and entertaining for the sake of garnering ratings. It allowed him safe passage (and temporary acceptance) in the straight world of American jurisprudence where LGBT citizens continue to be denied the same freedoms as heterosexuals. While the appearance of an out and gay TV judge may seem like evidence of great strides in gay rights, Whitney argued that the visibility of camp does not correlate with social change: "As LGBT politics continue to be represented in the mainstream by co-opted, campy imagery, the seemingly progressive social politics become dependent upon market values and continued consumption. What appears to be gain is no gain at all."[105] For *Judge David Young,* camping it up in the courtroom may have been counter-productive to audiences' accepting Young's authority and to his progressive aims of bringing compassion and tolerance to a national audience. By leading his brand with the comedy of camp, his courtroom became, more evidently than other TV courtrooms, a "quotation" of a courtroom. It therefore may have undermined its symbolic authority despite how kind and compassionate Young was as a TV magistrate.

Connecting to the judge

Reality courtroom TV's diverse benches appeal to millions of viewers. Jenny Hope suggested that part of the appeal is that audiences can live vicariously through the judges—especially when the judges resemble them:

> I do believe people look to television to live vicariously and especially to feel some sort of victory. And daytime television does skew to—the viewers are women. So they do identify more with the female judge. Judge Judy may be tough, but they love it, and a lot of people wish they could say those words.[106]

Hope remarked that viewers could indirectly experience the judge's authority when they relate to them. Studying television audiences in the 1950s, Donald Horton and Anselm Strauss described vicarious interaction as an "implicit enactment of roles." They wrote: "[T]he observer takes the roles of the various actors alternately and reciprocally. Unlike personal interaction, the taking of roles remains implicit or covert. . . . He exerts no direct control over the observed encounter."[107] In Horton and Strauss's model the viewer takes on multiple roles to feel as if he or she was in the actor's place, even without being able to change the course of the onscreen action. Hope described a similar phenomenon—a surrogating relationship between reality courtroom TV viewers and the judges. The judges say what audiences "wish" they could.

As the trajectories from their state benches to the TV benches illustrate—and the viewer demographics attest—the draw to reality courtroom TV is not *only* that it reflects images of powerful black, female, gay, and Latino/a judges. (Yes, reality courtroom TV judges embrace these identities and producers emphasize their difference.) But it is also *how* the judges perform their brands that draws viewers. Many of the successful reality courtroom TV judges' performances of law are defiant expressions that unapologetically turn away from a formalist legal methodology, a system and choreography of "justice" that historically excluded and did not protect people of color and women. Their symbolic "turn away" casts doubt on our institutions of justice—slow, bureaucratic processes executed with exclusionary legal language so complicated that the average person needs a professional to translate it.

Bourdieu wrote that "judicial space" requires a demarcation between "actors": "It divides those qualified to participate in the game and those who, though they may find themselves in the middle of it, are in fact excluded by their inability to accomplish the conversion of mental space—and particularly of linguistic stance—which is presumed by entry into this social space."[108] Reality courtroom TV offers entry to the uninitiated. The judges' decision-making logic stems from their personal connections to the issues producers bring onto their courtroom stages—connections that were established long before they sat down on their TV benches.

2

The Law/Theater Continuum: Performing Real Disputes on Courtroom Stages

When we talk about reality TV, court shows, in my opinion, are the ultimate unscripted drama because they are told with passion by the people directly involved in each case. It's drama at its finest.

Cristina Perez[1]

Reality courtroom TV relies on audience interest in the spectacle of "the law," the same curiosity that drew crowds to the gallows and keeps audiences clambering for seats in the courtrooms of celebrity trials and glued to their TVs and Twitter feeds. It promises to satisfy a similar appetite to observe the exhibition of state power meting out punishment and reward and does so within the regulatory space of a studio set, all in less than 30 minutes. Examining the overt theatrical strategies used by reality courtroom TV reveals the theater that is always already there in actual courts despite law's dissimulation of its presence. As numerous scholars have concluded, the courtroom is a judicial theater, a theater of law, a site where performance strategies are employed to persuade juries and jurists, to win cases, to enforce laws and to question them (see Friedman 2000; Hibbitts 1995; Ball 1975; Levinson 2007; Simonett 1966).[2]

The fulfillment of legal process requires its performance. Legal scholar Bernard Hibbitts wrote: "If we consider law as an enforced standard, rather than a written rule, it is clear that law cannot be brought into being but for performance. A rule which is not performed is arguably no law."[3] Trial choreography and its processes are ritualized, performed again and again in courtrooms across the country. The gestures and language used in courtrooms are codified practices taught to participants and repeated by them. The proper enactment of these rituals, these rules of engagement, is required for the trial to be deemed fair. Enacting them incorrectly—going off script—risks invalidating the process or being punished for contempt of court.

In addition to the requisite trial choreography, in actual courts the aesthetic of the various elements is essential (what the courtroom space looks like, what the judge, bailiffs, witnesses, and litigants wear, how they do their hair and makeup, walk, talk, and sit—their overall comportment). The formal processes are tightly regulated through scripts that lawyers and legal professionals learn, rehearse, and perform. Lawyers, court officers, and judges direct juries during selection and throughout the trials so even those unfamiliar with the courtroom codes are made aware of how they are expected to move, sit, listen, and deliberate. Like most theatrical performances, the participants perform these actions for an audience: the enactment of legal process is often done before a jury, judge, and the courtroom gallery. Although entertainment is not its primary aim, it may be its by-product. During public trials theater is in the service of law.

Entertainment norms are part of legal persuasion and do not disturb law's general credibility. As Richard Sherwin has written, pop aesthetics are a hidden presence in courtrooms even as law conceals this presence.[4] But the theater of legal process is a contentious proposition, and while there are parallels between the legal event and the theatrical one (both take place for an audience, participants play roles, follow scripts, and both have varying levels of drama for defined durations of time) the validity and efficacy of the legal field, as Bourdieu theorized, relies on its denial of cultural and aesthetic influence. Richard Terdiman summed up Bourdieu's argument:

> In Bourdieu's conception, the law is not by nature and by theoretical definition independent of other social realms and practices as the formalists claim. Instead, it is closely tied to these. But the nature of its

relation is often one of intense *resistance* to the influence of competing forms of social practice or professional conduct, for, as Bourdieu argues, such resistance is what sustains the self-conception of the professionals within the juridical field.[5]

Legal process borrows entertainment norms and is vulnerable to its influence despite its denial of doing so. Therefore, the difference between what happens on reality courtroom TV and in actual courts does not hinge on one using theatrical strategies and the other being immune to them. For example, if a juried trial was staged on a courtroom set in a theater or in a studio—say, one like *Judge Judy's*—the location alone would not disrupt the meaning or effect of that trial so long as all parties agreed to abide by the same rules and procedures of an actual court. The theater could be designated as an actual courtroom. This designation would not be in name alone, but in how the processes of law unfold in that space. So the proceedings may not be that different than if it took place in an actual courtroom. Lawyers would question witnesses, give opening and closing statements to a selected jury, and defer to the judge for review of the law and the lawyers' line of questioning. The jury's decision would decide the case, and the parties would have to follow the appropriate procedures to address this outcome with the help of other courts, court officers, police, and the penal system. Because of the systems and government apparatuses buttressing the trial, its effects could remain virtually the same.

However, if the judge violated codes of judicial conduct, or if the bailiff interrupted with witty remarks, or if the lawyers presented evidence without following the correct procedures, the proceedings could be declared a mistrial. So the critical difference in the type of justice produced on reality courtroom TV and in actual courts is not determined by whether or not the process takes place on a veritable stage or on a metaphorical one, or whether or not the participants put on costumes, use persuasive strategies, self-conscious gestures, or rehearsed behaviors. The disparity comes more from the *excess* of theatricality employed in reality courtroom TV's performances of binding arbitrations and the absence of the force of law that regulates and punishes this excess. Acting out on reality TV has different consequences than acting out in an actual court.

While in actual courtrooms theater is in service of the legal event, on reality courtroom TV, law is in service of the theatrical event. Entertainment is primary. This chapter looks at reality courtroom TV's excesses, the claims of this make-believe space, and the dramas actualized within reality courtroom TV's theatrical frame. It looks at how it is a layered performance—it is a social drama, a legal procedure, and entertainment—made to amuse and draw audiences, and, while doing so, frames the events and the people participating as entertainment and entertainers in order to generate the affect of popular TV justice.

Beneath the small claims: Casting the dramas

Reality courtroom TV shows' arbitrations can be both mundane and spectacular. They are often mundane because of the pettiness of the disputes, and spectacular because of the network of performance signs enlivening the argument. The cases are dramatically heightened because they are acted out in a TV studio and on a set, the litigants rehearse before going on stage, spectators watch the live event, the participants know they are being recorded, and in postproduction editors condense the case into its most remarkable moments. Because of all these factors, reality courtroom TV has established its own kind of recognizable "small claims" process, and current shows still copy the format established by *The People's Court* in 1981.

Reality courtroom TV reproduces reality courtroom TV's legal and theatrical practices—binding arbitrations mediated by former judges and legal professionals staged as if they were small claims trials. Like a snake biting its own tail, the programs are reproductions of themselves, cycling back onto each other for reference. There is no actual referent for the form, but a composite of theatrical renditions used to verify each copy. This mirroring allows new shows to add elements to the process while still seeming legitimate because rather than only looking to a real small claims court for verification audiences can look at other courtroom TV shows. Reality courtroom TV shows become their own frame of reference; they are what Baudrillard called hyperreal, "more real than real," and possibly more definitive than the thing itself.[6]

Casting is essential to making an entertaining episode, and producers can cull through over 1,800 cases a week to find interesting stories with good defenses involving family members, neighbors, or friends.[7] Viewers can also call into the shows or submit online requests to have their cases heard by a particular judge. As part of my research, I applied online to be on *Judge Judy* and *Judge Joe Brown*. A few days after my submission, I received a call from Randi Page, one of the producers from *Judge Joe Brown*. She asked me to go over my case. I explained that I had rented an apartment sight unseen, trusting that the advertisement for the apartment was accurate. Upon arrival I discovered the apartment was actually a dank room in an unkempt house that was in foreclosure. The lessor refused to return my payment. I thought the story had dramatic appeal, but the producer told me they were more interested in cases between people who were related to each other. She also told me that the program would not take my case unless I could present a copy of my lawsuit. I had a feeling she thought I was making up the story, and despite my best efforts on the phone, I did not make it past this initial screening.

In addition to uncovering details of the dispute, part of the phone call's objective is also to find out who actually wants to be on TV and who does not. Once that is assessed, it is important to find someone who can clearly and concisely tell his or her story. Jenny Hope, former producer on *The Tyra Banks Show, Judge Judy, America's Court with Judge Ross, Texas Justice, Power of Attorney, Divorce Court*, and others spoke with me about these initial phone calls:

> You just go over it. OK tell me your side. Do you have any evidence? You make sure they have it sorted in their mind. You practice. It's

like going in for a test. Just to make sure they have it, and you want them to tell the story: "It all started on this date and then dah da dah dah da." As long as they can do that, then they're pretty much a good candidate to be on a show like this. If they can tell it in a very concise and passionate way.[8]

The cases with potential are earmarked, and depending on the show's process may be shown to the judge prior to approval.[9]

Once accepted, producers invite the litigants onto the program, enticing them with appearance fees, the award payment, and a chance to be on TV. The financial incentives are particularly helpful if one of the litigants is judgment proof, meaning he or she is financially insolvent, which would make the small claims court's decision fruitless. If a litigant chooses to go on the program, she would receive the compensation she may have not have been able to collect (or would have been very difficult to collect) had she won in her local court. Even if the litigant has the money to pay the judgment, having the production company pay instead may be a more attractive option because the programs offer to settle the cases without financially burdening the litigants.

When one agrees to go on a reality courtroom TV show, she risks exposing personal and confidential life details in front of a national audience. Therefore, only people willing to risk being exposed and possibly publically shamed tend to agree to appear on the programs. (Of course some people agree to go on the shows because they want to be on TV—also an attractive proposition for many.) This automatically filters the applicant pool so that certain kinds of litigants appear again and again. Furthermore, and as I discuss in the following chapters, the cases are chosen to give each judge an opportunity to make the litigants models of how or how not to behave—exemplifying the judge's pedagogical message. Through the use of deliberate camera shots, on-set coaching and direction, and the postproduction editing (captions, audience reaction shots, inserts of the judge and bailiff), the litigants are often framed as needing the judge's guidance.

Because certain types of people appear repeatedly on these programs, the shows risk perpetuating stereotypes of certain individuals as always needing help. The danger of this approach is that audiences may understand these stereotyped performances to be indicative of the represented group as a whole.[10] But this is a key element of their storytelling strategy. Part of the genre's appeal is that the programs are easily understandable and that all the disputes can be solved speedily. Stereotypes circumvent intricate dramas, complex analysis, and uncertainties, making the judges' decisions seem unquestionable. Hope told me that it is necessary that the audience perceives a clear winner and loser: "It's always a black and white in terms of right and wrong or good and bad in the courtroom."[11] A nuanced character analysis would complicate the simplicity of reality courtroom TV's unambiguous judgments.

The framing of litigants as stereotypical representations emboldens audiences to believe they already know them because of the recognizable signs associating them with particular ideas about certain types of people. Therefore, the judge's snap judgments are readily supported by the knowledge the audience thinks it already has. It limits the litigants' self-presentation into simple and codified terms. Clint Wilson, Lena Chao, and Félix Gutiérrez wrote that stereotyping shortcuts character development, especially with portrayals of people of color in American mass media: "It is a means of quickly bringing to the audience's collective consciousness a character's preconceived value system and behavioral expectations. Audience members are then able to assess the character against their own value systems and characterize the character as, for example, 'the villain' or 'the heroine.'"[12] The same goes for class and gender.

Playwright and director Bertolt Brecht wrote and developed a series of learning plays, Lehrstücke, in the 1920s and 1930s that put these quick assumptions on trial. Brecht's learning plays are anti-Aristotelian and didactic plays that invite the audience to produce meaning with the performers. They do not merely "show the world as it is", but "show the world how it changes (and also how it may be changed)."[13] In this genre the theater is metatheater, aware and revealing of its own theatricality in order to provoke its audience to think critically. Many of Brecht's Lehrstücke use allegorical characters standing in for social and economic statuses to make the play's social critique more obvious.

The Exception and the Rule, a lehrstück Brecht wrote in 1930 with collaborators E. Burri and E. Hauptmann, ends with a trial. A rich and impetuous merchant (The Merchant) is charged with murdering his porter (The Coolie). Before the trial, the story follows The Merchant as he ruthlessly pushes The Guide and The Coolie to hurry through the desert in order beat his competitors to Urga. The Merchant's ill preparedness and impulsive firing of The Guide results in him and The Coolie getting lost with only limited supplies. The Coolie, who had been drinking his water sparingly, notices that The Merchant is out of water. Fearing that if he outlives The Merchant he will be sent to jail, The Coolie offers him his canteen. The Merchant, paranoid by how cruelly he had been treating his helper, mistakes the gesture for an assault and in defense shoots and kills The Coolie.

Despite the preponderance of evidence proving that The Merchant killed The Coolie when he offered him his canteen, The Judge acquits The Merchant. He reasons that The Coolie should have been angry with The Merchant because of the mistreatment he was forced to endure. The Court ruled that even if The Coolie was not angry, which would have made him the exception, The Merchant was justified in fearing him because of their class differences. The Court substantiated using stereotypes as a means to justify one's actions, even rationalizing The Merchant's violence.[14] The Court maintained the rule (and the status quo) without consideration of the exception.

In the final moment of the play, the chorus of players advises the audience to question what they accept as normal and to find the ordinary strange. They encourage the audience to find the abuses in sanctioned rules, and finally, to "Do something about it!"[15] The chorus requests that the audience think critically about what they saw and to question the authority and rationale of the Court, especially its assumptions about class. The story invites the audience to consider the relationship between economics and law and to observe how the courts are fallible, producing verdicts that favor some people over others. The court does not solve problems, but presents new ones. On the other end of the spectrum, reality courtroom TV does not invite critical reflection about its process. Rather, the shows rely on general rules, not the exceptions, to make their points. This will become evident in the following case.

Locating the dramas: The personal/social conflict

In the February 14, 2008, case *Kiana vs. Deon* on *Divorce Court*, Judge Lynn Toler used the litigants, a married young black couple, to model the root problems plaguing some poor communities. Though the program is called *Divorce Court*, the cases never conclude by finalizing a divorce, dividing a couple's assets, or assigning parental custody. Instead, the show's hook is that it only stages small claims arbitrations between married couples (or soon-to-be betrothed litigants), which ensures the interpersonal conflicts between the litigants are extremely emotional. The legal dispute provides an entry into the deeper struggles in the litigants' relationship. In this case, plaintiff Kiana Tillery wanted her husband, Deon Tillery, to repay her $500 for the value of a car towed while in his possession. This was the basis of the small claim; however, it only took up a fraction of the episode.

The proceedings began with Judge Toler asking about the money owed, but quickly moved to completely unrelated details about the litigants' marriage. After only a few sentences Judge Toler asked Mrs Tillery to tell the courtroom about their marriage because both claimed the other was cheating. With the studio's rapt attention, the plaintiff tells Toler the reason she came to court is because, "my husband is a liar and a cheater."[16] Right off the bat she admitted the repayment was secondary, so before any information was gleaned regarding the car's towing or how the plaintiff determined the amount owed, the judge urged the plaintiff, and she consented, to talk about her marital problems. After all, cheating spouses are much more interesting than an unpaid debt. Mr Tillery refuted his wife's accusations and then quickly detailed their history. They met when they were young and had a child when he was 15 years old and she was 14 years old. He described sticking it out with her despite his fear of being a father. He confessed that he sacrificed his college scholarships and his possible NBA career in order to be with his wife. His wife challenged his story, but Mr Tillery defended the veracity of his NBA future—a conjecture so clichéd that it sent the audience into a titter. At this point the small claims case was far in the background. What had taken center stage were the problems in the litigants' marriage, Mrs Tillery's teenage pregnancy, and Mr Tillery's shattered NBA dreams. These issues were flamed by Judge Toler's line of questioning.

After a commercial break, Judge Toler called Mr Tillery's witness, his sister, Leandra Lee to the podium. While attesting to the multiple children the plaintiff had both in and out of wedlock and her lying about their paternity, Ms Lee lost her composure and hurled insults at the plaintiff. To break up the chaos, Judge Toler ordered the bailiff to escort Ms Lee from the courtroom. Lee spewed a barrage of invectives all the way off set, and for the moment the scene broke down into the familiar territory of a trash talk show the likes of *Jerry Springer* or *Maury*. Rather than the host encouraging the unprofessional stage fight, on *Divorce Court* the outbursts gave Toler the opportunity to reprimand and instruct the out-of-control litigants, shifting her attention from the micro problems between the couple onto macro issues facing those like the Tillerys—black, uneducated, and poor—and the more pressing concerns that the case raised:

> **Judge Toler** Mr and Mrs Tillery, I see a vision of the future, and it isn't pretty. I see I don't know how many children who have parents who are arguing, fussing and cutting up. Having sex with various people. Bringing home children from different mamas and different daddies. I see a household full of kids with no stability. I see a household full of kids where nobody can pay for extra-curricular activities. Where

college is a distant dream and a bad joke. I see a place where people are worried about what they look like and who they're sleeping with, sex and cell phones, but not with intellect . . . or interests. I see a vision of a future that is dead. If you continue to do what you have done your children will not have the opportunity to do any better. . . . My blessings go out to your children because I'm afraid. My blessings go out to you because I have not given up. My blessings go out to all of you because we need to do better as a people just to have a future. And if you don't believe me, spend some time in a courtroom like I used to do and ask them what their story is.[17] Ask them what their mama and daddy were doing. And you're going to hear the story you just told me. I'm not in a position to give you five hundred dollars. . . . Good luck to you, and I sincerely mean it. There will be no recovery.[18]

Judge Toler directed her address to a collective of viewers—to "all of you"—pleading to "do better as a people."[19] She included herself so that her shaming speech also became a plea with personal resonances. The narrative she recounted of absent fathers and mothers, misplaced values, and lack of educational opportunities was harrowing, but it was the emotional tenor of her entreaty that was most compelling. The litigants' outbursts opened the door for Toler's compassionate and driven performance, and she used these opportunities in ways that made her advising appear rational and caring. Judge Toler secured her position as a figure of sensitive authority while shifting the magnitude of the cases from a petty dispute to a community crisis.

By giving the disputers a public platform, producing for the duration of the program the kind of attention on television usually reserved for media trials—courtroom TV shows elevate the paltry, small claims court-type of quarrel to the level of a social drama with broad, reverberating effects. Anthropologist Victor Turner categorized four phases of the social drama: breach, crisis, redressive action, and reintegration or schism:

> A social drama is initiated when the peaceful tenor of regular, norm-governed social life is interrupted by the *breach* of a rule controlling one of its salient relationships. This leads swiftly or slowly to a state of *crisis*,

which, if not soon sealed off, may split the community into contending factions and coalitions. To prevent this, *redressive* means are taken by those who consider themselves or are considered the most legitimate or authoritative representatives of the relevant community.[20]

Social dramas are "social" by definition; they involve groups, communities, and nations. Individual players enact the main roles, but the social dramas resonate through a whole community. In most cases, the TV judge appears to redress the crisis, assuming the role of powerful authority figure who has the advice that if followed will end both the current predicament and prevent future ones. Like in the Tillerys' case, Judge Toler stands in as a representative of the community she advises. She not only offers an end to the legal dispute, but she also dictates a remedy to problems plaguing black communities. This is par for the course with TV judges who all lecture their litigants in terms that recommend "correct" normative behaviors for all their viewers.[21]

At the end of the case the credits roll over footage of the Tillerys leaving the courtroom. The legal dispute had been settled, but the larger issues are far from remedied. Will the Tillerys' children grow up to be like their parents? Will they go to college? Become teenage parents? Will viewing audiences align their priorities with the ones Judge Toler advances? The episode leaves the cycle of the social drama incomplete, suggesting that the problems featured on the program are far from over. This point is drilled home as advertisements for the next episode present another couple in crisis awaiting Judge Toler's counsel.

The aesthetic drama

Casting is only part of what creates the aesthetics of reality courtroom TV. Directors, designers, camera operators, and editors contribute to the unified vision of each episode, emphasizing key dramatic moments, and sometimes creating them. In addition to the backstage support, during the tapings the performers have to use both simple and complex acting strategies to convey the impression that they are actually in court, to persuade the judge and the viewing audience that their position is both morally good and deserving of the requested award, and finally, to convincingly do so as if they are not acting at all. The live performance works with the edited product to craft the look and feel of reality courtroom TV.

Richard Schechner described unique attributes of aesthetic drama: "Aesthetic drama is almost entirely prearranged, and the participants can concentrate not on strategies for achieving their goals ... but on displays. Aesthetic drama is less instrumental and more ornamental than social drama."[22] In courtroom TV shows (and in many media trials, for that matter) aesthetic aims are in play with interpersonal conflicts and legal objectives. The litigants focus both on displaying themselves—looking good and performing well—and on strategies to achieve their goals—whether they are winning the award, having their side of the story heard by a national audience, or humiliating one's adversary. The attributes Schechner ascribed to each are difficult to separate during the live event of reality courtroom TV. Rather, the performance aims oscillate between winning the arbitration and displaying oneself for the audience. Sometimes these aims are in concert, and other times they conflict with each other. This tension between wanting to give a good performance and fulfilling a legal procedure has been the source of much debate around law and entertainment since the broadcasting of the first law related radio program (see Chapter 5). This is because certain fields like law and politics explicitly use theatrical and aesthetic strategies while hiding that they do so.

I observed this strain between the displaying and the strategizing from on set. Over the course of 3 years, I sat in reality courtroom TV audiences to study how they worked from the inside of the production. From on set, backstage and in the studio waiting rooms I witnessed the seams of production and how the reality courtroom TV performance was cultivated during the live event. I perceived moments of genuineness and surprise and also the crafted reaction sequences. I experienced being directed on camera, and I watched as the star judges stopped and restarted, altering their decisions and delivery at the director's command. I also understood what it was to be a part of the production and how my role as an audience member contributed to the drama. From on set I became familiar with the audience's contribution to the meaning making of the programs and how the audience experience is a vantage point from which to study the live event.

The audience role

Many media and communication scholars have theorized the role of the studio audience, especially on talk shows (see Livingstone 1994; McKenzie 2000; Annese 2004; Gamson 1998; Nabi and Hendriks 2003). While the formats share some similarities, there are fundamental differences that I experienced firsthand as both a studio audience member and a home viewer. Both positions informed my viewing. As a home viewer I looked at the televisual effects of courtroom studio audience shots, and as a studio audience member I studied how production staff directs the studio audience during tapings, making the audience another actor in the performance.

Unlike on talk shows, the reality courtroom TV studio audience is univocular, a chorus with no soloists. Audience members are rarely, if ever, distinguished from one another during the cases. They are shown as a group seated behind the litigants, and like a stage scrim they are background to the main event. Their background role certifies the authenticity of the disputes. Just as actual courtrooms have a gallery of viewers, so the TV courtroom reproduces this audience. But in addition, the TV gallery is extremely full, diverse, and active relative to what is mostly an extremely desultory actual courtroom (celebrity trials and show trials aside).

The audience's position in frame is strategic. On every reality courtroom TV show the audience is always seen in the background of shots featuring the litigants. The litigants stand behind podiums and face the judge. The positioning in the television courtrooms blocks the studio audience from seeing the litigants' faces during the case because the litigants' backs are to the audience. The only time audiences see the litigants' faces is during their quick exit from the courtroom stage. This means that the emotional or interpersonal cues the litigants use to convey and to convince are not visible to the studio audience—only to the judge. The visual positioning of the audience aligns them with the litigants and divides them from the judge and bailiff. The litigants appear as part of the audience, as if they could have emerged from it. The framing suggests that the litigants and the audience are alike. It is a harbinger; if the audience is not careful, they too could be standing behind those podiums. Thus it follows that from the perspective of the judge it appears as if the litigants could be audience members and vice versa—as if the litigants are emerging from the lookers and are part of the community represented by the studio audience. The judge is literally "on high," the sole authority, and the only one not on trial.

Because of this positioning, the studio audience only sees the judge's reactions. Sandwiching the litigants between the visual paths of the judge and studio audience forces the audience to experience the litigants through the judge's reactions to them. This firms the judge's role as superior judger—a status confirmed by the raised bench overlooking both litigants and studio audience. The studio audience and the litigants are "beneath" the judge spatially and in status. This relationship is quite different from the studio audience's role on a talk show where audiences are often arranged in a raked auditorium as in a theater. Talk show guests sit on couches or across a desk from the talk show host. A feeling of informality and equality is fostered between the guests and the host. By contrast, judge shows emphasize formality and inequality. Talk shows facilitate audience dialog; judge shows work from agonistic encounters—litigants challenging each other (or the judge challenging litigants)—and opinions delivered from on high. On talk shows the guests try to ingratiate themselves with the audience because so much of the show's allotted time is given to audience response.[23] On reality courtroom TV shows it does not matter if the audience likes one or the other litigant; they are there to like the judge.

However, the judges, stage managers, and audience coordinators cue and direct the reality courtrooms' studio audiences' reactions. The studio audience functions as the visible confirmation of the judge's actions and decisions. They support the judge, the program's leading actor. Directors and audience coordinators organize the audience to always be in agreement with the judge, to find the judge funny, and to appear persuaded by the judge's passionate discourse and moralizing: "The value that the programme producers assign to the judges' raw emotionalism is evident when one considers how closely both their performances and the studio audience reactions to these are followed by the camera."[24] Cameras track the judges' heightened emotional performance and the studio audience's unanimous and approving responses to it.

The studio audience community is intended to be representative of the viewing audience in the same way that an actual jury is intended to be representative of the defendant's peers: a broad sampling of the population. (Of course, the studio audience, unlike a jury, has no determination in the outcome of the case.) The studio audience models the correct reactions to the home audience. The viewer can always look to his or her TV "reflection" for response cues. In their 2003 study of host and studio audience reaction shots, Robin Nabi and Alexandra Hendriks concluded that TV viewing audiences create impressions based on attitudinal reaction shots, especially when in a passive viewing position: "As either motivation or ability is impaired, peripheral processing is expected to predominate, during which simple cues present in the persuasive setting are most likely to influence attitudinal response."[25] Studio response shots intend to influence the home viewing audience's interpretation of the episode. Because of the diverse demographic of the studio audience, the home viewer can almost always see someone like herself and check in with how that likeness reacts.

This is useful when trying to convey a particular image and brand of the star judge. In his study of interaudience reactions, Cal Hylton determined that home viewers who observed audience members in agreement with the program's host and approving of his or her position (with head nod and smiles) were "more likely to rate the speaker as authoritative and dynamic and to hold favorable attitudes toward the topic under discussion."[26] The same went for the converse: "... [T]hose who observed audiences reacting negatively held less favorable attitudes toward both speaker and topic."[27] Similarly, Hendriks and Nabi's study found that visibly representing group agreement with the host or emcee influenced home viewers' perceptions of that host as an authority. The studio audience functions similarly on reality courtroom TV; their collective agreement with the judge is intended to confirm his/her authority to the home viewing audience. To create this sense of agreement during the tapings, stage managers coach audience reactions, and the camera angles and the staging support the studio audience's role. During postproduction, editors cut reaction shots into the episode evidencing audience agreement. This marks a stark contrast with the critical responses Brecht's *The Exception and the Rule* intended to evoke.

While the studio audience is always univocular, some programs provide controlled outlets for viewer responses. *Judge Alex* asks home viewers to call in and share their opinions on the case. On *The People's Court* Harvey Levin, a lawyer, journalist, and TV producer who went on to be the star and creator of TMZ television, stands in Times Square with a selection of people who watch the cases with him. During the breaks, the show cuts to Levin and his guest commentators. He asks them a question and quickly passes the microphone to give a few of the bystanders time to voice their opinions. Some episodes of *Judge Joe Brown* featured a "polling the audience" section where the hired audience voted "yes" or "no" to questions about the progress of the case. Votes were compiled and became part of a statistic that had no impact on the outcome of the case. Across the board, studio audience members never express their opinions of the case as it unfolds during the episode, a device that ensures the judge's unilateral control over the courtroom.

Playing the audience

In their research on studio audiences in the 1950s, Donald Horton and Anselm Strauss noted that part of the reason the structure of audience-as-confirmer goes uncontested is because the studio audience's behavior is not only directed by the stage manager, but is also guided by their familiarity with the genre: "Within all the established forms of programs, there have evolved routine types of stage action to which audiences have grown accustomed." When new programs debut, audiences acquainted with the form already know what to expect: "Familiarity with the media prepares viewers for new formats."[28] Watching television familiarizes studio audiences with performance expectations so that they have some sense of their role before going on set.

While some reality courtroom TV programs have open audiences, meaning both hired background actors and ticketed guests compose the audience, other programs employ background actors exclusively.[29] These shows have closed audiences. *The People's Court, Judge David Young, Judge Hatchett, Judge Maria Lopez,* and *Judge Karen* had open audiences with both guest audience members and hired background actors. *Judge Judy, Divorce Court,* and *Judge Joe Brown* hired only paid background actors. By special request, shows with closed audiences will allow a limited number of visitors to sit in the audience without pay. This is how I was able to attend *Judge Joe Brown* and *Judge Judy*.

Regardless of whether one is paid or not, all audience members are directed to perform certain actions. Once on set, most of the studio audience experiences I had were similar in process. This was especially true for programs produced by the same company. Though the sets and judges were different, many of the production staff and the procedures were the same. Being a studio audience member is an all-day experience, and only after waiting backstage—sometimes for hours—does the on set experience begin.[30] Upon entering set, the audience coordinators arrange the seating, placing people with bright colored clothing among those wearing darker colors, peppering young audience members among older folks, and arranging the seating so the audience appears diverse.

After the audience has the right look, the rehearsal process begins. At Metropolis Studios in New York City, audience coordinators began by leading warm-ups with games and jokes to get the audience excited for the case. (These warm-ups were for the ticketed guests, and this was the only studio I went to where this happened.) At every taping I attended, we were reminded that our energy helps the judge give a good performance. Our performances, we were told, bears on the judge's. Then, a stage manager or audience coordinator introduced the audience to the rules of the set such as no loud talking, no sleeping, and no outbursts.

Whether or not the audience member was a guest or a paid actor, she was asked to do some simple acting during the taping such as give off the impression that she was interested in the case, smile, clap, look amused, show disdain, and talk to her neighbor using "courtroom conversation."[31] This last term described the soft and lightly animated chitchat one imagines people sitting in a courtroom gallery would have. Loud, boisterous talk was not permitted. At a *Judge Judy* taping, the stage manager warned audiences that outbursts would result in their expulsion from set, and she recounted a story of a woman so enthused by Sheindlin's decision she hollered, "You go girl!"[32] The woman was subsequently removed from the audience.

Once the taping began, the stage manager, or someone just off camera, would periodically give instructions to the audience. On *Judge Joe Brown* and *Judge Judy* the stage manager directed the audience with hand signals to smile, applaud, and look awake. On *Judge Joe Brown* there was an additional cameraman with a hand-held camera who zoomed in on coached audience reactions. No complex acting skills were needed.

The audience vantage point: Seeing the seams

The studio audience sees the judges and litigants when they are not on camera, and these breaks reveal the difference between the TV personas and the people playing those roles. Judge Hatchett, who on her program was quite serious and sincere, always entered set by strutting across the stage showing off her newest pair of shoes. Production staff coached us to stand up and applaud as she lifted the bottom of her robe to display her new pumps. Her celebrity persona, the one that lavished in the luxuries having her own show afforded her, did not mesh with her judge character. Only in these few moments before the cameras were rolling did Hatchett strut like a star. Judge David Young seemed to love his studio audience, and at several tapings I attended he came out into the audience to talk to us, waved to audience regulars who he knew by name, and appeared genuinely interested in meeting us. He looked like he relished these moments when he could be loose and funny. Young did bring his lightness and humor on to the program, but we saw a freer version before the show began, and the audience loved it. Judge David Young was gracious, kind, and funny. He won us over in his introduction, and by the time the taping began we were energized and excited to watch him hear the upcoming cases.

Young was also comfortable articulating the difference between what he did on his program and the legal obligations he fulfilled as a judge in Miami. When I asked if he thought what he did on the show was practicing law, he responded, "No, I'm performing it."[33] (Some judges are less willing to admit the difference.) He never tried to hide the performance aspects of his program when the cameras were not rolling. At a May 8, 2008, taping, Young ingratiated himself to us before the taping with his lively telling of how he was "discovered":

> For those of you who don't know anything about me, Google me. (*Audience Laughs*) No, I was a judge in Miami for almost fifteen years. I was in criminal court. The way I was discovered, I guess, was I was a judge—Guys, do y'all remember the case where the two America West pilots were flying the airplane while they were drunk? (*Audience says "Yes."*) That was my case. So that's how Sony pictures television found me. I've worked with Janet Reno. I was one of her assistants. I also worked for F. Lee Bailey—his law firm when I was

in law school. So I have a little bit of experience as a prosecutor and defense lawyer.... I'm just really happy you're here and decided to spend the day with us. Does anyone have any questions you'd like to ask? Yes m'aam.

A woman in the audience asked Young how long he had been with his bailiff Tawya. Young looked momentarily pensive before he wittily answered, "Let's see, it was a dark and cold night." The audience ate it up, laughing heartily. Before he could take another question the stage manager interrupted to tell Young the taping was going to start. As he was being pulled off set he made sure to tell the audience how much he appreciated us being there.[34]

Between takes Judge David would, at times, break character to entertain the audience. During an April 10, 2008, taping, a technical glitch stopped the filming at an inopportune moment—right before a specialist telecast in from Chicago was going to announce the paternity of the plaintiff's child. The monitors in the courtroom lost connection with the lab, so staff milled about the stage trying to fix the problem while the camera operators took a breather. I watched the plaintiff nervously take his wife's hand in his, squeezing it as he sheepishly looked around the set waiting to find out if the children he raised as his own were biologically his. The litigants' vulnerability was palpable as they waited for production to restart. Despite the intensity of the moment, Judge Young joked with the audience, "Let me tell you, this doesn't happen in real court." When the filming broke down, Young relaxed into his jovial self and was not concerned with maintaining the decorum of the courtroom or committing to what Konstantin Stanislavsky called the "given circumstances."[35]

This moment marked the difference in the taping for the judge and the litigants. While the taping allowed Young to take a break from the drama, the litigants did not have that same luxury. They were embroiled in an emotional situation that did not stop with the cameras. In fact, when production paused, the litigants looked even tenser because the break in the action highlighted the theatrical conventions of the program, which were details that conflicted with the reality of their predicament. This is not to say that Young did not care about his litigants. In fact, in our conversations he made it clear to me how much sympathy he had for the people in his courtroom. Rather, as a performer he broke character when the cameras were off, and these moments evidenced the friction between the personal drama and the way that drama is captured and made for TV.

After a few minutes the telecast was reconnected, the cameras rolled, and the doctor revealed that the plaintiff was the father to the second child as well as the first. When the case aired, the home viewing audience saw the case run smoothly, with the doctor seamlessly announcing the paternity of both children.[36] The technical malfunctions, the judge's asides, the breaks in the suspension of disbelief and acting in agreement with the given circumstances, and the defendant's nervous handholding were all beyond the cameras' scope and therefore not in the episode.

Audience members are privy to more than technical failures; they also witness the judges lose their composure. Judge Karen, the former star of her eponymous show, *Judge Karen,* maintained a professional demeanor when on set. She was all business and approached the cases with poise and control—except during the last case of the day during a June 17, 2008, taping. The plaintiff was a batty, elderly woman who presented what seemed like a bogus complaint about her young upstairs neighbor that concluded with a description of him drilling a hole in his floor so he could spy on her. Seemingly offended by the case's ridiculousness, Judge Karen Upped and left set, muttering loudly enough for the audience to hear, "I am not going to do this." The litigants looked stunned as the production staff left their posts to see what was going to happen next. None of us in the audience knew whether or not she would come back to finish the case, but after a few minutes, Judge Karen returned to set. The taping restarted and she heard the case without any trace of the anger or frustration that drove her off set a few minutes before. Whatever happened offstage convinced her to return and finish the taping. TV cases give judges an opportunity for do-overs, a luxury that actual courts disallow, but they also require the star judges to hear cases that they might have otherwise dismissed in an actual court.

In addition to the breaks in character, TV judges also have to follow the director's instructions in order to get both good footage and a good performance. During *Judge David Young* tapings one of the stage managers stationed off camera had a sign she would hold up to him that said, "Belly mark." This reminded the judge to position himself in a particular orientation to the bench so that he would be well placed in the shot. Whenever he was off his mark, she held up the sign. Young also had a phone on his desk that was used to deliver instructions from the director's booth. During several of the tapings I attended, the phone would ring and interrupt the taping in order to direct Young to bring up a particular bit of information or to revise his decision. Some TV judges wear ear buds to communicate with producers and directors. This means the star judges do not have to remember all the applicable state laws or details of the case because they are continuously being fed information by the production team. This, of course, helps in their appearance of being all-knowing. The information also assists in directing the cases toward more dramatic moments by offering the judges juicy details the litigants revealed to producers or in their complaints.

In a case involving a plaintiff suing her hairdresser for overprocessing her hair resulting in it falling out and the plaintiff losing her self-esteem, Young initially sympathized with the plaintiff. After listening to her describe how badly she felt about herself and then consoling her by telling the plaintiff she was beautiful, Young agreed to award her $2,000 for pain and suffering. Instead of accepting the amount, the plaintiff interrupted Young to ask for more. The plaintiff's disruptions violated the power structure of Young's courtroom, so to punish her for not complying Judge Young reduced her award by $1,000, warning her that if she interrupted again he would give her nothing. Seconds after his caveat, the phone rang. Young listened, hung up, and then told the plaintiff he would pretend she apologized and was not so rude. When the cameras rolled, Young restated his decision, awarding her the original amount of $2,000. The second take excluded the moment of discipline in the first, displaying a softer side of Young, and one that the director must have believed was better suited for the *Judge David Young* brand. The show's dramaturgical needs superseded Young's intuitive response.

Because reality courtroom TV is predominantly unscripted, the judges might miss a moment that the director wanted or that would help the editing team tell a particular story. During an April 10, 2008, taping of *Judge David Young* the director wanted to get reaction shots of Tawya Young, the bailiff, and Judge Young. After the litigants left the set, the cameras moved close to the judge. The stage manager whispered direction. The cameras rolled and Judge David raised his eyebrows, looked to the bailiff, and he said, "Well, how about that?" He said it again. Then he said it again. The stage manager listened on her headset for directions to relay to the judge. After the shots were approved the cameras moved over to the bailiff. The bailiff made some facial expressions to the camera, raised her eyebrows, and looked at the judge. She did it a couple of times until the stage manager indicated they could move on. When their pickups were complete, Young smiled at us and joked, "I smell an Emmy."[37]

Being in the audience also provided a vantage point from which to observe production staff and the directors rehearsing with the litigants, although the majority of the litigants' preparation happened backstage, far off set. Producers worked with the litigants once they arrived at the studio. Traditionally, the two opposing parties are kept separate from each other, arriving at different times and in different cars and placed in waiting rooms far from each other. The production staff tries to keep them from running into each other prior to the taping.[38] (There was always security around in case a physical altercation erupted.) In the waiting rooms producers go through the litigants evidence and walk them through their stories to make sure they can tell them clearly. They emphasize the importance of having a beginning, middle, and end. The producers ask the litigants to pretend they are the judge, and they rehearse their arguments.[39] The final instructions come right before the litigants go on set. Producers ask the litigants to tell them the three points they want to make.[40] Producers help the litigants craft their stories and the impressions they want to make by using the personal information the litigants told producers and wrote down in their complaints. The producers, like theater directors, help the participants piece together their motivations and objectives before going on stage. Unlike in text-based theater where actors turn to the script for information about the characters, courtroom TV participants' lives are the texts used to craft convincing impressions. Producers and directors mine the litigants' personal testimonies to find facts they can use in order to get the performances they want from the participants.

While the majority of the rehearsing happened off set, before the taping began the litigants were brought on stage to go over where their marks were (where to stand) and how to use the equipment, such as the projectors affixed to the litigants' stands on *Judge Karen's* set. Producers took the litigants on a walk-through, showing them where they would enter and exit. On some shows, the litigants recorded excerpts for the episodes prior to the case's taping. During the tapings of *Judge David Young,* the production staff always began by taking each litigant to a backstage area to tape an additional segment. Litigants stood against a green screen (a green backdrop that allowed editors to fill in whatever graphics and background they wanted in postproduction) while producers fed them lines to repeat. The litigants copied both the words the producer said and their inflection. At the taping of the hairdresser case outlined above, I could hear the staff and the litigants trying to get the right tone to the lines summarizing their complaints. Producers had the litigant repeat the lines until she said them to the director's liking.

Figure 1 Judge Karen set: The audience relaxes while production gets ready for the taping. Author's photo, June 3, 2008. New York City.

Figure 2 Judge Karen set: The stage manager shows the litigants around the set. Author's photo, June 3, 2008. New York City.

Figure 3 Judge Judy set: Audience leaves to take a break off set. Author's photo, October 1, 2008. Los Angeles.

Figure 4 Judge Judy set: A view from outside the courtroom set. Author's photo, October 1, 2008. Los Angeles.

Nonacting on reality courtroom TV

The judges', litigants', witnesses', bailiffs', and audiences' performances on reality courtroom TV shows are, for the duration of the episode, nonprofessional actors presenting themselves as characters in a courtroom drama where these characters are versions of themselves they would like others to see. They follow the staging assigned to each role by the producers and directors of the programs, and in addition to following the choreography, the participants have to give off convincing impressions. They do this with the awareness that they are being filmed and that they are performing for three different audiences: the other participants, the live studio audience, and the eventual home viewing audience who watches the show after it is edited. Their impressions take into consideration the given circumstances of the drama, which includes pretending to be in a real court and participating in a trial even though everyone knows the shows are being videotaped on a stage in a television studio.

Figure 5 Judge Judy set: The empty bench with cameras. Author's photo, October 1, 2008. Los Angeles.

Figure 6 The People's Court set: Empty bench with lights. Author's photo, May 26, 2009. New York City.

Figure 7 The People's Court set: The camera in the entrance. Author's photo, May 26, 2009. New York City.

Figure 8 Judge David Young set: Camera in the courtroom. Author's photo, April 10, 2008. New York City.

Participants have to fulfill their character's objectives (the plaintiff's, the defendant's, the bailiff's and the judge's) and compellingly portray their assigned roles. These objectives shift according to the role. The litigants, cast as defendants or plaintiffs, have to persuade the judge that they are right and deserve to win the case (or use their stage time to make a public declaration, get closure, or humiliate their opponents); the judge has to act authoritatively and decide the case while simultaneously being entertaining; the spectators have to act like they are in a courtroom and interested in the proceedings; the bailiff has to look like the judge's muscle and add supportive and funny affirmations when permitted; the court reporter has to continue the drama by asking the winning and losing litigants probing questions about the outcome of their cases.

Even though actors on reality courtroom TV may be playing the same roles they inhabited in their real lives, the circumstances of the production frames them differently. It is verisimilitude; it has the appearance of being true and real, yet it is not quite. And as Roland Barthes wrote, "verisimilitude is never anything but *opinable*: it is entirely subject to (public) opinion."[41] As discussed earlier, the reality of reality courtroom TV is organized around an idea of TV court process established by other reality courtroom TV shows that are loosely based on small claims trials. It is a constructed reality rather than a veritable one.

Producers control the gap between the performance and the arbitration by maintaining the fiction that the studio is a courtroom on and off the set. The litigants are told to "enter the courtroom" and not "enter the set." They go over their "testimony" and not their "lines." They get "sworn in." When in the courtroom they are seated facing the judge (as they would in a real court) and not the audience. The staff continuously reminds the audience and the litigants that they are in a court and to behave accordingly. The production staff's treatment of the circumstances as if they were real curbs the anxiety a nonactor might feel when having to perform in a theater and on a stage. By insisting that the stage is really a court, the producers draw on most people's common knowledge of what it means to be in a court. Some of this knowledge is doubtlessly derived from television with its many courtroom dramas, and even from viewing other reality courtroom TV shows. Once the production staff convinces the participants that they are entering a courtroom, everyone can focus on their performances of themselves trying to behave as if they were not acting at all.

The circumstances of production also drive multiple intentions. There is constant fluctuation between the litigants' desire to win and to display. As mentioned earlier, winning and displaying are not completely separate. Displaying requires deliberate, self-conscious, and planned self-presentation. For example, a litigant who when the cameras are not rolling is gruff and callous might try, when the cameras are on, to display herself as kind and thoughtful by standing upright, speaking clearly and softly, and dressing conservatively. These deliberate performance adjustments are tactics the litigant uses to convince the judge to take her side. Displaying and winning, in this instance, work together. Another litigant may care less about winning and more about using the opportunity to promote his new album or acting career, like when the Naked Cowboy (actor Robert Burck who is best known for standing only in his underwear, cowboy boots and a cowboy hat in the middle of Times Square, NYC) appeared on *Cristina's Court*, topless and with his guitar. In the midst of the case Judge Cristina asked him to play a song.[42] In this case, displaying trumped winning.

The acting on courtroom TV shows oscillates between the litigants' presentation of the version they want others to see and an uncontrolled explosion of feeling that emerges when fueled by emotions and the sheer excitement of being on "trial." For example, during the *Divorce Court* case discussed earlier in this chapter, the litigants broke character when Ms Lee took the stand to talk about her brother and Mrs Tillery's relationship. The two women started shouting at each other, and there even seemed to be danger of a physical fight. The frenzied tussle disrupted their initial calm presentations. Their behavior was wild and childish, inappropriate for the courtroom, but very entertaining for television.

The draw of reality courtroom shows comes, in part, from watching nonactors act badly. The bad acting of reality shows is convincing evidence that what's happening is real. For example, one could say of a poor performance on a scripted show, "So and so' is a bad actor," which is very different from watching someone doing something wrong, immoral, or against ethical codes. We say of the "real person," "So-and-so" acted badly, but we mean something very different by the word "acting" than we mean when discussing the work of a professional actor. In reality TV terms, the evangelical pastor and *Divorce Court* litigant Ted Haggard "acted badly" when he had a homosexual affair with his methamphetamine dealer because his behavior violated his contract with his wife and the morality he preached to his mega church congregation.[43] But when Haggard appeared on *Divorce Court*, he "acted good" by behaving as expected in the television courtroom. Reality courtroom show litigants can act badly while on set if they disobey the judge's orders and courtroom rules. Of course judges periodically goad the litigants into acting badly because it is not only entertaining, but also gives the judges the opportunity to discipline the litigants, demonstrating their authority. Judges also use these heated dramatic conflicts to teach the litigants (and the audiences) how they should behave—how to act good.

In these moments of acting badly on reality courtroom shows, nonactors demonstrate the qualities of great performers: full commitment and investment in the reality of the world being presented through heightened and dynamic self-presentation. Editors and producers bank on these breaks in character because they are fun to watch and dislocate the monotony of the predictable trial proceeding. Directors know the entertainment value in these behavioral lapses, and they urge the judges to ask the litigants provocative questions to create these moments of conflict and of true nonacting.

Michael Kirby distinguished different modes of acting by registering a matrix of performance from simple to complex. He drew a continuum from the "nonmatrixed performer" at one end, a performer who is not pretending to be someone or somewhere or in a situation he or she is not, to the "complex actor," a trained performer, on the other. He called this a "continuum of behavior."[44] Kirby introduced the concept of nonacting by saying it was the kind of performance enacted by participants in most Happenings, art events popularized in the United States in the late 1950s during which participants tended to complete a series of tasks[45]: "Although acting was sometimes used, the performers in Happenings generally tended to 'be' nobody or nothing other than themselves; nor did they represent, or pretend to be in, a time or place different from that of the spectator."[46] Kirby placed complex acting—the kind of technical acting advocated by Stanislavsky's "System"—on the opposite end of the spectrum from Happenings. The actor performing complex acting has to portray a character, convey an emotional condition, and do things that the character would do in his or her imaginary given place and time. These given circumstances are different from the place and time and circumstance of the spectator or the actor when not in character.

Kirby defined complex acting as feigning, representing, simulating, or impersonating on one end, and nonacting as just behaving, putting on no pretenses, and being in the same world as the spectator on the other. Participating in reality courtroom TV shows does not require actor training because the premise of reality TV is that the subjects on it are acting like themselves. (Even though this is the premise, some reality shows have writers and directors that help craft, coach and enhance the reality presented.) However, the contexts of the tapings demand that participants act like they are in court and sustain the intensity of their argumentation during interruptions due to production needs. Additionally, participants have to convince and persuade the judge to take a side while pretending to be in an actual courtroom. There is pretense involved, and this requires acting. This is not so far off from the kind of acting one might employ in his or her everyday life to give off a particular self-presentation.

Sociologist Erving Goffman's analysis addressed the techniques people use in everyday interactions to control how others perceive them: "... I assume that when an individual appears before others he will have many motives for trying to control the impression they receive of the situation."[47] He studied the techniques people used to make these impressions, calling them "dramaturgical problems" with the performance of self. Like the reality courtroom TV litigant, the individual is also aware of being judged. Goffman conferred that "in the capacity as performers" individuals tend to be driven less by their moral compass and more by the desire to create the impression that they have a good moral compass. On reality TV, participants are not only concerned with conveying a particular impression to each other, but also to audience members they do not know.

Like in social situations, saying someone on reality TV is acting has a negative connotation. The epistemic grounding of reality TV is that the events and people captured are performing as normal and natural versions of themselves. Even though the viewing audience probably knows that what they are seeing is carefully edited, the suspension of disbelief is such that the behavior in the TV courtroom is *as if* real. Reality TV shows are premised on the belief that it is possible to see people as they are, an ontological position diametrically opposed to what an actor does—pretending to be someone else through any number of techniques. Acting is the craft of intentionally presenting a character, even when the actor's technique may be to access and express truthful reactions and personal details in order to reveal a character (like Lee Strasberg's Method.).[48] On reality TV, there is supposed to be no separation between self and character, and when there is, when audiences see the subject acting inorganically and violating the premise of the format, their performance is read as insincere. The challenge to reality TV actors is *to act as if they are not* acting. The same conditions of sincerity that apply in social interactions also apply to reality TV performances.

Barthes wrote of this conflict of self-presentation when having his portrait taken: "I lend myself to the social game, I pose, I know I am posing, I want you to know that I am posing, but (to square the circle) this additional message must in no way alter the precious essence of my individuality: what I am, apart from any effigy."[49] Barthes wrote of the double-consciousness experienced when facing the camera's lens: the self I *believe* I am, and the self that I *want to express* in and for the record. Though professional actors and models, regulars in front of the camera, may also experience this anxiety, it is particularly acute for those not used to crafting an image for the lens. It takes practice to master one's portrait. The very act of having someone watching changes things. Furthermore, this lack of control does not mean the subject ceases trying to assert control over her or his image. Rather, the act of capturing someone on film or videotape motivates the act of trying to portray "the one I want others to think I am."

Allan Kaprow knew the impossibility of letting reality go un-crafted once it is framed as performance. He discussed this tension in regard to Happenings: "When you do life consciously, however, life becomes pretty strange—paying attention changes the thing attended to—so the Happenings were not nearly as lifelike as I had supposed they might be. But I learned something about life and 'life.'"[50] Participants on reality TV tend to "do life consciously." Their self-consciousness guides their performance for an audience and cannot help but make "doing life" a little bit strange. It is lifelike, but it is not quite, not exactly, life.

Baudrillard connected this recognizable strangeness to a burst of excitement in the viewer, to a "frisson":

> In the "verité" experience it is not a question of secrecy or perversion, but of a sort of frisson of the real, or of an aesthetics of the hyperreal, a frisson of vertiginous and phony exactitude, a frisson of simultaneous distancing and magnification, of distortion of scale, of an excessive transparency. The pleasure of an excess of meaning, when the bar of the sign falls below the usual waterline of meaning: the nonsignifier is exalted by the camera angle.[51]

Baudrillard described the experience as kinetic. He attributed it to seeing the nonextraordinary, the unrepresentative, exalted by a "camera angle," and from seeing what seems to be an exact replica, the "phony exactitude," of the everyday on screen. This causes a crisis of perspective: everything feels both magnified and completely distanced, normal and spectacular, familiar and also strange.

This kind of tension is not unique to reality TV. During the mid-twentieth century, American and European avant-garde artists began to open up and experiment more radically with what Allan Kaprow called "lifelike art" as distinct from "artlike art." Kaprow:

> Simplistically put, artlike art holds that art is separate from life and everything else, whereas lifelike art holds that art is connected to life and everything else. In other words, there is art at the service of art and art at the service of life. The maker of artlike art tends to be a specialist; the maker of lifelike art, a generalist.[52]

Kaprow played and experimented with the art/life divide. These investigations challenged the "frame," or how the context of place and time determine what something is, such as how viewers read objects and performances in places such as museums, concert halls and theaters. Kaprow worked against these "frames of mind," the way that viewers' preconceptions about a place informs the viewers' understanding of what is inside them: "In fact, museums, concert halls, and theaters needn't have a thing in them; they are still the signs for art. Like the dog in Ivan Pavlov's conditioned-reflex experiment, we spontaneously salivate a million artworks when they are even mentioned."⁵³

Just as Marcel DuChamp in 1917 challenged the meaning of art by submitting a urinal as the "readymade" piece "Fountain" for an exhibition of the Society for Independent Artists, many performance artists and theater experimenters in the 1950s and 1960s challenged the meaning of theater by expanding the possibilities of the theatrical event. They said that life, real life, is theater even if it does not happen in a designated theater building. Art performances took place in storefronts, apartments, streets . . . anywhere. The theater also became a place where real life could happen and where the performances had consequences beyond any fictional circumstances. In Richard Schechner's *Dionysus in 69*, performers invited audience members to participate in the Total Caress, during which actors and audience members would touch, fondle, kiss each other, and more. Performance artist Chris Burden put pressure on the art/life divide in his 1971 piece "Shoot" in which his assistant shot him in the left arm with a 22-caliber rifle. The Living Theatre members lived communally, and their 1968 touring production of *Paradise Now* was a partly improvised and audience participatory expression of the core beliefs they lived by in Paris.

Reality TV also promises audiences that life can happen, really and truthfully, even within the context of television. It may be more than a coincidence that Craig Gilbert's production of *An American Family*, known as the first reality TV show, was filmed the same year Burden's assistant pulled the trigger and only a few years after *Dionysus in 69* and the Living Theatre's *Paradise Now* played in cities all across America in 1968. Experimental theater and performance art as well as the cinéma vérité movement helped lay the groundwork for reality TV.

The editorial wink

Once the taping is completed and the footage goes into postproduction, the courtroom TV shows' dramas take on a new life. The raw material of the studio courtroom is edited and manipulated by the postproduction staff. They cut the footage down into 3 to 5-minute segments, add interstitials, music, and graphics, and they shape the arc of the case. Some moments are added, while others are excised. The final cut is a composite of parts, and therefore what the studio audience saw at the taping might be presented differently to the home viewing audience.

Postproduction is a creative process. Editors and producers control how they want the characters on the programs to be perceived. Tim Sullivan, Senior Vice President of Core Media Group, says: "Editing plays a huge role in all of these shows.... One of the more surprising things about reality TV was how much storytelling is involved, and that you can tell any story you want."[54] The tendency on courtroom TV shows is for editors to hunt for the juiciest bits of material to make the episode interesting. Editors exploit the mishaps and the bumbles of the participants, such as when during a *Divorce Court* episode the litigant's dentures flew out of her mouth while yelling at her husband. For the rest of the episode all the interstitials replayed that moment again and again.[55] The interstitial for the Tillerys' case on *Divorce Court* reran the fight between Mrs Tillery and Ms Lee. Editors profit from these outlandish moments, especially when the seams show—the unguarded "real moments" in the participants' performances. Exposure to these interstitials and the commercial breaks are part of what differentiates the live viewing experience from the home audience's.

Graphics and added captions also shape the episodes. For example, during the Tillerys' case on *Divorce Court* the editor's additions sent a clear message to the audience about the program's view of the plaintiff. Though Mrs Tillery admitted she had four children fathered by men other than her husband she put Mr Tillery's name on the birth certificates, pinning him with child support. Mrs Tillery denied this accusation, telling the judge that she never misled Mr Tillery or tried to make him think that the children were his. Then Judge Toler asked Mrs Tillery the names of her children. Cameras moved in to a close-up on Mrs Tillery as she listed the names of her seven children, and one by one they appeared sequentially along the right side of the frame: Deona, Deon Jr, Deonvey, Deonte, Demonte, Deondrus, and Myana. Mrs Tillery's face, pursed into a grimace, looked just off camera as her children's names boxed her into the frame. The image confronted Mrs Tillery with the lies she told her husband. Each child whose name began with "Deon" and was not her husband's child seemed to validate Mr Tillery's complaint that his wife was a fraud who tricked him into paying for child support. The editing helped build the case against Mrs Tillery that she was an irresponsible mother having too many children with different fathers. But within this configuring, the scenario was comedic because of its excess, and this excess was punctuated by the listed names captioned in the close-up frame. The audience laughed at Mrs Tillery's seemingly endless list of children. As this editing choice illustrated, the program used technical elements beyond the purview of the testimonies to entertainingly create visual support for the parenting lessons Judge Toler offered at the end of the case.

Along with the edits, the graphics add to the episode's narrative. Most often these are short descriptions of the material complaint, but occasionally the blurbs are more colorful, such as this one from a different episode of *Divorce Court*: "Jason Tjapkes: Wants a divorce from Jennifer after 6 years of marriage" and "Jennifer says he's a bigamist."[56] At the time of the taping, the litigants are unaware of what phrases will run under their images. During the taping the defendant might have been saying how much he tried to please his wife, as in the May 14, 2008 case of "Mary Steele vs. Todd Steele" on *Divorce Court*, while the subtitle contradicted the defendant's statements. The phrase that ran under the defendant's close-up read: "Mary says he's a big mama's boy."[57] These subtitles create a visual schism between the litigant who is representing him or herself in a certain way and the caption's explanation. The caption may express something different from the impression the litigant is trying to make. This Brechtian relationship between the actor's performance and the caption describing it makes it so the audience has to negotiate two impressions at once: one made by the litigant and the other by the production team—although the production's angle is usually more persuasive.

Home/studio

As it has already been established, the performance for the studio audience is different than the one for the home audience. The studio audience has more freedom to choose how to interpret the cases and on what aspects he or she wants to focus. The home viewer is at the mercy of the camera operators and editors. Although, as Philip Auslander wrote, "The multiple-camera set-up enables the television image to recreate the perceptual continuity of the theatre" and that "Switching from camera to camera allows the television director to replicate the effect of the theatre spectator's wandering eye," the home viewer does not have the agency to decide when and where to look.[58] The camera's eye is the viewers' surrogate, and though the intention of the multiple cameras may be an attempt to "replicate the effect of the theatre spectator's wandering eye," the viewers have no choice but to assume the camera's perspective. It is not the viewer's eyes that are wandering freely, but the cameras', hinting at the freedom the studio audience has. Contrarily, the studio audience member has the autonomy to construct his or her own narrative outside of the production's intent. In my experience, I found myself drawn to simple gestures hidden behind the podiums, like tender touches between guests, or the snarky remarks whispered to the audience as an angry litigant left set. These moments were beyond the purview of the cameras and were just for us, if we so chose to look at them.

Reality courtroom TV is a layered performance: It is a social drama, a legal exercise, and entertainment. To make the reality courtroom TV drama complete, there is no single artist in charge of crafting the episode from the live experience. An array of participants contribute to its making, and the postproduction team harmonizes these elements into the aesthetic, made-for-TV episode that cogently expresses each judge's brand. The legal claims hover in the background to legitimate the performance, giving an illusory weight to the judge's opinions about life, behavior, and morality. The magnification of the litigants' quotidian problems, and the resulting excitement that comes from watching the normal become spectacular, serves the judges' pedagogical aims. The performance drama shapes our understanding of the social conflict so that the way the show is produced magnifies and orchestrates the lesson each judge aims to teach, which is the subject of the following two chapters.

3

The Compassionate Courtroom

The small claim in the end has to be ruled on. But if it's not the broken TV set that is really at the issue, then let's get to what really is. It's very therapeutic.

Peter Brennan[1]

It's never about the white towels; it's about how you made me feel.

Jenny Hope[2]

Over the past 30 years, reality courtroom TV has grown along with the therapeutic trends in reality and talk television, developments modeled in shows like *Dr. Phil, Celebrity Rehab,* and *Intervention.* The premise of these programs is not only to watch guests expose their personal problems, but also to offer an entertaining glimpse at their healing process. Several reality courtroom TV programs follow this model. Those that do weave together legal and life lessons for the express purpose of making the litigants feel better. Because of these programs' emphasis on the litigants' emotions, the legal disputes tend to take the backseat. As Jenny Hope, a former reality courtroom TV producer told me, "Court shows are talk shows in a courtroom."[3] These programs use familiar talk show tropes of self-help and self-improvement, offering bits of personal advice disguised as a legal decision.

Although small claims cases have low legal stakes, emotions tend to run high—especially the cases chosen by producers to be argued on the programs. Rarely is the unpaid loan, ruined t-shirt, or dog bite the reason the litigants are in court, but rather it is the social drama between the litigants that drives them to air their dirty laundry on the courtroom stage. Peter Brennan, the former executive producer of *Judge*

Judy, Judge Joe Brown, Cristina's Court, Last Shot with Judge Gunn, and several others spoke with me about the personal problems animating the legal issues:

> It's amazing how many epic family tragedies and human heroes turn up in the smallest of cases in small claims. We get families with brothers and sisters who haven't spoken in thirty years because of some misunderstanding or some unfortunate incident and the entire two or three decades of bad feelings pours out and people are weeping in the courtroom. It's quite amazing. You think of small claims as a broken fence or a dented car. No, no, no. The reason people go to small claims is because of some deep wound and conflict, and finally they reach out for resolution. And amazingly they use small claims or a lawsuit to force that person to come face to face with them. Extraordinary stories are played out both in Judy's court and in Cristina's Court. It's amazing.[4]

With the help of their programs' research teams, TV judges are experts at getting the litigants to talk about their "deep wounds." Like talk shows, the guests on reality courtroom shows expose personal details for various reasons. Some may want to exculpate themselves or be publically forgiven or exact revenge on national television. Others may want to put on a good show or make money or attract publicity. Regardless of their motivations to talk on TV, the judges use probing questions to get to the root of their social dramas, eliciting emotional responses from the litigants so that the conflicts continue to be played out on stage. Litigants fight, expose themselves, forgive each other, and are exonerated or punished by the judges all within the staged trial's choreography. And unlike in conflicts transpiring outside of arbitration, the format promises a definitive end (which they may or may not agree with): the judge's decision about who is right (the winner) and who is wrong (the loser).

Both talk shows and reality courtroom TV shows make claims that participation is a step toward amelioration. Talk show strategies frame social and interpersonal problems as psychological dysfunction and promise that talking about problems and exposing oneself (subconscious thoughts, feelings, and past actions) will be therapeutic—meaning it will have a good effect on the participant's psychological well-being. Janice Peck wrote: "The programs' personalization strategies, parasociality, and therapeutic framework organize social conflict within narratives of individual and interpersonal dysfunction. Within those confines, all problems seem to be amenable to therapeutic intervention—to treatment via the 'talking cure.'"[5] However, as Stuart Fischoff warns, this is often not the case: "Talk shows exist to entertain and exploit the exhibitionism of the walking wounded. If you want to explore your problem, you go to counseling. If you want to exhibit your life, attack and humiliate your spouse, or exact revenge for some misdeed, you go on a talk show."[6] Like talk shows, compassionate reality courtroom TV judges also borrow psychoanalytic strategies and promise that their advice and judgments will be ameliorative. But within each genre the participants' self-exposure and public display of interpersonal conflicts operate differently. Talk shows focus on the guests talking to each other, to the host, and to the audience. On reality courtroom TV, the episodes focus on the advice the judges give the litigants. While talk show hosts are expected to treat all guests objectively, TV judges make sweeping and quick assessments of the litigants. They lecture the litigants. They boss the litigants. They are in every way superior to the litigants. This is the underlying structure of "court." The judge is the presiding officer, the top dog, the one in charge. The litigants appear "before the bench," and this staging dramaturgically reinforces the judge's status by placing him or her physically above the audience and the other performers. This differs from talk shows where the host sits with the guests, and the audiences tend to play the hypercritical role. In writing about talk shows, Jane Shattuc noted: "[I]t is usually the audience's role to reveal outrage and/or moralism over guests' ideas and behaviors."[7] On reality courtroom TV, that privilege is reserved for the judges who invoke symbolic state authority to validate their instructions and proscriptions. In other words, these judges usurp the talk show audiences' role as the guests' figurative juries in order to pass judgments in both the legal and moral sense.

TV judges who strategically use compassion as a means to address social and legal problems tend to have the following in common: (1) They prioritize the litigants' personal histories and emotional responses over details of the case; (2) the judges focus on reconciling the social rift more than settling the case; (3) the cases last longer than the ones conducted by TV judges who practice a more rigid, disciplinary style; (4) the judges enact a parental role as they express their concern for the litigants' well-being, offer physical and emotional affection, and distort the temporality of the case by treating the litigants as if they had known them before and will continue to be in touch long after the taping. While some TV judges perform their role punitively, compassionate TV judges use reparative tactics to amend both the civil disputes and what the judges perceive as their underlying causes.[8]

The compassion and mercy that justice brings

In a case that aired January 28, 2009, on *Family Court With Judge Penny* (2008–9), 31-year-old Greg Matyjasik sued his brother, 26-year-old Eric Matyjasik, for $1,100 in unpaid car repairs he made to his brother's vehicle. The brothers are both white, polite, and neatly dressed young men from Cleveland, Ohio. Judge Penny spent the first few minutes of the case gathering facts about the incident. Greg told the court that he did extensive work on his brother's 1981 Cadillac and charged his brother a fair rate. However, the defendant, Eric, sold the car for $2,000 and refused to pay Greg for the job. Once the basic facts of the case were on the table, Judge Penny shifted the narrative trajectory by asking the brothers about their emotional responses to the case:

Judge Penny How did you feel when he wouldn't give you the money?
Greg Your honor, of all people I wouldn't expect to do that to me—my own brother. You know, I might expect it from a stranger off the street, but your own . . . you know. He's my blood.

Judge Penny You also share another concern you have for your brother.
Greg My concern is his drinking.⁹

Judge Penny relocated the focus of the case onto the litigants' emotional status: "*How did you feel* when he wouldn't give you the money?" By turning her attention to feelings, the material conflict (the unpaid car repairs) was set aside to explore the root cause of the defendant's behavior. The voice-over during the interstitial iterated the shift: "Judge Penny has discovered that the real issue may be [Greg's] little brother's drinking problem." The judge proceeded:

Judge Penny Do you have a history of alcoholism in your family?
Greg Yeah we do. That's the problem. I see a lot of the traits my father has, or had. . . . But I see those same traits with him.
Judge Penny Well Eric? Do you drink?
Eric Well, looks like I have a best friend now and that's alcoholism 'cuz it's not my brother anymore.
Judge Penny Have you been struggling with it for a while? When was the time you took your first drink?
Eric Probably about nine.
Judge Penny How did you do that, baby?

The judge's mouth drew downward into a sympathetic pout as Eric described his father's bout with alcoholism and then detailed his first taste of beer, given to him by his father's friend at a Cleveland Brown's football game. Her question anticipated Eric's struggle, and she soothingly encouraged him to reveal more about his history, moving the heart of the case farther and farther from the unpaid bill. Judge Penny's sympathetic response to Eric's admission of his addiction transferred the responsibility for his actions away from his irresponsibility and put the onus on his alcoholism, the disease that was passed down from father to son.

The program's emphasis on feelings and Eric's inherited addiction as the determining factors in how the litigants behaved echoes the way expert psychiatric testimony operates in state and federal courts. Michele Foucault wrote that the introduction of psychiatric opinions into twentieth-century courtrooms had profound effects on the legal understanding of criminality:

> First, expert psychiatric opinion allows the offense, as defined by the law, to be doubled with a whole series of other things that are not the offense itself but a series of forms of conduct, of ways of being that are, of course, presented in the discourse of the psychiatric expert as the cause, origin, motivation, and starting point of the offense. In fact, in the reality of judicial practice they constitute the substance, the very material to be punished.[10]

On *Family Court with Judge Penny* none of the performers were psychologists or medical experts; however, Judge Penny employed a pseudo-medical evaluation that mimicked the displacement that takes place when expert psychiatric opinion bears on a case in actual courts of law. Judge Penny's line of questioning doubled Eric's offense so that it was not only that he did not pay his brother, but also that he suffered from alcoholism. His excessive drinking became the conduct under scrutiny, dealt with as the underlying cause of the unpaid bill. As Foucault wrote, this conduct becomes the subject of the judge's admonishment, superseding the offense "defined by law." Eric's deviations from normal behavior (which Foucault wrote is, "defined on the basis of administrative regularity, familial obligations, or political and social normativity") were read as symptoms of his sickness—his alcoholism.[11]

Judge Penny's eyes widened as she raised her eyebrows: "You touch my heart, Eric. Doesn't take a whole lot to touch my heart, I mean, I've seen it all, but I can feel the sincerity.... Do you know you have a problem?" She did not merely state, "You have a problem," but asked it. Her question was a diagnosis that anticipated Eric's cooperation in affirming it. Requiring Eric to publically admit he has a problem is reminiscent of the First Step in Alcoholics Anonymous' "Twelve Step Program." The first step is: "We admitted we were powerless over alcohol—that our lives had become unmanageable."[12] Judge Penny's rhetorical strategy prodded Eric to divulge details of his binge drinking, of blacking out, vomiting on himself, and drinking alone—particulars that confirmed her analysis. Judge Penny affectionately rewarded him for his compliance in the process:

> **Judge Penny** I have to tell you, I want to run out there and put my arms around you. Do you know what it takes for people to admit what you're admitting? To come out here in court and tell me the truth?

By offering positive affirmation in exchange for Eric's truth-telling, Judge Penny's adjudication process demonstrated the reciprocity of what Foucault termed "pastoral power," a system of compassionate government that reproduces the mutuality of church leaders' (the pastorate) power over their congregants (their flock) that is founded on the organization of confession. The representational construct of Judge Penny's show illustrated a courtroom that was similarly organized. Her stage was not a site of punishment, but a place for transformation and forgiveness of the individual who came before her.

In every episode Judge Penny focused on the litigant and on the modifications that can be made through her compassionate performance, rather than, as I discuss in the next chapter, holding the litigant up as an example to demonstratively teach the viewing audience how to behave. Judge Penny, standing in as the representative government official, invited litigants to confess in order for her to forgive and advise them. Foucault wrote that both the pastorate and the "flock" get something from confession: the leaders come to know their congregants while the congregants, unburdened by the confession, receive forgiveness from their leaders: "[F]or one does not confess without the presence (or virtual presence) of a partner who is not simply the interlocutor but the authority who requires the confession, prescribes and appreciates it, and intervenes in order to judge, punish, forgive, console, and reconcile." The ritual of confession, as Foucault theorized it, "produces intrinsic modifications in the person who articulates it: it exonerates, redeems, and purifies him; it unburdens him of his wrongs, liberates him, and promises him salvation."[13] This episode staged the ritual of confession in a courtroom context.

Certain rituals have at their heart the aim to transform. Deeply influenced by anthropologists Victor Turner's and Arnold van Gennep's research on initiation rites, performance scholar Richard Schechner wrote, "An initiation not only marks a change but is itself the means by which persons achieve their new selves; no performance, no change."[14] The ritual of reality courtroom television confession similarly promises modification in the individual confessing. And every episode of a reality courtroom program is a determining performance, whether it is in the matter of "right" or "wrong" according to state law, or "good" or "bad" as factored by the judge's personal preferences. Furthermore, while confession informs the person being confessed to about the confessor's inner condition, it also sets up a system of exchange where the confessor expects something in return for his or her openness. In this case, Eric envisaged that his confession to Judge Penny (and her millions of viewers) would, in some way, be beneficial to him. Because Eric was on a TV show and a party in a binding arbitration, the benefits are multiple. He may have wanted public forgiveness from the judge, he may have wanted to put on a good show for the audience, he may have wanted to win the award money from the production company, and he may also have hoped that his confession would help him overcome his alcoholism.

This episode emphasized the latter, Eric's "intrinsic modification," despite the other benefits that may have come from appearing on the show:

> **Judge Penny** I know you all came for one thing, but as usual it never ends up that way. Everything is for a reason. And maybe the point has come in your life when it's time. An intervention is happening now.... Would you consider going to AA? (*Eric nods.*) ... I can't jump over there to hug you. So come over here! Come on.

When Eric consented to Judge Penny's course of treatment, she offered to embrace him. Breaking the formal choreography of the courtroom stage, she called Eric up to her bench. He approached and stood on an elevated platform that put them at eye level with each other. Judge Penny took his hands in hers and looked deeply into his eyes.

> **Judge Penny** Let me say this to you. It's going to be alright.... Just go [to AA] one time and see how it goes because I don't want to see you hurting anymore ... I don't want you ashamed going in that dark place.... You got places to go. And you've got a woman to go find.... You've got a life to live, right? I feel a connection with you in that way, almost like a son. Because I wouldn't want to see my son go down that way. And I'm not judging you.... You need somebody to just talk to. You're going [to go to AA] for me?
>
> **Eric** Yes.

Judge Penny pulled Eric into a hug. She patted him on the back, and they stayed holding each other for several seconds.

Judge Penny's distortion of the temporality of the case, telling Eric "I don't want to see you hurting anymore" as if she had known him his whole life instead of 15 minutes, reimagined their relationship. Her posture shifted from judge ("I'm not judging you") to advocate, caregiver, and supporter ("It's going to be alright"). The physical rearrangement—Judge Penny holding Eric's hand and comforting him with hugs instead of sitting steadily above the litigants—complimented this variation. After a moment's pause, Judge Penny reinforced their relationship by framing it as a parental one. By telling Eric he is "like a son", Judge Penny situated herself as "like a mother." Her advice as a concerned mother was more pronounced than her juridical opinion. As such, Judge Penny diminished the complexities of Eric's alcoholism both by infantilizing him (she called him "baby" several times) and counseling him with broad instructions to direct his future behavior and overcome his addiction. Foucault wrote that this over-simplification is inevitable when the medical and legal are joined and the court becomes a site to normalize abnormal behavior:

> That is to say, joining together the medical and the judicial implies, and can only be brought about by, the reactivation of an essentially parental-puerile, parental-childish discourse that is the discourse of

parent to child, of the child's moralization. It is a childish discourse, or rather, a discourse basically addressed to children that is necessarily in the form of the ABC.[15]

Although this case transpired on stage, Judge Penny's compassionate adjudication style sheds light on the legal process of normalization that takes place in actual courts and the inexorable roles medicolegal discourse demands participants play.

After the hug, Eric went back to his litigant's stand and Judge Penny returned to the case: "Now for the bad news." She told them that she did not believe Eric was trying to cheat his brother; however, he owes him money for the repairs, which according to the receipts was $859 (Greg did not provide receipts for the break pads so Judge Penny deducted it from the reward). Of course, the production company, and not Eric, paid the $859, and Judge Penny was licensed only to arbitrate the financial dispute between the brothers, which meant she could in no way guarantee he would go to AA. Her extralegal sentencing was a suggestion framed within the symbolic context of a trial. It is what she would have liked him to do and what she thought was the right course of action to prevent further problems she predicted would be caused by Eric's alcoholism.

Family Court with Judge Penny followed a restorative justice model, one that "entails solutions that promote, repair, and reconcile victims and offenders with each other and their communities" by resorting to forgiveness as "an emotion-focused means of coping with [injustice]."[16] However, Judge Penny modeled the mercy and forgiveness that the litigants should grant each other by offering forgiveness to them first. Her role as the "giver of mercy" was even a part of her program's slogan: "It's about the compassion and mercy that justice brings." This set her procedure apart from state and federal courts' criminal process, which Staphanos Bibas critiqued for its "interests in deterring, incapacitating, and inflicting retribution" while leaving "little room for mercy."[17] Judge Penny's reparative model of justice was implicitly a Christian model, especially in its implementation of confession as a vital part of her legal performance. Her commitment to the healing power of confession embraced the message in John 1:9 in the King James Bible: "If we confess our sins, he is faithful and just to forgive us *our* sins, and to cleanse us from all unrighteousness."[18] I would argue that this was more than coincidence because Judge Penny is actually an ordained minister and associate pastor at Midway Missionary Baptist Church in Atlanta, Georgia. She even told reporter Rodney Ho that when she sees herself on TV, "All I see is God, what God has done for me. I stand before you as God's representative."[19] Her TV role quite literally conflated her legal profession with her religious faith, and nowhere was this more evident than in her commitment to confession as a means to forgiveness. No matter what was said on the courtroom stage the *Family Court* model of justice turned the other cheek so that the defendant, even when found guilty, did not lose anything; instead he was offered to the viewing audience as an example of how apologizing for one's wrong doings on the courtroom stage would lead to a positive emotional outcome. Every episode of *Family Court with Judge Penny* followed this script, demonstrating that justice, embodied in the role played by Judge Penny, could be a spiritual force for self-transformation.

Judge Penny's courtroom was in no way extraordinary. Rather, it made explicit what already happens in legal decision making despite the First Amendment's Establishment Clause protecting the separation of church and state. In writing about how religious ideas about the body have been enforced through state and federal law, Ann Pellegrini and Janet Jakobsen wrote:

> [S]ecularization has not so much meant the *retreat* of religion from the public sphere as its *reinvention*. This reinvention is accomplished through a conflation of religion and morality, in which morality is assumed to be the essence of religion and, conversely, moral proclamation can be a means of invoking religion without directly naming it. In other words, under cover of an official secularism, particular religious claims about "the good life," the way things are or should be, can still remain operative.[20]

Judge Penny did not directly name religion in her opinions, but religious claims about the life she wanted Eric and her other litigants to have were covertly delivered through her decisions. While this is acceptable for a TV show that is not bound by the same constitutional restrictions or codes of conduct that govern actual courts, it becomes more problematic when thinking about what motivates judicial decisions in actual state and federal courts. As discussed in Chapter 1, most TV judges do not change their adjudication style drastically when they come on television, but rather they exaggerate the tendencies they already exhibited in their state courts. As such, the reality courtroom stage can be looked at as a site that magnifies the habits of legal professionals. In other words, studying these programs also gives us a glimpse of the varying and extralegal processes taking place in courts across the country. Theater has always been prized for the way it reflects back onto its viewers a picture of the society in which it is produced—as it is, how it wishes to be, or how it fears it will become.

The reality courtroom morality play

Because of its religious undertones, its method of instruction, and Judge Penny's concern in saving the individual more than settling the legal issue, her program functioned in many ways like a contemporary morality play. Medieval morality plays were Christian dramas that featured an everyman character tasked with resisting temptation and expiating his sins in order to be granted salvation. In one of the few remaining plays, *Everyman*, the story follows the title character who finds out he is going to die and has only a short period of time to atone for his sins. After searching for comfort in his family, friends and material goods—to no avail—he goes to Confession, an allegorical character, to whom he atones for his misdeeds and sins.[21] Confession offers Everyman penance, and Everyman scourges himself so that God will forgive him and award him salvation. Through Everyman's entertaining journey audiences learned what kinds of behaviors were moral, church sanctioned, and guaranteed them entry into heaven—and which kinds did not. Dorothy Wertz wrote that the morality plays were used as vehicles to resolve "both social and intrapsychic conflicts among the uneducated or partially-educated bulk of the population."[22] Unlike in the liturgical dramas of that period, characters in moralities spoke in everyday vernacular and the plays were staged in village centers, inns, bars, and at carnivals to large and diverse audiences expressly to teach and spread the gospel in interesting and amusing ways.

Of course there are vast differences between the moralities and reality courtroom television, but they are similar in the ways they serve their viewing audiences by providing entertaining, moral, and religious lessons that resolve internal conflicts through a popular format performed in locations outside of the institutions they support. The moralities provided explicit instructions on how to be good Christians and were staged in public places, not in churches. In the *Family Court with Judge Penny* episode discussed above, Judge Penny addressed Eric's struggle with alcohol and family problems in ways that both seemed to help Eric and also spoke to audience members who may be going through similar struggles. In other words, Judge Penny resolved the social dispute between the brothers (the unpaid car repairs) by addressing Eric's intrapsychic conflict (his depression and alcoholism). Judge Penny's process enumerated how to deal with difficult familial conflicts, and Eric endorsed this lesson in his postshow interview. Eric said to the camera, ". . . [I'm] trying to working on cutting out the drinking completely because I have learned this isn't the way to go." This all took place under the auspices of a legal process staged not in a court, but in a television studio.

Judge Hatchett's intervention: "I Got My Eye on You"

While the Christian gospel provided the scaffolding for the moralities' allegories, reality courtroom programs have no agreed upon instructional central text. And not all TV judges follow a Christian logic of forgiveness like Judge Penny. Different judges moralize and instruct differently in both tactic and message. Judge Hatchett, the star of Sony Television Production's *Judge Hatchett* (2000–8), used hope as her guiding principal. In her 2003 advice book, *Say What You Mean and Mean What You Say! Saving Your Child From a Troubled World,* Hatchett wrote: "I had to operate on the simple premise that, no matter how bleak a family's prospects, I would approach my work from a place of hopefulness, from an unshakable belief that all could be set right with the appropriate mix of justice and compassion."²³ Judge Hatchett described this method in handling a young overweight boy whose father brought him onto the show for stealing. During the episode Hatchett determined that the boy's actions were caused by his low self-esteem, so she "sentenced" him to attend a weight loss camp for children.²⁴ Hatchett differentiated her work from what happens in actual court: "Call it fraud, call it embezzlement, call it plain old stealing . . . a prosecutor could have made a case on all counts, but in my role as a television judge it fell to me to see a hopeful resolution alongside justice."²⁵ She described spending the episode helping the father and son reconcile by letting the boy know what he did was wrong, but also that his father loved him. Her focus was not on the boy's thievery, but on lessening "some of the conflict that had pushed him to this place."²⁶ Hatchett constructed meaning outside of an analysis of the social forces determining the family's or the boy's problems. Instead, she invoked a "therapeutic ethos": what Janice Peck described as reasoning that uses "the individual psyche to explain social phenomena, and the belief that social problems can be resolved with psychological management."²⁷ Hatchett framed the boy's criminality as a symptom of his hopelessness, his lack of self-esteem, in order to feel compassion for him, repositioning him from delinquent to child-in-need, and prescribing a motivational/emotional-centered solution: therapy via weight-loss camp.

Hatchett developed her judicial philosophy while serving as the chief judge of the Georgia Fulton County Juvenile Court from 1991 to 1999, a county known for its largely poor, uneducated, and minority populations. During her tenure Hatchett implemented several programs that extended aid (both state funded and volunteer) to families and children between court dates. One such organization was the Truancy Intervention Program founded in 1990 as a response to the high dropout rate in Fulton County schools. The program staffed volunteer lawyers to mentor and advise teenagers who otherwise may not have stayed in school until graduation. After only 1 year on the bench, the National Bar Association's local affiliate named Hatchett the "Outstanding Jurist of the Year" for her "pioneering leadership in revolutionizing the Fulton County Juvenile Court system."[28]

In addition to her work with children and young adults outside of the courtroom, Judge Hatchett also developed a unique approach to handling cases involving drug-addicted mothers and their children. After Georgia passed a law in 1997 that stated the finding of trace amounts of drugs in newborns constituted child abuse, the number of child abuse cases coming into her Fulton County Courtroom shot up exponentially. The increase was so drastic that in order to handle the upsurge Judge Hatchett designated every Wednesday morning to what she called "Baby Court." On these mornings Hatchett would only hear cases dealing with mothers who had babies born with crack cocaine in their systems.[29] In many cases Hatchett did not see the child's permanent removal as the best option and instead worked with the Department of Family and Children Services to advocate for residential drug rehabilitation programs for mothers so that families could eventually be reunited.[30] Judge Hatchett followed up with these mothers in scheduled court dates.

A 1998 article by Jane Hansen of *The Atlanta Constitution* chronicled one of Hatchett's "Baby Court" sessions. Hansen reported that during one of the cases, a young woman stood before the bench holding her child. After Hatchett asked how she was doing, the woman replied that she was better and did not realize how bad things were before. Upon hearing that, Hatchett congratulated her, telling her that she looked wonderful and offered words of encouragement: "See what it's like to be in touch with life? This is a long road, but you can do it."[31] The woman agreed, and with that Hatchett called the young woman up to the bench so she could see the baby, but before the woman could reach the bench, Hatchett met her on the floor with a hug. While embracing, Hatchett told her, "I'm real proud of you."[32]

Hansen's report of Hatchett's Baby Court exhibited the judge's adjudication style—a performance of justice as compassionate, invested and caring. Hatchett did not mete out justice with an "iron fist," but offered second chances and support. Judge Hatchett's strategy of congratulating the woman for her successes, exhibiting empathy for her struggle, and expressing interest in her achievements in "Baby Court" was unique enough to be noticed by the local press and eventually by producers who contacted her after she stepped down from the bench in 1999 due to a public dispute with Governor Zell Miller.[33] Reporter W. Walsh of *The Atlanta Constitution* wrote a complimentary farewell, crediting her not only with doing a good job, but also for raising the court's standing: "For the past eight years, the murky, troubled waters of juvenile justice have had a remarkable beacon in Judge Glenda Hatchett. Her creativity, vision and commitment have been an inspiration to all who have come in contact with the Fulton County Juvenile Court."[34] When Judge Hatchett moved onto the television bench, she took this model with her. Working with her producers, they came up with a reality courtroom format that would focus primarily on family issues. Judge Hatchett told Tom Walter of *The Commercial Appeal*: "I want to do a court show where we could deal with some of the hard issues facing families today: teen pregnancy, drug abuse, family violence. . . . We try to deal with these issues directly on the show."[35]

One of the unique aspects of the *Judge Hatchett* program was segments called "interventions." Hatchett described the development in her 2003 advice book:

> Over time, I began to look for teachable moments in my courtroom, the points of pause in the hearing of a case . . . where I could offer a child a leg up or a lifeline or a second chance. . . . Lately, these moments take dramatic shape in my television courtroom, pretty much on a weekly

basis. My producers call them "interventions," and I mean to intervene in life-changing ways. After all, if you're going to shake things up and set kids straight, you might as well get results, right?[36]

Hatchett's interventions worked like creative sentences, methods of punishment that do not use prisons, jails, or monetary penalties. Creative sentences are alternative ways that judges handle someone who has committed a crime or wrongdoing that they think will be more rehabilitative than traditional modes of redress. Judge Hatchett's interventions facilitated experiences for the troubled litigant that first scared and then inspired him or her with lessons in self-improvement.

Alonzo Mourning saves a troubled teen

On a 2009 episode of *Judge Hatchett,* Judge Hatchett staged an intervention to straighten out a delinquent teenager named Jahon. The case opened with a voice-over that announced: "A troubled teen gets a life lesson from basketball super star Alonzo Mourning. Jahon's dream is to play in the NBA, but the way things are going he's got no shot."[37] Jahon, a straight faced 16-year-old dressed in a baggy shirt and trousers, entered through the back door of the courtroom and walked to the podium as the voice-over continued: "Even worse, Jahon's fast breaks come after he's committed a crime. So Judge Hatchett asks an NBA All-Star to show Jahon how to make his hoop dreams come true." To punctuate the narration the footage cut to a staged shot of Jahon sitting on a bench outside of a courtroom as if he was awaiting trial for one of the many misdeeds that cluttered his juvenile record. The episode then cut to inside the courtroom where cameras followed the defendant's mother, Stephanie Henderson, and his great aunt, Kaylynn Trotter, as they walked to their podiums. As the litigants settled into their places and the courtroom audience took their seats, the voice-over recounted Jahon's criminal past which included an arrest for stealing a car, expulsion from high school for failing a drug test, and expulsion from another school for pulling a knife on a female classmate.

The bailiff called the courtroom to order and Judge Hatchett began. Judge Hatchett first addressed Ms Henderson: "Tell me what's happening." Standing at the plaintiff's podium and positioned in opposition to her son who stood behind the defendant's, Ms Henderson testified to the trouble Jahon caused. She described how difficult it had been to figure out how to handle him especially because he was kicked out of the district school system. Then, Judge Hatchett turned to Ms Trotter, Jahon's great aunt, for her assessment. She told the judge that the family had a history of weapons violence, with one brother fatally shooting the other brother, and that Jahon should know better than using a knife. Judge Hatchett recoiled, "Oh my goodness!" Then, without prompting, Ms Henderson began to confess about her own troubled past, referring to herself in the third person: "Also he has a mother who was a crack addict, a runaway from the age of thirteen, and he knows what I've been through." Jahon stared vacantly at the judge while the plaintiffs described how their warnings were falling on deaf ears.

Up to this point the case established that Jahon's guardians could not control him. This was the first part of Judge Hatchett's intervention. The rest of the case demonstrated how Judge Hatchett could succeed where they failed. This next segment began with Judge Hatchett engaging Jahon, first by asking him about what he has done wrong in his past, and then by asking him about what he would like to do well in the future. Jahon talked about playing basketball, so Judge Hatchett asked: "How good are you?" Jahon told her he averages 40 points a game, but got kicked off the team. This provided Judge Hatchett an entry to the next step of this intervention. Her tone shifted:

> Let me tell you how this works. Let me tell you how this works. (*She indicates to Jahon's mother.*) What I see is a woman that is standing here asking for help. That's what I see. (*To the bailiff*) You know what, Tom? He needs a reality check. (*To Jahon*) Because you are wasting

your dream. There's a dream with your name on it and you don't even understand that you are missing out.

The "reality check" is a pedagogical exercise through which one learns what he or she needs to do in order to achieve his or her goals—much like what Judge Mathis described as the "wake-up call" as discussed in Chapter 1. Jahon's "reality check" took place over the 2 days between the first taping and the second taping. The program sent Jahon from the New York City studio to the Overtown Youth Center, an after-school and recreational facility for at-risk youth in Miami, Florida. A professional camera crew went with Jahon to document his trip.

After a brief recap of the previous episode, the second segment began with a screening of the film that was broadcast on a small television in the courtroom. Home viewers not only watched the movie, but they also could see the litigants watching it. The video opened with establishing shots of Miami: streets, beaches, and highways. Then it showed Jahon outside a community center located in a large grassy field. The center's coordinator led Johan into the basketball court where NBA player Alonzo Mourning was shooting hoops. Jahon looked shocked when Mourning said, "What's up, man?" He held up the basketball: "Do you know what to do with this thing?" Jahon said, "Yeah." Mourning responded, "Better yet, do you know what to do in the classroom?"[38]

Mourning took Jahon on a tour of the facility, and once they were outside Mourning told Jahon that when he was young he too got in trouble with the law, but decided his bad behavior was not worth risking his dream of playing basketball. Back inside on the basketball court Mourning made this deal with Jahon: "We'll play to five. If you win you can do anything you want to do.... If I win you gotta listen to me. You gotta go to school." The episode cut together excerpts from the game, mostly highlighting Mourning dunking the ball. Mourning won, and slightly out of breath told Jahon, "I wanna see you do well, man. You got the potential to do it, man. God gave you the ability, man. You take advantage of it, all right? Make me proud, all right? Make your momma proud." They shook hands and Mourning threw Jahon the ball: "Practice. You need to practice."

The video faded to black and the cameras caught the litigants on the courtroom set looking content and happy in a way they were not the first day. Hatchett asked Jahon, "So, what did this mean to you?" Jahon said that Mourning got in trouble with the law, so he knows now, "If he can make it, then I can make it." Judge Hatchett asked him what he was going to do now, and Jahon replied that he would go to school, quit being disrespectful to his mom and obey her orders. *Judge Hatchett's courtroom performance appeared to have succeeded where Jahon's parent and family failed. Mourning and Hatchett were able to motivate Jahon by supporting and fueling his dream of being a basketball star. They gave him hope that he could become a professional ball player no matter how unlikely the attainment of that dream might be. Reality courtroom TV is, after all, the world of entertainment and not a site of real reality checks. Regardless of how impossible it may be for Jahon to play in the NBA, witnessing a young man go from assailant and crook to aspiring sports star in under an hour makes for good television.

At the end of the case Judge Hatchett got up from behind her bench and asked Jahon, "Are you too big for a hug?" She embraced him and then orchestrated a group hug with the plaintiffs. The gesture aligned them all together, adding Hatchett as another parental figure watching out for Jahon. And as Jahon hugged his mother and great aunt Judge Hatchett said, "If I even hear about you acting up I'm coming to find you. We clear?" Hatchett's managing of this case recalled her methods in her Fulton County "Baby Court." Like she did then, she still got down from her podium to embrace her litigants while offering them effectual guidance, support, and advising. And by the time she met Jahon, her compassionate approach was firmly set.

Using compassion

Compassionate courtrooms are rarely sights of punishment. The questions raised by the programs are not ones of guilt or innocence but if early intervention can prevent a more catastrophic future. Judge Hatchett lightly reprimanded Jahon, but the episode focused on necessary future actions and used the "intervention" as inspiration to stay in school and obey the law. Both Judge Penny's and Judge Hatchett's courtrooms enacted a parental-puerile relationship between the judge and litigant, regardless of age. Their caring courtrooms modeled television justice as a rehabilitating and forgiving process where everyone has the potential to succeed. These TV judges were shown (via the editing process, the musical cues, and the cut together narrative) to have the power to bestow on the litigants insight and motivation to succeed where religious institutions, school, and family have failed. The compassion they exhibited affirmed their positions of power.

"Experiencing compassion for" is an emotion with a directional flow from the person feeling sympathy (the sympathizer) to the person needing sympathy (the sympathized), and the gratitude the sympathized may experience backflows to the sympathizer. The person experiencing compassion is in the more powerful position: to give or withhold sympathy with a resulting benefit or lack thereof to the sufferer. But the sufferer also has some goods to dispense: awarding or withholding thanks. To that effect Lauren Berlant wrote:

> In operation, compassion is a term denoting privilege: the sufferer is *over there*. You, the compassionate one, have a resource that would alleviate someone else's suffering. But if the obligation to recognize and alleviate suffering is more than a demand on consciousness— more than a demand to *feel right*, as Harriet Beecher Stowe exhorted of her white readers—then it is crucial to appreciate the multitude of conventions around the relation of feeling to practice where compassion is concerned.[39]

Compassion can be political—especially when the demands to be compassionate are more than a demand to "feel right." Because compassion structures a power relation between sympathizers and sympathized, the authorization of compassion is not only a demand to feel but also a marker of status. The danger of this structure, as Berlant wrote, is that the feeling of compassion lends itself to grouping individuals into a representative whole: "When we want to rescue X, are we thinking of rescuing everyone like X, or is it a singular case that we see?"[40] This slippage extends the sympathizers' compassion from one person to a group of people perceived to be like that person. A poor person stands in for "the poor"; an abused woman stands in for "battered wives/women." But even as these individuals and the groups they represent are placed in a position of need, those bestowing compassion on the needy are elevated above the needy. The trade-off is compassion in exchange for status. Structures of feeling—of how feelings are used, bestowed, and traded—are not only emotional experiences, but also sociopolitical acts.

Reality courtroom TV's compassionate judges guide this structuring of feeling. For the litigants and for the audience, the judges inscribe themselves as the highest authority—both in the legal sense (the courtroom) and in the feeling sense (dispenser of compassion). For several reasons the shows participate in what Stuart Hall classified as media's "ideological work": Certain types of litigants appear repeatedly, and these litigants are met with the judge's compassion; compassion structures a power relationship between the judge and the litigants. Within this relationship the individual sympathized can slip into the role of group representative, which structures a power dynamic between the sympathizer(s) and a whole group of people (the sympathized). Stuart Hall:

> In the broadest sense, the work of ideologies is to represent historical contradictions as *natural;* as immutable *differences* (between men and women, blacks and whites, "them" and "us," the "successful" and the "idle"; as rich or amusing *variety* ("it takes all sorts," "*vive la difference*"); as mutual *dependency* ("different but equal," social contract, a share of the profits); or as mere appearances subsumed in a larger *unity* (the family, the British people, "we're all human beings").[41]

Hall wrote that the media is an ideological field that reproduces social relationships, gender and sexual divisions and class distinctions as normal and natural. Jahon is not just Jahon, but representative of troubled young black men with no father, a lack of financial resources and an NBA fantasy. Eric represents alcoholics (or substance abusers) and their destructive patterns. As types they will appear again and again, episode after episode.

A bad night at Woodforest: Anatomy of a hate crime

In 2009, *Cristina's Court* (2006–9) won the Emmy Award for Outstanding Legal/Courtroom Program from the National Academy of Television Arts & Sciences 36th Annual Daytime Entertainment Creative Arts Awards for a two-part episode, titled "Bad Night At Woodforest: Anatomy of a Hate Crime." On December 27, 2005, Kyle Allard and Joshua Guthrie, two white 17-year-olds, attended a party in the Woodforest neighborhood in south Houston, Texas. Both young men were part of a group of teenagers (boys and girls) who had been committing acts of vandalism in the neighborhood and documenting them. Guthrie was the camera operator and Allard the driver. On this night, Lloyd Sams, a 27-year-old black man, was jogging near the party and ran into, according to his autobiography, a barrage of golf balls pelted at him: "Before I could make it to the bend of my street I was hit by fast flying golf balls thrown by a fraternity of racist baseball players at a local 2-year college."[42] Sams said he was assailed with racial slurs and then, when he tried to leave, Guthrie and Allard got into a car, chased him into Sams's driveway, and hit him with the car.

The police were unable to arrest Sams's attackers until Guthrie's parents found the videotape and turned their son in to the police. The police linked the tape to Sams's assault. Other participants were identified, but were released after making a bargain with the police and testifying against Allard and Guthrie. On May 18, 2006, Guthrie and Allard plead guilty to the assault and both were sentenced to 6 months in jail, 6 months of boot camp (a military-style disciplinary program),

8 years' probation and $9,000 each in restitution to the Woodforest community.[43] Because of their age they were given a plea bargain and the case was settled out of court. The *Cristina's Court* episodes reopened the case.

The episode began with the sound of a heartbeat. It pumped steadily over footage that Guthrie shot in 2005 of kids hitting cars with baseball bats, throwing rocks through car windshields, kicking dents into cars, trenching lawns, and setting off firecrackers. The announcer set the scene with his deep and portentous voice: "This is a video of a wilding spree that terrorized the Woodforest neighborhood of Houston in the weeks before Christmas 2005, and the prelude to a hate crime that would wreck families and lives and leave a stain on the soul of a city."[44] The episode cut to an interview with one of the neighbors, an older woman with disheveled blond hair and a pouty face. She looked into camera and said in a southern drawl, "Mean because they could be, and mean because no one stopped them."

The voice-over continued: "And then two nights after Christmas they raised the stakes." Footage cut to Lloyd Sams playing the piano. "They turned on a young black man, a teacher and a classical pianist named Lloyd Sams as he walked towards his home." The episode cut to daytime footage of Sams talking directly to camera as he walked through the neighborhood where the assault took place. The camera angle was low, looking up at Sams, who, as he walked reenacted Guthrie's and Allard's verbal attack. Whenever he said a curse word the editors inserted a dull bleeping sound: "They started screaming at me.... You better get off our block. You better get the [bleep] off our block, you [bleep]." Sams grew more intense: "You Kanye West, Snoop Doggy Dogg mother [bleep]! I'm gonna kill you! ... Man, get out the car I'm gonna run over this mother [bleep] monkey. I'm gonna run over you, [bleep]!"

The scene cut back to more footage of the spree, and the images were menacing: groups of angry kids smashing and burning neighbors' property. The voice-over amplified the balefulness of their vandalism and the emotional torment it caused Sams. The segment cut to police photos of Guthrie and Allard along with three other arrested boys whose faces were blurred. For impact, these mug shots were juxtaposed with a photo of Sams on what looked like a European cobblestone street. Sams was in a gentlemanly pose, leaning against his umbrella like it was a cane, with his long coat opened to reveal a pale blue button down shirt.

Sams's piano playing underscored the voice-over: "Because the two young men made a plea deal, Lloyd Sams never had his day in court, never got to question his attackers about why they caused him the terror that has affected his life until this moment. But today in a special *Cristina's Court* he'll come face to face with his tormentors." Sams's dissatisfaction with the Texas legal process was that it punished the defendants but did not provide an explanation as to why Guthrie and Allard attacked him or give him the chance to face them. Settling out of court failed to give Sams the emotional closure he needed. While the plea deal handled the legal matter with sentencing, *Cristina's Court* promised to handle the emotional one.

The scene returned to Cristina's courtroom. Sams stood behind the plaintiff's podium, and Guthrie and Allard stood behind the defendant's. Sams wore a slightly over-sized dark gray suit jacket buttoned over a pale yellow shirt with a checkered yellow tie. He perched his glasses high on the bridge of his nose. He held tension in his lips, slightly pursing them when he was not talking. Allard and Guthrie were in button down shirts. Allard's dark blue striped shirt was open revealing the top of his black undershirt. His eyes darted around the courtroom as he rocked from foot to foot. Guthrie wore a pale blue button down cinched at the neck with a black tie. Guthrie hung his head as Cristina asked Sams to describe the events.

Sams said that when the group of boys started to chase him he felt "hunted like an animal," afraid he was going to be "lynched." Sams's deliberate invocation of lynching automatically situated the crime as a hate crime, and the evocative nature of the word instantaneously cast a negative light on the defendants before they had a chance to speak. (This maneuver echoed one of the best-known invocations of the word; when during Justice Clarence Thomas's confirmation hearings he told the all-white senate committee that the sexual assault allegations Anita Hill brought against him had turned the proceedings into a "high tech lynching.") When Cristina asked Guthrie and Allard to describe what happened, Guthrie tried to clarify his motive: "I'm gonna go ahead and get this off my chest now before it goes any farther. This was not about race. I'll tell you that. It is not about race. There were two black people there at that party." Sams interrupted: "If it's not about race why were you using racial epithets?" Guthrie never responded—at least in the edited episode—because it quickly cut to a commercial. The editing elaborated Sams's understanding of the defendants' motives by piecing together excerpts that aligned with his version of events. The two episodes framed the attack as a hate crime, even as Guthrie and Allard tried to explain it differently.

The second part of the episode aired on November 11, 2008. After a short summary of what happened the previous episode, Cristina gave Allard the floor to describe the December 27 events. Allard told Cristina, "I don't like to be set here and perceived as a liar and as a racist person for something that I've done one time."[45] Then Allard's testimony took a turn: " I didn't have the money a lot of the other families did. Everyone else was bonded out. I spent my whole court term, six or seven months, I spent in the county. Didn't have a lawyer. Didn't have no help. I plead guilty because from the get-go alls I was offered was twenty-five to life." Allard claimed that he plead guilty not because he was admitting to committing a hate crime, but because his family did not have the resources to bail him out of jail or hire a lawyer. Pleading guilty was the best choice he could make to avoid a lengthy jail sentence, and it also may have been the reason he and Guthrie agreed to appear on the show. The compensation the production company paid must have been an attractive offer considering the hefty fine the court gave Allard and Guthrie. While Allard's statement momentarily refocused the case onto the injustice of a legal system that privileges the wealthy, this issue was beyond the pale of what could be resolved in an episode of reality courtroom television. Therefore, the cameras stayed focused on Allard just long enough to establish his emotional distress and then they cut away to the next moment. The content of his statement went unremarked and the episode quickly returned to Sams's emotional state.

Concentrating only on the litigants' emotional states avoids a more critical evaluation of the events and issues the episode raised such as class inequity, teenage vandalism, and racism. The program limited reflection in order to present a television version of justice that could explain and solve problems quickly. Janice Peck wrote about a similar phenomenon in talk shows:

> ... [T]hrough the mechanism of "intimacy at a distance," the programs discourage critical engagement with and reflection on those problems in favor of immediate identification and catharsis, and undermine the ability to take these problems seriously in the service of making them entertaining. The intimacy structure of these shows, which establishes their encoded and decoded fields of intelligibility, is both the source of their appeal (and profitability) and the locus of their ideological work. It permits viewers the pleasure of identifying with guests' problems without obliging them to do so, and without demanding they do anything collectively about those problems.[46]

The editing resisted Allard's derailment of the case onto a systemic critique of the legal system and cut to a video of Sams's wife, Ladonica Sams, who spoke to camera in a pained tone: "I saw Lloyd digress into moments of solitude, unacceptance, feeling unworthy of himself because of what happened." Mrs Sams once again returned the case to familiar territory.

After the commercial break, Cristina invited Sams's father, Kelton Sams, and Guthrie's mother, Melissa Crouch, to come to the respective podiums. (Like in *Judge Hatchett's* courtroom the parents are always implicated in their children's bad behavior. The litigants *and* their parents are on trial.) Cristina asked Ms Crouch how she felt about Josh's behavior. After admitting her feelings of failure as a mother, countering that she did not raise him to act like this, Josh's mother brought up the problems in his life and his suppressed emotional responses to them as possible causes of his delinquency: "There are no excuses, but his dad and I divorced, and I think that deeply devastated him. And his best friend was killed. . . . Josh is usually not an emotional person. He holds his emotions in. He held it in for so long. After that he started going down hill." Unlike in the *Family Court with Judge Penny* case discussed at the beginning of this chapter, Ms Crouch located her son's intrapsychic distress without Cristina's prompting. She was already inducted into the compassionate judges' process of blame displacement; the defendant should not be blamed because his actions were motivated by his emotional distress following his parents' divorce and his best-friend's death.

Ms Crouch continued, telling Cristina that other parents warned her about Allard's bad reputation. Cristina turned to Allard, who looked uncomfortable after Ms Crouch's statement, and asked if he was close with his father? Allard paused for a moment and then spoke: "No. He beat my mom up until I was about six, and she finally got up and left him. I don't associate with my family any more. My family at certain points are very dysfunctional." Prompted by Cristina's question and following Ms Crouch's lead, Allard also disclosed traumatic family events and personal details about his brothers and parents. But he did not articulate these issues as cause for his actions; he left that up to the trial's narrators: Sams and Cristina.

When Allard finished, Mr Sams, a former Civil Rights activist, interjected: "I don't think it's really race." A sound cue of a shimmied symbol lightly underscored Mr Sams's statement, an editorial punctuation of the "Aha!" moment. The tone shifted:

> I think there are programs for everybody. . . . But there are a lot of alienated, disaffectioned [sic] young people—white—who don't have these programs. And these young people are hurting. The only way it comes to anybody's attention is when they do something like shows on the video. I have hope, that's the type of person I am, for both of these young men.

Like Ms Crouch, Mr Sams also read Guthrie's and Allard's vandalism and attack on his son as an expression of pain: "And these young people are hurting." His choice to phrase their actions in terms of psycho-emotional distress and to have compassion for them instead of anger was a sociopolitical act that resituated white children as not having enough resources or the same access to mentor and volunteer programs as black children. Mr Sams's comment described a situation where black youth, not white, are advantaged; his discourse of injustice reimagined the status quo, and this continued in his assessment of Guthrie and Allard as underprivileged white teenagers who the system failed. (His argument rehearsed the same tropes used to justify bad behavior in minority youth.) Using them as examples, Mr Sams explained that racism is a symptom of emotional distress. Then he argued that the roots of prejudice can be traced to psychological anguish and therefore can be cured with mentorship, love, and good parenting. Judge Cristina agreed:

> **Judge Cristina** I think Kyle needs somebody to be proud of him.
> **Kelton Sams** Yes.
> **Lloyd Sams** I totally don't have any animosity for the first time since the incident. The reason they did not give him twenty-five years to life—because the DA came to me with thirty years to life, and he says, "What do you think, Mr Sams?" ... The DA did not want to accept that plea. (*To Allard*) I pled for you. I did that. I'm also the same person who brought us to this point because I believe in healing and I believe in forgiveness and I believe in redemption.

In the episode's final moments, Lloyd Sams forgave the defendants. Sams's forgiveness was different than the forgiveness offered by Judge Penny in the case discussed earlier because while her litigants confessed their wrong doings, Allard and Guthrie refused to accept the charges Sams brought against them. In fact, Sams's forgiveness seems less about the defendants and more about him asserting his status over them as retribution for the way they tormented him that night in Woodforest. In this public forum and in front of millions of viewers Sams positioned himself as Guthrie's and Allard's savior from both a long jail sentence and a life of sin, and this repositioning appeared to make Sams feel better.

This performance gave Sams a platform to expiate his bad feelings in the way that the Texas court's retributive/punitive model could not. For the Sams family, their *Cristina's Court* performance was the "trial" they wanted, but the state system was unable to provide. Indeed, Lloyd Sams reasoned he came on the show because settling out of court denied him the catharsis he wanted—the catharsis he anticipated would come from facing his tormentors and the kind of catharsis reality courtroom TV promises. And this is one of the guarantees reality courtroom TV makes. In our interview, Cristina Perez stressed her program's cathartic function:

> If somebody actually hears them out, and you give somebody the opportunity to unload their feelings, then that's it. A "healing" begins. They've said it. "Oh my God, somebody actually heard me." That's how I am on my court shows. I approach those cases with, "Tell me all about it," giving all an opportunity to be heard. I can't even begin to tell you how it happens. You begin to talk. You forget about the cameras. . . . It's really an open forum where people feel very comfortable. The moment they start talking, I'm listening to both sides. We try to make it work. We try to resolve the issue since I think that's what we all want—to be heard and vindicated.[47]

Like in Judge Penny's courtroom, resolution has little to do with the legal dispute and everything to do with feeling better. Perez: "My director said to me, 'You know people come in here and they're just so angry. They're so angry all the time. And when they walk out of your court room . . . they're not.'"[48] Feeling good feels good, and when both parties in a dispute feel good, not only does the dispute cease, but also the emotional turmoil driving the argument is quelled. The emotional care is the extralegal work of compassionate reality courtroom TV.

Conclusion

Compassionate judges' courtrooms locate psychological distress as the cause of social misdeeds and illegal acts. They explain that bad behavior can be attributed to sadness, depression, lack of self-confidence, or other character deficiencies. Aligning harmful acts with character faults and weaknesses configures the perpetrator as a victim of his or her condition and asks the plaintiff to feel compassion for him or her. What's on trial is not just the individual, not his or her behavior as such, but the emotional causes of and responses to the dispute. Therefore, the remedy is not only legal redress, or a monetary award in TV land, but forgiveness, mentorship, nurturing, and advice.

While this strategy has sociopolitical resonances, it can also simplify complex problems into terms of feelings. Participants anticipate compassionate judges will resolve conflicts using a therapeutic ethos, and as audiences become familiar with the programs' ideological work they can make psychological evaluations without help from the judge. (Ms Crouch and Mr Sams illustrate their proficiency in applying this ethos.) Jane Shattuc suggested that the dictums of psychological health reverberating across programs become internalized so that the audience can identify illness and asocial behavior before any expert chimes in. Reality courtroom TV judges and their litigants exhibit the same phenomenon. The audiences' knowledge of both the judge's brand (and how he/she feels about certain issues) and familiarity with the judge's therapeutic assessments creates a circle of affirmation. The judge affirms the audiences' already embedded belief in what makes someone a moral, ethical, and psychologically healthy individual, which is affirmed by the decisions and actions judges made before, which are affirmed by audiences' beliefs, and so on and so forth.

In her research on talk shows, Mimi White argued that therapeutic inundation is at the service of dominant culture. Jane Shattuc summarized White's position: "TV as an agent of the dominant culture exercises its power over unwitting viewers by naturalizing therapeutic psychology as a neutral method to free the self, when it is in fact the very opposite: a form of social control. Talk show viewers learn to police themselves in the name of 'mental health.'"[49] This can be applied to reality courtroom TV as well. TV judges who practice compassionate justice urge—even oblige—the litigant to admit that his/her behavior is unhealthy. The judges' decisions reinforce middle-class values and dispense these social values within a legal framework, albeit a make-believe legal framework, designed for daytime American television. This is not to overlook the values of these lessons. Learning and embodying these values is part of how one attains a middle-class lifestyle. Conforming to social codes also has its benefits.

But this is not the only work of these programs. The model compassionate reality courtroom TV performs does more than actual small claims process and gets closer than actual courts to the needs and lives of the parties involved. While small claims trials must adhere to the objective of determining the legality of the dispute and assigning culpability, the compassionate TV model has the time and resources to attend more to the individual's emotional needs while also resolving the dispute. This restorative justice model aspires to make participants feel good by going beyond the legal claims; it also seeks to mend damaged personal relationships. Compassionate judges see past the defendant's alleged crime: the person who steals is not merely a thief, and the person who uses racial epithets is not just a racist. The therapeutic approach to legal disputes reveals the complex person (not the complex social issue) beneath his or her actions, and with care, gentleness, a desire to heal—and to make good television—the judges advocate for the person's betterment instead of their punishment. Like Judge Hatchett wrote, compassionate TV justice provides hope with justice. These judges approach the cases not as a prosecutor would, finding ways to convince and prove the defendant's guilt, but as caring authority figures that use the lawsuits to make the litigants face their problems so they can become better people and live more fulfilling lives. The transformation on compassionate courtroom TV shows is not only from innocence to guilt or vice versa, but shifts in attitudes that could, if all goes according to plan, change the participants' lives—and maybe even the viewers'— for the better.

4

Rehearsing Citizenship: Exercises in Tough Justice

While compassionate judges work from a basis of empathy, of Aristotelian catharsis by means of identification, there are another group of TV judges who propagate messages in self-responsibility by using punitive tactics. These tough judges cast their litigants as examples of model or failed citizenship and use them as characters to illustrate the moral and behavioral lessons they teach to their viewing audiences. Compassionate judges model their courtrooms after the therapist's office, and the tough judges treat their courtrooms as a sternly monitored classroom. Rather than attending to the litigants' emotional lives, locating feelings as the source of bad behavior, "tough judges" examine the litigants' conduct and use raw discipline to address it. They hector, yell at, shame, and insult litigants they deem as acting stupidly, immorally, or ignorantly. They aim their sights at bad behavior, and from on high prescribe new courses of action. These prescriptions most often have no formal legal basis, and each tough judge directs the litigants to behave in ways that fulfill that specific judge's ideal of what constitutes a healthy, productive and good citizen. Every tough judge orders their litigants to do the "right thing" even when it does not feel good. Like Judge Judy told *Variety's* John Dempsey in 2008, ". . . I'm making the right thing happen at the end of the trial."[1] They do this by employing disciplinary measures available to them within their shows' framework.

The main qualities of tough TV judges are (1) The judges can be cruel, sarcastic, and funny; (2) they yell at and reprimand the litigants, using shaming and scapegoating to modify behavior; (3) the litigants neither correct their behavior during the show, nor do they ask for or receive forgiveness; (4) the cases are mostly small claims cases already filed in small claims courts; (5) the cases are quick; (6) and the judges depersonalize the cases, evading deep analysis for snap judgments that position the litigants as examples of what not to do.

Bad Boys and Girls: Gender policing in Judge Joe Brown's courtroom

The tough, punitive judges use comedy and ridicule, not to make the litigants feel better or to rehabilitate them as compassionate judges profess to do, but to hold them up as examples. Nowhere is this more evident than during the "Bad Girls" and "Bad Boys" episodes of *Judge Joe Brown*. Organized as "Bad Girls Tuesdays" and "Bad Boys Thursdays", producers grouped episodes that featured defendants who modeled similarly defiant behavior. A press release from CBS described "Bad Boys" as litigants who were "waiting to be straightened out by the Judge, from unruly teenagers, spoiled 'mama's boys' to deadbeat dads with every excuse in the book."[2] The same release described "Bad Girls" episodes as ones that "will feature a 'Bad Girl' viewers will love to hate, including thieving sisters, scandalous best friends, opportunistic mothers and greedy girlfriends, who will say anything to try to persuade Judge Joe Brown to rule in her favor."[3] These litigants, as the press release boasts, were delivered to audiences prejudged.

But what made these litigants bad? The behavior that earned these litigants their title did not always predate their court appearances. Their actions on set helped them obtain this badge. Bad girls and boys tended to challenge Judge Joe Brown and the proceeding's validity, refusing to take it seriously or show respect for his authority. They were unwilling to suspend their disbelief that the courtroom stage was a court of law. Instead of welcoming the judge's criticism, they talked back, they cursed, they returned insults, and they fought to get their points across. Their insubordination won them a place in the catalog of "bad" where they were held up week after week as problem subjects that only Brown's advice could fix.

During an October 29, 2009 episode that aired on a New York City Fox affiliate, WNYW-TV, college student Lezerick Murphy brought a case against his former friend, Michael Eggleton, who punched him in the face and broke his jaw. Murphy was seeking $3,000 for his medical bills. The plaintiff, Mr Lezerick Murphy was a 21-year-old black man. He wore a light purple polo shirt and neatly pressed khaki pants. He had a stylish short haircut, walked confidently, and stood steadily at the podium. The defendant, Mr Eggleton, presented a style counterposed to the plaintiff's. Mr Eggleton was also a black man in his early 20s, but he moved down the aisle with a lateral swagger, holding onto his oversized pants with his right hand. He wore an extra-large untucked, long-sleeve bright blue shirt; two large silver chain necklaces hung to just above his mid-section, and his hair was done into thick, short braids that fell onto his forehead.

Moments into the episode a graphic of a crumbling brick wall spray-painted with graffiti that read "Bad Boys" popped up along the bottom of the screen. The graphic told the audience that what they were about to see were not recalcitrant white, prep school boys, but urban ones, ghettoized young men whose badness was emblematized in the graffiti tag—an act of vandalism historically associated with inner-city black youth. But more than that, calling the litigants "boys" indexed a history of its use to subjugate black men. The term "bad boys" cannot escape its citationality. This time, however, it was a black judge orchestrating the titling, and his performative use of the word designated not only the litigants as certain kinds of subjects, but also illustrated how Judge Brown strategized his performance of blackness as a way to discipline and demean his litigants. Calling the litigants "boys" would not be as readily accepted if a white judge were sitting in Brown's shoes. Being called "boys" (and "girls", for that matter) denies the litigants their adulthood. They are cast, unwittingly, as perennial children in need of parental care and state assistance, discipline, and direction. The tag also recalled the chorus of the TV show *Cops'* theme song by the band Inner Circle: "Bad boys bad boys, whatcha gonna do?" The track played at the beginning of each episode over gritty footage of police arresting mostly poor, Hispanic and African American individuals in American suburbs, cities, and small towns. With what seemed like a strategically Brechtian placement, the sign below the litigants indicated how the story would go despite the litigants' best efforts.

Like in every episode, former Tennessee Shelby county criminal court judge, Judge Joe Brown, recapped the events. He described how the defendant arrived drunk at the plaintiff's house, and upon entering poured liquor on the floor. When the plaintiff, Mr Murphy, asked the defendant to stop, the defendant got angry, insisting: "It's for my dead homies," referring to the tradition of pouring libations for dead friends resurrected by American gangster rappers in the 1990s.[4] When Judge Joe Brown repeated, "It's for my dead homies" he let the word "homies" linger, over-enunciating each syllable, making the defendant's word choice sound quite silly. Then he paused, cueing the audience to react, which they did, and the cameras cut to the mostly female gallery laughing, heads tilted back in humorous (and perhaps a bit exasperated) disbelief at the defendant's clichéd tribute.

When the laughing quieted, the plaintiff gave his side of the story, one that detailed a hard-working college student who was sucker punched by his former friend. When he finished, Brown turned his attention to the defendant. He said, "Now you have the floor," an offer he quickly rescinded. As Mr Eggleton described being in college, Brown interrupted by telling the audience he dropped out. The audience, charmed by Brown's tenacity, laughed at how easily he undid the impression Mr Eggleton tried to make. By denying the defendant his narrative, effectually silencing him, Brown restricted Eggleton's use of language to formulate the impression he wished to make. The case continued with the defendant and the judge talking over each other until Brown stopped their verbal volleying with an insult:

> **Judge Joe Brown** You went to college and you talkin' like that? Why you trying to act like a hood rat? What's your problem? You tryin' to perpetrate like you're a hood rat? You talkin' over me. See there's one difference. I'm not him. (*He points to the plaintiff.*) . . . See you cold-cocked him. You sucker punched him.

Mr Eggleton Yeah, win lose or draw I fights. Yeah.

Judge Joe Brown I'm trying to help you out so someone doesn't kill your fool self.

Mr Eggleton And I'm trying to tell you my story-

Judge Joe Brown You have a cloud of death hanging over your head because you've been failing. Somebody tried to get your tacky-head self off in college and you running around here trying to perpetrate that you're an ignorant hood rat that got as far as college, but you can't talk anymore.

In this brief excerpt Brown positioned himself as the person who would save the defendant from imminent death by illuminating the dangers of playing the hood rat. Brown extended his counsel to an unwilling defendant while silencing his protests against the impression of him Brown painted. Brown told Eggleton that he "can't talk anymore" as a means to invalidate his testimony, but the assault on Eggleton's language also suggested that the defendant's use of black vernacular made him unable to communicate—but to who? Brown clearly understood him, and the judge's code switching from the professional speak of legalese to the street lingo he shared with the litigants was a badge of his street and legal smarts. Brown adopted the same dialect he criticized: "Why you trying to act like a hood rat?" However, the defendant's unwillingness to switch in the same way classed and raced him inferiorly.

Brown's play with language, and how language races (or erases) the speaker, may have played differently to different audiences. Some of the popular colloquialisms Brown used were unremarkable in their mainstream popularization, but at points his use of particular forms of speech seemed to be directed at those Umberto Eco called his "Model Readers," the audience members "supposedly able to deal interpretively with the expressions in the same way as the author deals generatively with them."[5] However, the heterogeneity of Brown's audience ensured there would also be misreadings because, as Eco wrote, meaning making is a collaboration between text and reader: ". . . [W]hen a text is produced not for a single addressee but for a community of readers, the author knows that he/she will be interpreted not according to his/her intentions but according to a complex strategy of interactions which also involves the readers, along with their competence of language as a social treasury."[6] Eco detailed the complexity of model readership. He wrote that it is a series of interactions between language, its grammatical construction, the readers' histories, and the culture produced by that language. Meaning is made discursively and transpires between the text (in this case the performance text) and the individuals in the audience who bring to the text their particular histories and cultural affiliations.

The nonmodel reading audience, what Eco called the "Empirical Reader," may not share the same reference points as the author and therefore may interpret the text more liberally: "Empirical readers can read in many ways, and there is no law which tells them how to read, because they often use the text as a container for their own passions, which may come from outside the text, or which the text may arouse by chance."[7] As an empirical reader of *Judge Joe Brown*, and not one of his model readers, I found myself misreading and reading against his performance text. As this chapter illustrates, I experienced his performance from an outside position, so instead of buying into his message I used it to expound upon my own passions. Brown's use of language located his model readers, and part of my feeling of exclusion, what made me an empirical reader and not a model one, comes in large part from feeling like he was not talking to me. Brown's language drew a cultural distinction between us. And that is one of the benefits of reality courtroom TV because while Judge Joe Brown may not have been speaking to me, there is most likely another TV judge who does.

While Brown risked being misunderstood by some audience members, he intended to be understood by others. He appealed to these audiences by using language to express affiliation and validate his claims as someone who knows the litigant and those like him. Critical race theorist Mari Matsuda wrote, "Your accent carries the story of who you are—who first held you and talked to you when you were a child, where you have lived, your age, the schools you attended, the languages you know, your ethnicity, whom you admire, your loyalties, your profession, your class position: traces of your life and identity are woven into your pronunciation, your phrasing, your choice of words."[8] Brown's linguistic leveling authorized his character assessments as from someone within the community. Brown's accent was a claim to his insider status, and as the case proceeded he used it to assert his familiarity with the difference between what he saw as the litigant and what he perceived as the litigant's performance.

Brown painted this gap with simile. Why you trying to act *like*. Brown oriented Mr Eggleton's performative deployment of the "hood rat" in an arrangement that set Eggleton at a distance from the role (hood rat). A hood rat is a slang term for someone who loafs about or engages in scandalous or gang activity in his poor, urban neighborhood. Brown located Eggleton's performance at the level of a racialized stereotype while ignoring the politics of race within this illustration. This separation implicated Eggleton in the performance of hood rat, insinuating that it is a role he chose to play, which meant he could just as easily play something else. He made this claim without considering the social and economic circumstances that produce hood rats. But this was strategic. Identifying the defendant's behavior as an "act" licensed Judge Brown to turn the role, the hood rat, and ultimately the person who chooses to play that role into the joke. It simplified the complex issues of truancy, poverty, and systemic inequality by making the defendant a caricature the audience could hate. This depersonalized Brown's criticism: it was not just about Eggleton, but everyone like him who chooses to play that role.

Making a litigant easily identifiable at the expense of a complex presentation is, of course, par for the course in trial law. As Lawrence Vogelman writes:

> The talented trial attorney is a student of human nature, all too often concentrating on its dark side. That is, she will exploit stereotypes. For example: Colombians sell cocaine, Nigerians sell heroin, Dominicans sell crack, Jamaicans sell marijuana, Jews cheat on taxes, Italians

belong to the mafia, Albanians carry guns, the Irish are all drunks and "Big Black Men" defile our women. Trial lawyers often evoke these stereotypes to obtain an emotional response from the jurors.[9]

Stereotyping circumvents complex character development by invoking signs that audiences (and jurors) already recognize. By painting the litigant as a stereotype, the audience may feel that they already know who this person is. Judge Brown, however, was not the plaintiff's legal advocate. He was supposed to be playing the impartial arbiter and magistrate, but his performance redefined the role so it looked more like what a lawyer representing the plaintiff would do—cast the defendant in a negative light in order to persuade the jury that his client is not guilty or deserves a particular reward. This ultimately left the defendant lawyer-less. He had to be his own advocate, which was impossible to do when Brown denied him his chance to speak. At this point the case had devolved into an exchange of insults, and not between the litigants, but between the defendant and the judge. In the few short moments the case had been on air Judge Brown usurped the adversarial role that should be played by the plaintiff. The issue that brought the litigants to court, the plaintiff's medical bills, had taken backseat to the verbal brawl between the two.

He's real girled up

Frustrated by this positioning, the defendant resisted. In what felt like an insult he had been cooking up the whole case, the defendant attacked the judge's masculinity by way of his appearance. Mr Eggleton said, "At least I'm not the one walking around in a dress." Of course the attack was not directed at Judge Brown's robe, but what was hidden underneath it: his masculinity. Brown paused before perking up: "Ohhhh, we're going there." The "oh" was drawn out for dramatic effect. Without breaking eye contact he retorted, "Let's take what you've got on." The audience hooted and hollered, thirsty for the deluge of insults Brown prepared to deliver. The judge leaned over his bench and pointed his finger at the litigant's necklace, looking down his arm like it was the barrel of a shotgun. The camera slowly panned up the defendant's torso, hovering on his chain. Brown asked: "You've been listening to your forty-year-old aunt talking about how she wants bling. What's a man need jewelry for?" Brown deduced that the only reason a male would want to wear jewelry is because the women in his life have been asserting too much influence. In Brown's hypothetical scenario this would be Eggleton's imaginary and bling-loving aunt. Brown's message was that without a man in the house women misdirect males to have unmanly objectives, which results in the production of boys who do not know how to be men. Black women as presented in Brown's courtroom were in what scholar Robert Staples described as a triple-bind: "Black female dominance is a cultural illusion that disguises the triple oppression of black women in this society. They are discriminated against on the basis of their sex role affiliation, their race and their location in the working class strata of this upper-class dominated country."[10] Brown concluded that women are the root cause of the problems with black men, so even though none were present, they were still on trial.

Their attacks on each other's manhood by way of their costumes and accessories refocused the courtroom lesson on heterosexual citizenship, black fatherhood, and gender performance rather than the plaintiff's medical bills. This was magnified when the defendant mistook Judge Brown's wedding ring for "bling":

> **Mr Eggleton** Wait ... what's that on your finger? (*He points to Judge Joe Brown's hand.*)
> **Judge Joe Brown** That, my man, is a wedding ring. It means I have a wife. It means I don't have a problem.

Judge Brown took Mr Eggleton's inability to identify his wedding ring, a symbol of a legally sanctioned heterosexual union, as an indication that Eggleton has a problem. Though Brown did not come out and say it, he implied that Eggleton has a problem with heterosexuality, which is a failure that within the rules of Brown's courtroom made the defendant a boy, not a man. Brown's logic connected gender performance, acting like a man, to traditional heterosexual bonds (being married) to responsibility as an ideal mode of citizenship. Brown modeled this ideal not only by his wedding ring, but also by the primarily female audience, a casting choice that positioned Judge Brown as both the object of these women's desires and also as the man, manly enough to fulfill all of theirs. Brown's focus on performances of masculinity was even included in the show's marketing. A marketing image on his website from 2008 showed Brown dressed in his robe, smirking into camera and holding his left hand outstretched while a quotation beside him read "It's about being a man."[11]

Brown's assault on the gender performance of his male litigants was a frequent occurrence. In a different "Bad Boys" case that aired on October 22, 2009, *Ellison v. Williams*, the plaintiff, former girlfriend Debony Ellison, began her plea by explaining to the judge that she stopped seeing the defendant when she discovered he was still pining for his ex-girlfriend. She described his heartbreak as being so painful that the defendant was reduced to fits of vomiting. This struck the judge as unfitting behavior for a man, and to make it clear to the audience that a real man stays stoic in the face of heartbreak, he acted out part of Ellison's story, performing the part of Williams as a wilted lily. Doing what looked like a Scarlett O'Hara impression, Brown limply lifted the back of his hand to his forehead, reclined in his chair while looking up and said in a high-pitched and quivering timbre: "Oh, I hurt so bad. Oh, that's so wrong. Oh, how could she do that to me."[12] Williams interrupted Brown's clownish performance by asking what the relevance was of bringing up his past relationship when the case was about the money he owes to the plaintiff. Brown pressed on, and like with the previous case, the defendant and the judge talked over each other, vying for the floor:

> **Judge Joe Brown** Don't roll your eyes like you're a woman. You're a man. Stand up straight. I hope you're a man. Stand up straight—
> **Mr Williams** That's disrespectful, judge.
> **Judge Joe Brown** I don't know. A lot of folks are down low these days.

Mr Williams You're not acting like a man by coming at me like that.
Judge Joe Brown Oh, but I am.
Mr Williams Oh, but you're not, folks. This is unreal.

Like with Eggleton, Brown fixed his authority to his masculinity, stabilizing his position by emasculating his defendant and attacking his sexual orientation. He told Mr Williams he was acting like a woman by the way he was standing and moving his eyes. He extended this observation into an assumption about Williams's sexuality, suggesting, on national television, that he may be on the "down low," which is a term used to describe black men who identify as heterosexual, but secretly engage in homosexual activity. Men on the down low live double-lives, hiding their homosexual activity from friends, loved ones, and even spouses. Down low culture is stigmatized because of its frequent association with the higher rate of HIV transmission and AIDS related illnesses in the black community in the United States.[13] Brown's insinuation that Williams is a man on the down low was meant to elicit an emotional response. Men on the down low disturb conventional identity categorization. They are abject, and as Julia Kristeva wrote, abject subjects' resistance to easy categorization is unsettling: "It is thus not lack of cleanliness or health that causes abjection but what disturbs identity, system, order. What does not respect borders, positions, rules. The in-between, the ambiguous, the composite."[14] Brown did not really believe that Eggleton and Williams were queer subjects, but by positioning them as such he did two things: he appealed to the audiences' emotions by trying to make them not like the defendants, and he used queerness as an insult to discipline the defendants into behaving according to the terms of manhood Brown defined. If they did not, then Brown would accuse them of being gay, which they clearly did not want to be called. Thus Brown shamed his defendants by associating them with abject subjects. (Brown said Williams is acting "like a punk girl unmanly little chump," and when Williams got angry Brown said to the audience, "He's real girled up." Brown's choice of using the word "punk," which is prison slang for a passive homosexual, deepened his attack on the defendant's manhood, especially for audience members who understood Brown's references.)

Williams responded by suggesting that Brown was not acting like a man by making baseless accusations, to which Brown retorted, "Oh, but I am." Brown continued:

> **Judge Joe Brown** I have noticed an interesting transition. The boys are starting to act like the girls used to in terms of their body language: rolling their eyes, head up, hand on hip, moving their head around. Women since time immemorial have talked over somebody who is trying to address them and you talking over me just like you're a woman. So when you start acting like one sounding like one moving like one then I'm gonna put it out there. Man don't sit up there . . . (*Brown looks up and rolls his eyes and puts his hand on his hip. The courtroom audience laughs.*) Now see look at you.

Brown participated in the policing of gender performance by using the litigants' failure to comply with the norms he defined as male or female as the reason for their conflicts. Eggleton would not have punched his friend and Williams would not have broken the contract with his ex-girlfriend had they followed Brown's prescriptions. But Brown's discourse also pointed to the performance of gender as much as the performance of hood rat, destabilizing the assumption that it is what Judith Butler wrote, "ontologically necessitated":

> Performing one's gender wrong initiates a set of punishments both obvious and indirect, and performing it well provides the reassurance that there is an essentialism of gender identity after all. That this reassurance is so easily displaced by anxiety, that culture so readily punishes or marginalizes those who fail to perform the illusion of gender essentialism should be sign enough that on some level there is social knowledge that the truth or falsity of gender is only socially compelled and in no sense ontologically necessitated.[15]

It is the instability of the litigants' gender performance that, in Brown's mind, required him to police it and punish those who perform one's gender incorrectly. This is because he located poor gender performance as a dire problem in the black community.

It is interesting to note that while Butler's analysis applies particularly well to cases of gender bending, on Brown's courtroom stage he targeted instances of hypermasculinity, in particular litigants who pose as violent or threatening. Take, for example, Mr Williams. When Brown referred to him as a young man, Williams countered: "I'm not a young man, I'm an O.G. [original gangster]." The defendant linked his manhood to the streets. He called himself an "O.G.", a way of indirectly posing a threat by invoking the fierce image of a gangster. While Brown played the role of the judge and asked Williams to abide by his rules, Williams assumed what he saw as a more powerful role in this setting in order to challenge Brown's hold on the courtroom stage—a violent criminal. (This recalls the moment when Eggleton told the judge, "Yeah, win, lose, or draw, I fights.") As far as this performance goes, both Williams and Brown (and Eggleton, for that matter) were equally O.G. and equally judge because they were playing these roles on a stage. All they had to do was perform the posture suitable to their respective roles, even if it was not the role each intended to play when they walked on stage.

In both episodes, two simultaneous performances come to the fore: one is the legal narrative the defendants were trying to tell, and the other is the TV narrative and theatrics of law the judge performed. During the *Eggleton v. Murphy* case, Judge Brown embraced the theatrical moment of conflict (perhaps exhibiting the same kind of excess that got him in trouble as a Tennessee judge) by caricaturing the thug walk, a comic display that brings our attention to the "performance" of this performance.[16] He stood up behind his bench, rolled his eyes up to the ceiling, and did a bouncy walk back and forth behind his desk. He paused and said:

Judge Joe Brown You can't even stand up straight. You're going (*Brown prances behind his bench*).
Mr Eggleton It's not even a case any more. It's about me.
Judge Joe Brown (*Standing*) Yeah it's a case. I'm just deciding how much punitive damages I'm going to hit you with. Jack you up.

Brown finished his demonstration and sat not behind the bench, but on top of it. He held the gavel, patting it into his palm menacingly as if it was a stand-in for the club he would use on the defendant if they were on the street instead of on a courtroom stage. In this moment, Brown invoked the hood rat's and the O.G.'s violent and threatening nature. He too can play their game. (Of course this threat was all demonstrative—just part of the show.)

The audience could see this posturing, and Brown knew the quickest way to take the feet out from under it was by emasculating his litigants and then using that as an opening to expound upon the problems of acting like a girl and the troubles that come from the absence of black fathers—a point he explicitly made in *Eggleton v. Murphy*:

> **Judge Joe Brown** And you running around talking about what you can live off of and you have no job and you're not in school and you have all that women's jewelry hung around your neck because in your subconscious when you weren't but five or six and nobody has seen a man in four or five generations and if you ask your mother why you don't need a man to help raise him—
>
> **Mr Eggleton** (*He burps at the judge.*)
>
> **Judge Joe Brown** (*Mimicking a woman's voice.*) "I don't understand judge, what's a man for?" (*In his own voice.*) There you go, little lady. You don't even know what he's supposed to be good for. How you going to raise him to be a man?
>
> **Mr Eggleton** Get to the case.
>
> **Judge Joe Brown** There ain't no case. You've already done it.
>
> **Mr Eggleton** Hit the gavel then. You feel me? Because I'm fittin' to walk out, man.

Brown readdressed his oratory to the black mothers who are not on set: "You don't even know what he's supposed to be good for. How you going to raise him to be a man?" Brown transferred the responsibility of Eggleton's misbehavior to an imaginary audience of women who have failed as mothers because they did not keep a man in their lives. Brown's answer to the absent woman's question, "What's a man for?"

was that only men can raise boys to be men because as Brown has used his litigants to illustrate, women cannot.

Far from being a direct response to the case at hand, Brown's imaginary conversation illustrated Anna McCarthy's Althusserian avowal that reality television participates in the production of terms of citizenship by amalgamating the state, the family, and the cultural text: "... [I]t would seem that reality television is something of a privileged site, annotating transformations in the institution of the individual (citizenship's raw material) through its consolidation of connections between three discursive apparatuses for the formation of citizen and self: state, family, and cultural text."[17] As a show with the primary aim to entertain, Brown's criticism of the black family in the midst of a binding arbitration compounded the work of the state, the family and of reality television while policing gender performance. And as Brown was prone to do, he decontextualized the situation so that the complexities of race and class were omitted from his blanket criticisms. This allowed him to address a large group of people without attending to the particularities of each person's circumstances:

> **Judge Joe Brown** But you see the bottom line is this. These young boys are so desperately in need of men to give them "man training."
> **Mr Eggleton** Don't talk about me like you know who my parents are—
> **Judge Joe Brown** I know you! I can see you! How many thousands of you do you think I've not seen? So what makes you any different from the other thug idiots trying to perpetrate they're men.

He repeated this performance with Williams:

> **Mr Williams** Where you know me from, cuz? You don't know me, bub! (*Slapping the podium*) You don't even know me man!
> **Judge Joe Brown** I don't have to. I've seen a thousand of you over the years. See I know you. You fit into a pattern. Look at you. You doing girl stuff. ...
> **Mr Williams** Shut up.

Judge Joe Brown Excuse me, foolish one.
Mr Williams You're not even listening to me.
Judge Joe Brown I am.
Mr Williams (*He barks.*)

Brown set Williams and Eggleton among the "thousands of you" he has seen over the years in both his Tennessee courtroom and on stage, and it was a grouping he used to justify his snap judgments. (And because Brown refused to listen to the defendants' counterclaims, their language broke down. Williams barked at the judge and Eggleton burped.) Of course these remarks are also disheartening. The "thousands of you" reminded viewers that black men have the highest incarceration rates, an alarming statistic that points to a systemic problem—one that Eggleton annunciated in this moment:

Judge Joe Brown I'm trying to keep you from dying, foolish one.
Mr Eggleton I don't care about dying, sir. You feel me? That's one thing about me and you. You probably care.

Eggleton's admission that he did not care whether or not he lives or dies is arresting, but goes ignored. Why does he not care whether he lives or dies? Might this by why he acted violently with his friend? And what does it mean that he was pouring out liquor for his dead pals? How many of them have died? Why are they dying? Brown's script did not warrant forays into an individual's unique circumstances, so he bowled over Eggleton's reflection about the dispensability of his life. Judge Brown, with the help of the postproduction staff, controlled Eggleton's depiction as a stereotypical thug. This licensed Brown to critique, ridicule, and make fun of the defendant not as an individual, but as a representative of all thugs. The defendant recognized Brown's maneuver, but within the television courtroom's dynamics there was little he could do to change the trajectory. The few protests he made were talked over by Brown's bellowing voice, ignored, or edited with commercial breaks. This was, of course, improper behavior for a judge because it was not representative of fair legal practice, a point both Eggleton and Williams try to make. Williams reminded the judge that his personal attacks were improper judicial behavior, and Eggleton, surprised by Brown's conduct kept pleading to "get back to the case."

But it is this theater of law that produced Brown's pedagogy. It reiterated tenets of the 1965 Moynihan Report, Assistant Secretary of Labor Daniel Patrick Moynihan's sociological study titled *The Negro Family: The Case For National Action*, an influential piece that attributed black poverty and underachievement to the welfare system and its effects on the black family—most evidently the lack of father figures.[18] The report's findings were taken up as part of a white liberal agenda, one that Judge Brown replicated in his program. Brown embodied the white liberal position and offered himself as the missing father figure by treating the litigants as his disobedient children. But this also became a lesson that his future guests internalized. In the case *Dixon v. Dixon* that aired September 14, 2012, Juanita Dixon sued her daughter Camisha Dixon for $4,500 in car repairs. Juanita Dixon opened her plea to the judge by saying, "I need Papa Brown." The daughter quickly responded, "That's the problem. There is no Papa Brown." They asked Papa Brown to be the stand-in for the missing "Black father," an apt appellative for the judge. Judge Brown looked sternly at the litigants and responded, "You know the saying, 'It takes a village to raise a child?' Consider me part of the village."[19]

The Dixons did Brown's work for him, reproducing his assessment that their problems stemmed from the absence of black father figures just like Brown's opinions repeated principles of the Moynihan report. Brown relayed the report's edicts just as the Dixons passed down Brown's. The passage of these lessons from government document to television performer to audience member elucidates how power is exercised through networks. Foucault wrote that "individuals do not simply circulate in those networks; they are in a position to both submit to and exercise this power. They are never the inert or consenting targets of power; they are always its relays. In other words, power passes through individuals. It is not applied to them."[20] Reality courtroom TV shows are an extension of these networks.

Bad Girls you love to hate

Toward the end of the *Ellison v. Williams* case, Brown told the defendant that "One of the things I was always taught is that you try to take the next generation and make men of them, and if you're a man that's your obligation." One way Brown did this was by enlisting the services of the women on his stage and in the audience. This becomes clear in the "Bad Girls" cases. In the case *Jones v. Jeffries* that aired May 7, 2013, plaintiff Latoya Jones sued her cousin's ex-girlfriend, Latanya Jeffries, for vandalizing her home in retaliation for helping her cousin move out of her apartment. The case culminated with Brown advising the women how to be mothers, saying that they should exhibit "lady-like behavior" for the benefit of their sons: "Maybe the boys will grow up with the idea it's their job to protect their areas and make them more economical and prosperous to secure order, safety for the women in the area, for the children in the area . . . so it becomes a nice place to live instead of hell." Whereas during *Eggleton v. Murphy* Brown addressed an imaginary mother, "Bad Girls" cases placed the women he was chastising right in front of him. They became direct targets for his sermonizing about how to raise men without paying any attention to the lives of women. When Brown said he is "protecting womanhood", he did not mean he was protecting women, but rather the characteristics he thinks they should display. Of primary importance are the traits that best help men be "men."

In another case, *Allen v. Reid,* Brown made apparent his belief that women are in the service of making men.[21] Plaintiff Monica Allen sued defendant Racquel Reid for vandalizing her car when it was on loan to her friend Miranda Stevens. Through a lengthy testimony by both parties we found out that Stevens and Reid were competing over the same boyfriend, and Stevens accused Reid of keying the car out of jealousy. When the judge found out that the man they were both fighting over was a repeat offender he asked the women, "Why don't you reward the men for doing right and withhold for doing wrong?" Though not explicit, Brown's invocation of "withhold" and "reward" had a specifically sexual connotation, one that resonated with the theme "Bad Girls." Unlike "Bad Boys," "Bad Girls" is less of a racialized term and more of a sexual one. Adina Nack wrote that "easily identifiable members" of the bad girls' tribe are prostitutes, porn stars, and exotic dancers.[22] Bad Boys are bad at being men. But bad girls conjure images of loose and rebellious women untethered to conventional, societal, and more aptly, sexual expectations. Good girls are demure, complacent, and chaste. Bad girls transgress social norms. Like a scene from Aristophanes' *Lysistrata*, Brown recommended with a verbal wink that the women use sex as incentive to keep men out of jail. His extralegal sentencing regulated these women's sexuality, performing on a courtroom stage the kind of pathologizing and criminalizing work usually left to medical, legal and social science discourse.[23]

Brown was not alone in pathologizing female sexuality. Judge Judy has a penchant for using unmarried and unemployed mothers on state assistance as a means to get across her "take responsibility for yourself" message.[24] In the *Judge Judy* case *Ross v. Ross*, Shawna Ross brought a case against her cousin, Pauline Ross.[25] Both litigants were young black women. Shawna wore a t-shirt and khaki pants and stood gripping the plaintiff's podium. Pauline wore a strapless maternity shirt that bulged out at her belly. Her hair was tied into a high ponytail that hung down along the backside of her head. Judge Judy began by directing her address to the plaintiff, Shawna Ross, giving a chronology of events. After Child Protective Services threatened to remove the children from Pauline's custody, Shawna agreed to take care of them. Pauline promised her state assistance check as payment, but never paid Shawna. Pauline claimed that Shawna did not watch her children and therefore was not owed the check. Pauline filed a counterclaim against Shawna for calling Child Protective Services and making false allegations.

Judge Judy turned to Pauline for questioning. "Pauline, how many children do you have?"[26] (To note: *Ross v. Ross* is the final case of the episode, preceded by four others. During every other case Judge Judy referred to the litigants by their last names, but here she referred to the defendant by her first name, "Pauline," or "madam.") Pauline responded, "Three," and the questions continued:

> **Judge Judy** You're expecting another one?
> **Ms Ross** Yes.
> **Judge Judy** How old are you?
> **Ms Ross** Twenty-one.
> **Judge Judy** You have enough children, Pauline.
> **Ms Ross** Yes.
> **Judge Judy** Did anyone ever tell you that?
> **Ms Ross** Yes.
> **Judge Judy** Who else told you that?
> **Ms Ross** Everybody.
> **Judge Judy** So add my voice to the rest of the pack. You have enough children. There are other things to do in your spare time. How old are your children?
> **Ms Ross** They're...
> **Judge Judy** You have to think about this?!
> **Ms Ross** No. One, two, and three.
> **Judge Judy** And who's the father of your one-year-old?
> **Ms Ross** Deon.
> **Judge Judy** And who's the father of your two-year-old?
> **Ms Ross** I don't know.
> **Judge Judy** And who's the father of your three-year-old?
> **Ms Ross** Deon.
> **Judge Judy** And who's the father of this one you're going to have now?
> **Ms Ross** His name is Nick.
> **Judge Judy** And how long have you been with Nick?
> **Ms Ross** Um, nine months.

Someone from the studio audience audibly sighed a disdainful, "Oh God." Judge Judy raised her head and with a severe glance gave a "Shhhhh," short and quick like the sound of an air pump filling a tire. Judge Judy did not need to say anything because her questioning already exposed Ross as an irresponsible young mother with too many children to keep track of to an audience familiar with Judge Judy's feelings on the matter. As the case continued, Judge Judy painted a picture of a useless mother while the defendant stood still, responding monosyllabically to the questions asked: "Yes. Yes. Yes." Each "yes" confirming the judge's snap judgment. (Of course Judge Judy looked over the cases before coming on set so she knew details of Pauline's life. Her line of questioning, however, made her knowledge look intuitive.) When Judy said, "Stop having children," her directive was not just aimed at Ross, but to all women in a similar position.

This kind of case is Judge Judy's bread and butter. Sheindlin has been honing her dislike of the welfare system and what she perceives it doing to an entire population dependent on it since sitting on the New York Kings County Family Court bench in the 1990s. She wrote in her 1996 book *Don't Pee on My Leg and Tell me It's Raining*:

> The only difference between a deadbeat father and a deadbeat mother is a nine-month gestation period.... They are teaching their children nothing, and unless they are forced to become more self-reliant—and I do mean forced—they will continue to labor under the misconception that when you have a baby, somebody else pays. Those habits have been ingrained over a lifetime, and it is no surprise that the child who grows up in a welfare household learns nothing about adult responsibility.[27]

Sheindlin argued that welfare dependency does not foster self-responsibility or promote education. She attributed the rate of unwed mothers in poor communities to a welfare system that financially rewards single-parenthood. Unlike the compassionate judges who look to emotional distress as the cause of the litigant's actions, Brown and Sheindlin exposed what they perceived as the larger social and systemic causes. They attack, through punitive measures, the litigants who evidence the bad results of these poor systems.

After her critique of Pauline's sexual behavior, Judge Judy zeroed in on the litigants' use of their welfare checks, exposing their misallocation. Judge Judy wittily made it clear Pauline was abusing Michigan's support money, money paid to keep her in the job force and "out of the baby producing business," by spending it on herself. Then Judge Judy's voice intensified, and she leaned over the bench:

> **Judge Judy** Ms Ross! Pauline! This is a scam! . . . I got it. You work three weeks and got checks for $1,152. . . . If you people don't think that I understand that this is just another scam on the state you're wrong! . . . You know what I'm doing with this case? I'm sending it to the state of Michigan so they can come after you and take the money from your welfare money. You are not entitled to keep that check! . . . You don't get it. Why didn't you send the money back to them. You don't move into your own apartment, madam. . . . That's not what the money is for. . . . That's what Deon is for.
> **Ms Ross** Well Deon don't help.
> **Judge Judy** (*Yelling*) Well that's your problem. That's not Michigan's problem.

Judge Judy's critique was no different than the one she made in her 1996 book, and, *Ross v. Ross* was case in point. Because Pauline's behavior fit so neatly into the pattern Judge Judy deplores, she addressed the Rosses as "you people." Judge Judy's rant widened the scope of her critique beyond the Rosses and the case at hand.

Judge Judy's method of attack differs from Judge Joe Brown's. Brown put himself in character to make fun of the way his litigants presented themselves; Judge Judy humiliates them. And though both Judge Judy and Judge Joe Brown are passionate about their messages, their TV courtroom limits them. In the above case, Judge Judy could not do anything to punish the litigants (beyond her reprimands), though she wanted to. Rather than tell Pauline to pay her cousin the money she owed or for her cousin to never work for Pauline again, Judge Judy sentenced Michigan to redeem the money from Pauline's welfare checks and then decide to whom that money is going: "That's what the state of Michigan ought to do. So they have to get the money back and then they're going to give it to you." Judge Judy's hands were tied in this matter, and there was no way for her to effectively handle the case the way she would like to. This case illustrated the limits of the legal power invested in a TV judge.

While a compassionate judge would hope for and forgive the litigants to inspire them to change, Judge Judy treated the litigants as flawed products of an infantilizing welfare system that failed to teach self-responsibility. Spreading this message is a large part of her objective, and she does so by publicly shaming litigants so they become examples of what not to do. This is because redemption is not Judge Judy's goal. Judge Judy's aims as a jurist have never been redemption-for-all. In a chapter titled "For Some Kids No Redemption" in her book *Don't Pee on My Leg and Tell Me It's Raining*, Sheindlin recounted a case in Family Court of two young boys who attacked an 86-year-old Vietnamese woman. She believed she knew their future: "For them, there would be no redemption, no rehabilitation. Their sociopathic behavior was fixed."[28] Not a licensed medical professional, Judge Judy classified the boys as sociopathic, writing them off to future incarceration. Unlike Judge Hatchett who approached every litigant from a position of hope, Judge Judy dismisses some people as criminal by nature. They cannot be changed, and therefore forgiveness and second-chances are useless.

Tactical comedy

While some judges use compassion as an instructive strategy, tough judges utilize comedy in the same way. They tactically employ humor to structure the power dynamics of their courtrooms, and the resulting laughter has socio/political meanings. Sigmund Freud wrote: "One can make a person comic in order to make him become contemptible, to deprive him of his claim to dignity and authority."[29] Judge Joe Brown's humiliation rituals relied on the joke; the organization of laughter determined status by using the joke to declare the judge's authority while stripping the litigant of his/hers. In his examination of how jokes orient emotional responses, Freud wrote that jokes are a means to surmount an enemy. He said that "By making our enemy small, inferior, despicable or comic, we achieve in a roundabout way the enjoyment of overcoming him—to which the third person, who has made no efforts, bears witness by his laughter."[30] By laughing on cue the audience participated in humiliating the defendant. Unlike shaming, Brown's acts of humiliation were degrading and injurious. Shaming may evoke self-realization on the part of the person shamed, and the feeling of embarrassment comes from realizing one's wrongdoing. In the above examples Brown's litigants never came to realize the identities Brown narrated; they refused them. While shaming can be an effective tool in catalyzing transformation, humiliation is more for the audience's benefit and entertainment. It draws a gap between the person humiliated and those enjoying it by denying any affiliation to them. Their audience's laughter, and whom it is directed toward, not only identifies the antagonists in the story, but also creates a representational enemy. In the examples in this chapter, it is hard not to see how laughter can firm up preexisting tendencies to identify certain people who exhibit certain types of speech and dress as problematic citizens.

Of course, this is intentional. With their insults and impersonations, the judges direct the studio and home audience to laugh at the litigants in order to teach lessons about certain types of people. (On *Judge Joe Brown* the stage manager also encouraged audience reactions and camera people captured these reactions in close-ups edited into the episode in postproduction.) Freud perceived the invitation to laugh *at* an attraction to pleasure that supersedes critical reflection: "It will further bribe the hearer with its yield of pleasure into taking sides with us without any very close investigation, just as on other occasions we ourselves have often been bribed by an innocent joke into overestimating the substance of a statement expressed jokingly."[31] Freud described how the desire to experience laughter might replace an evaluation of what is being laughed at. J. Jerome Zolten wrote:

"The tacit and instant rapport of humorous acts is as responsible for winning audience support as actual argument content itself."[32] The joke is a shortcut to convincing the audience of an idea, perception and impression of someone, some action, or some idea. (Compassionate judges use their therapeutic ethos similarly.) Jokes are an effective tool on reality courtroom TV where most cases are heard in less than 15 minutes (not including commercial breaks and interstitials). The joke circumvents the need for full explication, attracting audiences to align with the judges' agendas through the very human desire to be in on the joke.

Summoning "The Judge"

Tough judges' comedic performances cannot resist citation. While Judge Judy's "no nonsense" performance recalls Dr Ruth Westheimer and Joan Rivers, both older, petite, tough talking, Jewish, white females with acerbic styles, Judge Joe Brown's strategic employment of comedic impressions, rambling diatribes, and colloquial verbal play conjure up one of the first performances of the black judge: Pigmeat Markham's satirical vaudeville routine "Here come de judge." In 1928, Pigmeat Markham created "The Judge", a character he performed in the "Chitlin' Circuit" for primarily black audiences. Sammy Davis Jr performed "The Judge" on the variety show *Laugh In* (1967–73) bolstering the character to fame among white television audiences. After his appearance on *Laugh In* in 1968 the routine's intro song aptly titled "Here Comes The Judge" rose to number 19 on the Billboard charts evidencing the reach of the character's popularity. But unlike white comedian Walter Kelly's vaudeville performance of "The Virginia Judge" (1928), a white southern judge hearing ignorant, slow-talking black litigants "perpetually on the wrong side of the law," Markham's "The Judge" was created by and was played by him, a black comedian.[33]

Vaudeville comedians often used explicitly racist and ethnic stereotypes for comedic effect, and no group was targeted as callously and unrelentingly as African-Americans. One of the primary critiques of black face vaudeville performances like "The Virginia Judge" and "Amos and Andy" was that they "created symbolic hierarchies through comic routines wherein African Americans were characterized as socially inferior."[34] These "symbolic hierarchies" reverberated beyond the theater walls substantiating preexisting prejudices. While white comedians played black face roles, black comedians had limited access to white audiences. When they did, actors were confined to roles fitting white audience expectations: "the shuffling, no-account 'coon.'"[35] (Bert Williams, one of the first black comedians to play for white audiences, suffered this fate in the 1890s through the 1920s.) But Markham's "The Judge" broke the mold by putting a black comedian in the white role of the judge.

Markham's "The Judge" was bombastic and foolish, drunk with power, and ignorant. As one of the lawyer's in the routine said: "Listen, you're going in front of a very dumb and very ignorant judge."[36] Armed with a gavel and bladder sacs "The Judge" made each court case a riot of misunderstanding and ridiculous innuendo. Fairness was not part of his practice, and he famously opened his cases by saying, "The judge is evil this morning. And when I'm evil everyone is going to do time that day."[37]

Markham played "The Judge" in an era when Jim Crow laws disenfranchised black Americans who had slim to no chance of becoming legal professionals let alone a judge. (President Taft nominated the first black judge, former slave and Harvard graduate Robert Heberton Terrell, to the District of Columbia Municipal Court bench January 15, 1910. Justice Terrell was the only black judge until Harry S. Truman appointed William H. Hastie to the Federal bench in 1949.) As much as Markham's buffoonish comedy tied him to vaudeville's racist legacy, "The Judge" had satirical resonances. By playing into the stereotype, but playing it in a white role, many of Markham's fans interpreted his performance as a critique of white authority. In his autobiography, Markham wrote:

> The Negroes in the audience loved it—the whites, too, I guess—probably because the judge, the pompous oppressor of the Negro in so many Southern towns, was bein' brought down a peg by a Negro comedian. They made me play that sketch over many times, and finally I got the idea that I could turn the character into a full act.[38]

White audiences enjoyed the familiarity of his minstrelsy, and black audiences enjoyed how his humor made the judge, a symbol of oppressive white authority, into a joke. As a black comedian playing a white role foolishly, Markham was able to speak to the corruption of a racist legal system.

Judge Joe Brown's impersonations of black litigants summons "The Judge." Both Markham's and Brown's performances employed stereotypes to satirize the characters they perform. Markham's judge is a fool; Brown's judge imitated the fool. Markham's judge wants to be laughed at; Brown's judge directed the audience to laugh at the litigants. Judge Brown's performance of his litigants maintained a critical distance. Like Brecht's Verfremdungseffekt or "alienation effect", Brown commented on the roles as he played them. His impersonations (like Mr Eggleton's lumbering walk) and uses of black vernacular ("I'm going to jack you up") were strategic portrayals during which he seamlessly swapped courtroom decorum for street talk to present his litigants' behavior as foolish while still maintaining his authority.

Freud wrote, "A joke will allow us to exploit something ridiculous in our enemy which we could not, on account of obstacles in the way, bring forward openly or consciously; once again, then, the joke *will evade restrictions and open sources of pleasure that have become inaccessible.*"[39] The joke makes the comment seem less cruel. It buffers the criticism with a veil of lightness so as to permit the joke-maker access to people and qualities that in other forms are guarded from critique. As Freud noted, the comedic allows us to cut through social laws and obstacles limiting what we can say or publicly acknowledge about somebody. Brown's enactments hyperbolized what Brown perceived as problematic behaviors lauded by certain groups of black men. By performing these behaviors foolishly he demonstrated their ridiculousness. Judge Brown stood in relation to his impressions: the judge next to the fool. The juxtaposition clearly and quickly exemplified what kinds of behavior the judge condoned.

Both Judge Judy and Judge Joe Brown use punitive strategies to position their litigants as models in their demonstrations of what not to do and how not to behave. However, scholar Laurie Ouellette criticized these programs for their regulating discourses, writing that they "implicitly criminalize" individuals who deviate from social norms:

> Within the space of the television courtroom, individuals who make "bad" choices (such as dating the wrong person) or who fail to conduct themselves according to particular social norms (such as holding a job and practicing family values) are implicitly criminalized. Similar to the suspects profiled on true crime television, the "failed" citizens of the popular court genre are disproportionately poor, Latino, and African American.[40]

But Ouellette's analysis does not consider the nuances of each judge's stance. Judge TV litigants are not failed citizens because they deviate from social norms, but because they deviate from a particular TV judge's code of ethics or behavior. Judge Judy held up the Ross cousins and Judge Joe Brown held up Mr Eggleton as "failed" citizens. The Rosses failed to "take responsibility for themselves" and Mr Eggleton failed at being a man. (He lacked "man training.") They failed for different reasons.

Ouellette pointed to the symbolic implications of casting poor, black, and Latino litigants as representatives of failed citizenship. In fact, a lot of criticism of reality courtroom TV fixates on the judges' castigation of minority litigants.[41] Though welfare dependents may be Judge Judy's bread and butter, these kinds of cases are not in the majority on *Judge Judy's* dockets. *Ross v. Ross* was the only case with black litigants (and the only case with black litigants on welfare) during the May 26 episode. All the rest of the cases were between white or Latino/a litigants who seemed to be from lower and middle class backgrounds (*Milbourn v. Clark, Cavender and Challice v. Fitzgerald, Hohnke v. Isdell, Herring v. Chavez,* and *Ross v Ross*). In fact, of the 42 cases Judge Judy heard during ten episodes airing from May 6 to June 6, 2008, only five featured black litigants and only *Ross v. Ross* involved black litigants on government support.[42]

There is no doubt that Judge Judy espouses a "take responsibility" message; however, on her program the message is predominantly directed to white litigants who also compose the largest percentage of her viewing audience. (*Judge Judy* draws the largest average percentage of white viewers and has the smallest percentage of black and low-income viewers of any reality courtroom TV show I analyzed from 2000 to 2010.) The fraction of cases like *Ross v. Ross* may have something to do with producers trying to appeal to *Judge Judy* viewers by presenting relatable litigants, a casting decision that embroiled the production in a 2007 legal suit. Jonathan Sebastien, a former senior producer on *Judge Judy*, filed a lawsuit in Los Angeles Superior Court on December 26, 2007 against the program and its supervisor, Randy Douthit, claiming, "He was fired from the show not because ratings were down [the official reason] but because he opposed the racial screening that occurs on the show."[43] The case was settled out of court and the details were not made public.[44]

Because ridicule and impersonations are essential to Judge Judy's and Judge Joe Brown's execution of their television justice, producers have to cast litigants who they can ridicule and impersonate in a way that transmits each judge's agenda without getting too overshadowed by racial politics. As I wrote earlier, because humor and comedy organize a hierarchical relationship between the jokester and the person or people made into the joke, the litigants' and the judges' race are factors in how the joke will go over. If most of Judge Judy's litigants were black and Latino and she ridiculed all of them the way she did the Rosses, her "take responsibility" message would get lost in accusations of racism. By humiliating and ridiculing white litigants Judge Judy's "take responsibility" message can take the fore.

While Judge Judy's "take responsibility" message is not race-specific, *Judge Joe Brown's* "manhood" messages are directed at black men and women. Casting black litigants (especially black male litigants) gives Brown the opportunity to perform his entertaining impersonations while broadcasting his message. But the composition of the litigant pool reflects another aspect of reality courtroom TV that I have discussed throughout this book: its lack of a centralized value system. TV judges are marketed and branded based on their differences (not in spite of them). Reality courtroom TV projects a landscape of judges with various values and morals, and tough judges use punitive and comedic tactics to attract their unique audience base. These judges use their comedy, their sharp tongues, and their biting wit to symbolically enforce their particular views of moral order and citizenship obligations. While not all viewers will like or agree with Judge Joe Brown's or Judge Judy's tactics or messages, those that do may discover their allegiances by what and who makes them laugh.

5

The Judiciary's "Lonely Splendor": Courtroom TV and the Battle for Ideological Influence

At some point during every reality courtroom TV show the announcer or a title card will remind the audience that what they are about to see is real. *Divorce Court* boasts, "Real couples. Real disputes." *The People's Court* announcer says, "Real cases. Real litigants. In our forum: The People's Court." *Judge Judy* begins, "The cases are real. The rulings are final." However, the limits of the real on the programs are left unarticulated. The elements of staged performance that go beyond what Richard Schechner termed, "scripts of behavior," the twice-behaved social behaviors we regularly enact performed by actual lawyers, judges, litigants, and court officers, are masked by the veneer of reality insisted upon by the programs' production.[1] Only at the tail end of the closing credits can a determined viewer pause to read the quickly passing one or two sentence disclaimer about appearance fees and the limits of the judge character's jurisdiction.

The programs' dissembling about their explicit theatricality, performance elaborations, and entertainment aims in order to convince audiences of their realness encapsulates the root of the contention American legal professionals have had with the presentation of legal process on television since the 1950s. Once within the camera's grip, critics worried that actual courts would bend to the whimsical passions of public reception and the dramatic, and sometimes salacious, drive of the entertainment industry. As the 1950s television lineup swelled with scripted courtroom dramas that hired legal professionals to imbue the fictions with an air of legitimacy, the American Bar Association's distaste for the genre grew.

As early as the 1960s, the appearance of legal professionals on television incited debates about judicial conduct. After an editorial appeared in the Los Angeles newspaper *Metropolitan News* on February 18, 1960, criticizing lawyers who performed on courtroom dramatizations, the Los Angeles County Bar Association (LACBA) tried to ban lawyers from acting on Courtroom programs.[2] LACBA cited that lawyers' appearances were self-advertising, a direct violation of California's legal code of conduct for lawyers (Canon 27 of the ABA 1908), a code that provided lawyers may only advertise their business through business cards. The Legal Ethics Committee first invoked this Canon in 1943 in regard to lawyers' appearances on radio programs. (Over 30 years later it was overridden by *Bates v. State Bar of Arizona 433 US 350* [1977], which decided that an attorney's right to advertise was protected under the First Amendment of the US Constitution.)

The LACBA also declared that the appearances of real lawyers risked "bringing the courts and the administration of justice into disrespect and reproach."[3] During the 1960 annual National Conference of Bar Presidents' panel discussion on courtroom dramas and television appearances of Bar members, one of the members of the Committee on Judicial Ethics noted that the subjects of litigation leaned toward the "sensational and bizarre" and that the episodes' objectives were "to see which attorney could reduce which witness to hysteria the quickest."[4] When asked if audiences mistake the programs for real trials, former Bar president, Herman F. Selvin, responded that audiences are led to believe they are real and so believe them to be: "These programs are advertised to be programs in which real lawyers appear; but again without being guilty of expressly fraudulent advertising, they come as close as possible to suggesting to the public that what they are going to see is not a simulation or a recreation, but a real trial." Mr Selvin protested that the programs sold viewers a bad bill of goods, and their deceitful promotion would inevitably brew discontent while dashing the public's expectations for the courts.

Presiding Bar president Grant Cooper played the devil's advocate by reminding members that television could do "a good public relations job for the Bar."[5] He asked those present to consider the advantages of having legal professionals take advantage of the medium. Mr Selvin contested Mr Cooper's optimism and responded that the programs' necessary inauthenticity posed a problem that could not be overcome. Selvin warned that because their primary aims were entertainment, their exaggerations in the service of "dramatic effect" would constitute and fix the public's impressions—both substantive and procedural—of the law.[6] Selvin's complaint was not only that the needs of TV could not be reconciled with the Bar's, but also that the attractiveness of TV's sensational portrayals (as opposed to the dullness of actual legislation) would offer such a persuasive picture of legal process viewers would read them as truthful depictions.

Judge Evelle J. Younger, the TV judge of *Traffic Court*, disagreed with the Bar presidents' complaints. Younger, who would later go on to become the Attorney General of California, reluctantly resigned from the show once *Traffic Court* got sponsorship in 1958 because its association with an advertiser put into question Younger's judicial ethics according to LACBA.[7] When asked to step down from his television bench on *Traffic Court* Judge Younger responded to his critics with an opinion that echoed Mr Cooper's. He argued that actual legal professionals would better represent the law than entertainers, and that legal professionals were responsible for ensuring and improving the reputation of law on TV. He said that they could use the medium to educate as well as entertain: "Have judges the right to refuse to use television to the fullest extent—or is it our duty to utilize this tremendously effective medium to better explain our laws and system of justice? . . . I do not believe that the judiciary can forever hide behind its robes in lonely splendor."[8] Younger's passionate rebuttal to the Ethics Committee warned that without the input of legal professionals television would continue to malign the judiciary with inappropriate representations. To counter this damage, Younger averred that legal professionals would represent the judiciary more responsibly than television producers, and in the right hands, could use television for the public good.

Younger connected the potential of courtroom dramas to the public service television programs popular at the time. In writing about these programs, Anna McCarthy gauged how in America's Cold War climate the television industry's structural separation from the federal government "made the medium seem like an ideal tool for nondirective persuasion; it could be used to educate (or reeducate) viewers' attitudes surrounding problems in a range of areas, from industrial relations to the Jim Crow South, while keeping them at a safe distance from the tentacles of the state."[9] This led to campaigns for "citizenship education on television," a way for TV to "bring its audience members into the domain of governance without subjecting them to direct state control—embodying, in other words, the ethos of liberal democracy as 'government at a distance.'"[10] Younger was positing the same claim while criticizing the Bar's disinclination to use media as an educational tool. He blamed this reluctance on the bench's separatist desire to remain in "lonely splendor."

The Bar Association never succeeded at banning lawyers from appearing on these shows, and legal professionals-turned-TV-stars continued to defend their appearances. The aforementioned Edgar Allen Jones, Jr, a UCLA law professor who also played the judge on *Accused* and *Day In Court*, justified his starring role in an article he wrote in *Virginia Law Weekly* (June 6, 1961) with Formal Opinion 298 issued by the American Bar Association on April 15, 1961. The opinion allowed for lawyers to appear on commercial programs as long as they were not identified as lawyers, the programs were clearly labeled dramatizations and the performances "conform[ed] to the proper standard of the bench and Bar in their participation in judicial or other proceedings."[11]

The Bar Presidents discussed two primary concerns that continue to irk critics of reality courtroom dramas today. The first complaint over depictions of the courtroom process summarized the fear that the programs would shed a poor light on the American Bar Association and the legal system—especially when the motive behind the broadcasts was entertainment and not education. The second was a concern over the public's misconception that justice is served like it is on television. In a 2001 article in *The American Journal of Trial Advocacy* Kimberlianne Podlas wrote that reality courtroom TV has damaging effects on juries: "Negative opinions about television judges may be extended to a negative view of the bench generally, the outcomes with which they are associated, and the justice system that they represent."[12] Citing documentation on media's pedagogical influence and the effects of juror exposure to syndi-court (syndicated reality courtroom TV) justice, Podlas proposed that during impaneling, lawyers and courts need to amend potential jurors' misconceptions that reality TV courts are like actual ones. She concluded that in addition to a more extensive *voir dire* session, jurors should have an orientation that addresses popular misconceptions about judge behavior and the legal process that stem from reality courtroom TV.[13] Her assessment asserted that the influence of reality courtroom TV is detrimental to the administration of justice in real courts and therefore the court system must address the discrepancy in juror expectations by creating programs to reeducate jurors on what to anticipate from the justice system.

Similarly, in his essay written in *The Journal of American Arbitration* in 2005, Philip Kimball echoed Podlas's anxiety and asked for congressional regulation of reality courtroom TV's "exploitation of arbitration":

> At this point, Congressional regulation of these programs is perhaps the only available recourse for trying to protect against the effects of syndi-courts' exploitation of arbitration. There is obviously no way or no reason for syndi-court shows to be taken off of the air. However, the effect of these shows upon the general public's attitudes towards the legal system is enough of a concern to require the attention of Congress.[14]

Kimball wanted Congress to pass a law requiring reality courtroom TV shows to announce in the credits that they are not actual courts. (None of the programs explicitly explain in the opening or closing credits that the proceedings are taking place on a stage.) Kimball won the 2004 American Bar Association award for his study; a win that suggests his theories coincided with the ABA's trepidation over reality courtroom TV's influence. Like Podlas, Kimball voiced concern that reality courtroom TV misleads potential jurors: "The danger is that the public perceives these shows as how trials are supposed to work, which, in turn, warps potential jurors' approach to acting as impartial tryers of fact."[15] Both authors regarded reality courtroom TV as impediments to legal operations.

The 1950s courtroom dramas aired in an age that predated the televising of trials. Audiences had limited experience with trial broadcasts.[16] Even though credits rolled at the end listing the actors and the production staff, critics worried that audiences had no other model with which to compare them. By the time reality courtroom TV hit the market, the presence of cameras in courtrooms was on the rise, an escalation spurred by the 1981 Supreme Court *Chandler v. Texas* decision in which Chief Justice Burger's majority opinion suggested that cameras could be in the service of "appearances of justice" (see Introduction). A decade after the decision, the Court TV channel dedicated round the clock coverage to trials and legal issues. Home viewers had more access to courtroom proceedings on TV than ever before. So reality courtroom TV programs were appearing simultaneously with broadcast footage from actual trials.

When new reality courtroom programs came on air in the late 1990s, filling daytime lineups across noncable channels, it would have been likely that viewers with and without basic cable subscriptions could have more readily found a reality courtroom program on the dial than footage from an actual one. When that happens, as Podlas and Kimball both asked, would viewers be able to distinguish between the two? Would they prefer the entertainment format to the actual one? Or worse, would they expect legal process to be like it is on TV? These points of criticism spanning over 50 years not only mark an enduring fear of the media's influence over public perceptions of law and shared arguments in favor of them, but also reveal that the arguments against depictions of law for entertainment have existed regardless of the format: whether it is presented as a scripted drama or as reality TV.

While these aforementioned critics aimed their sites on audience reception, Richard Sherwin also critiqued the effects from the inside out, contending that law "seizes on the same putatively self-legitimating images and forms of persuasion as the commercial mass media themselves."[17] Sherwin assessed that the danger of implementing pop cultural strategies of emotional manipulation in legal process—especially on the part of lawyers—is that it impedes complex thinking and critical reflection: "What we find instead are artificially heightened and strategically manipulated urgencies of emotion—the disguised, and at times unconsciously displaced, compulsions and needs of irrational fury, retribution, fantasy, and illicit desire."[18] This is, as I have illustrated, what reality courtroom TV does. It appeals primarily to the emotions—both the audience's and the litigants'. Its cathartic aims trump all others. Sherwin suggested that when legal professionals borrow entertainment norms the process of legal persuasion elides the necessary complex approach to the presentation of facts that ensures fair process. The problems of legal representation as a cultural product can be contested on both sides of the gavel.

What this also suggests is that pop cultural representations of law might not be so different from what transpires in actual courts precisely because legal professionals cannot help but borrow entertainment norms as tools of persuasion. If this is indeed the case, it becomes more complicated to locate what separates reality courtroom TV proceedings from the small claims trials they emulate. While on its face this assertion seems to have a simple answer: small claims are actual trials held in courthouses and reality courtroom TV programs stage arbitrations on a courtroom set. However, as the preceding chapters have demonstrated, the dynamic of reality courtroom TV's straddling of theater and law obfuscates this divide. Reality courtroom TV does not only *represent* small claims court; it also creates another entity that produces similar effects—and more—as small claims courts. It is more than a copy; it is a simulation.

Jean Baudrillard alleged that a simulation produces the symptoms of the thing simulated while not producing the thing itself. The simulation does not dissimulate, but neither is it "really so." Baudrillard wrote: "To simulate is to feign to have what one doesn't have."[19] He went on to write that simulating something is fundamentally different from faking it. He used the example of an illness: "'Whoever fakes an illness can simply stay in bed and make everyone believe he is ill. Whoever simulates an illness produces in himself some of the symptoms' (Littré). Therefore, pretending, or dissimulating, leaves the principle of reality intact . . ."[20] Dissimulating, lying, is plain dishonest. The lie can be exposed, the truth known. Simulation, on the other hand, changes these conditions and "threatens the difference between the 'true' and the 'false,' the 'real' and the 'imaginary.'"[21] It does this by producing the *same* symptoms as the (true) event simulated; it is a "disease" consisting of pure symptom, a malady without an underlying infection.

Baudrillard used the example of a bank robbery to flesh out the distinction between truth, lie and simulation. He wrote that a simulated bank robbery and a real bank robbery would have virtually the same effects assuming that the patrons of the bank and the bank employees were unaware that the robbers were merely simulating the hold up. Thinking the event was real and the guns were loaded, a patron might have a heart attack or experience panic and an employee might hand over money to the "robbers": "[T]he network of artificial signs will become inextricably mixed up with real elements . . . in short, you will immediately find yourself once again, without wishing it, in the real, one of whose functions is precisely to devour any attempt at simulation, to reduce everything to the real—that is, to the established order itself, well before institutions and justice come into play."[22] Because the effects of the simulation and the real event are indistinguishable, simulation has the potential to supplement the thing or process simulated. Because reality courtroom TV can settle disputes and reconcile some legal claims, it is not unreasonable for some people to prefer to have their cases heard on a courtroom set—especially if the latter produces a more desirable emotional and financial experience.

Absences

Baudrillard wrote that every simulation has absences, the missing pieces that distinguish it from the object or process simulated. In Baudrillard's example of a bank robbery there were no bullets in the guns. This absence confirmed the robbery's status as simulation because pulling the trigger would not result in the firing of the weapon. The promise was there—that the gun could shoot to kill—and unsuspecting participants reacted according to that promise, but the ability to follow through with this promise was lacking. The guns needed the bullets to execute the act cued by pulling the trigger. Looking at reality courtroom TV, what are its "missing bullets"?

Of course there are a lot of "false" or "theatrical" elements in reality courtroom TV simulations: the bailiff and judge are in costumes given to them by wardrobe and approved by the producers; the makeup and wardrobe staff offer to dress the litigants and do their hair and makeup; the production pays the awards and appearance fees; the actors and ticket holders comprise the studio audience; the cases take place on a professionally designed set lit by lighting designers; camera operators move around set to capture the action; and stage managers and directors cue the stops and starts of the cases. These theatrical elements alone do not address the critical absences in Baudrillard's sense, but they pave the way for it: the taped arbitrations lack the force of law that oversees small claims trials, and more specifically, the judge's behavior and the litigants' conduct. On TV the judges do not have to adhere to judicial codes of behavior, rules of evidence, or rules of procedure. They do not even have to be licensed to practice law in the state where the shows are taped. For example, in 2010, former *Judge Joe Brown* litigant, Mark Schweninger, sued the show's star for fraud and slander.[23] Despite signing a waiver, Schwinger claimed that producers misled him into believing Brown was a legitimate judge when Brown was actually retired from the bench and unlicensed to practice law in California. Schweninger also charged that during the 2008 case Brown humiliated him by mocking him on national TV. The Los Angeles Superior Court dismissed both charges because, according to the superior court judge, Brown's behavior was subject to the "litigation privilege," a California Civil Code 47(b)(2) that "protects parties in litigation from subsequent tort liability for any statements made during litigation except those that give rise to a claim of malicious prosecution."[24] This code is most often applied to protect lawyers during arbitration hearings who are afforded different safeguards than judges.

Concurrently, the repercussions for a lawyer's presumed malicious actions during arbitration are different from a judge's during a trial. Because Brown was not an active judge, his conduct was safeguarded. The same goes for the reality courtroom litigants. A TV litigant can behave outrageously without legal ramifications. Assigning legal penalties to their conduct is beyond the scope of the reality TV arbitration. Although the judge may threaten it, there is no chain of legitimation to substantiate or enforce punishments beyond the awards the programs offer. The judge's commands, in the words of speech act theorist J. L. Austen, are infelicitous, meaning they do not have the illocutionary force to constitute the claims made.[25] On TV, only the arbitration and the contract the litigants sign are enforceable. Beyond this, the force of reality courtroom TV law is symbolic. This becomes unmistakable when lawyers attempt to use reality courtroom TV proceedings as evidence in an actual trial.

In 2010, Justice Francois A. Rivera heard the case *Kahn v. New York Department of Housing* in the Supreme Court of Kings County, New York. The case and Justice Rivera's comments locate the boundaries of reality courtroom TV. In this case the petitioner, Ellen Kahn, tried to invalidate a decision made by Francis Lippa, an administrative hearing officer for the New York City Department of Housing Preservation and Development (HPD) regarding succession rights to her mother's apartment in a Mitchell-Lama housing development.[26] According to HPD rules a successor must have lived in the apartment for at least 2 years immediately prior to the primary tenant's vacating the apartment. Kahn claimed that she was living with her mother during that time; however, Lippa countered Kahn's claim by citing testimony she gave during her appearance on *The People's Court* in 2009. Kahn appeared on *The People's Court* as the plaintiff in a case against her mother's in-home aid. During the episode Kahn told Judge Milian that she only visited her mother on weekends. She "testified" on *The People's Court* that she was too busy to see her mother during the week.

Prosecuting attorney Lippa used a DVD recording of the episode as evidence that Kahn did not live with her mother. Kahn's counsel, Lee Nigen, asked the judge to dismiss this evidence. Nigen argued that testimony on *The People's Court* is not actually sworn testimony regardless of what it appears to be to the average viewer. Judge Rivera agreed: "'The People's Court' is not a court, body, agency, public servant or other person authorized by law to conduct a proceeding and to administer the oath or cause it to be administered."[27] Justice Rivera's claim denuded *The People's Court* of legal authority despite the fact that it is an actual arbitration hearing, and in most states arbitrators have the ability to administer an oath if they so choose. However, on reality courtroom TV the bailiffs administer the oaths to make it look like a trial, and, as Justice Rivera stipulated, this is at the expense of the oath's validity.

Justice Rivera then took his analysis a step further, drawing extensive parallels between what is said on the program to what is said on stage in a theater:

> The words or statements uttered by these participants are not testimony. They are neither sworn nor reliable. Furthermore, the statements made on the show have no more probative force than the words of an actor reading from a script in a play. The only difference between the two is that the participants of the show may freely ad-lib their lines. Here, AHO Lippa gave tremendous weight and probative force to words and statements allegedly uttered by the petitioner on "The People's Court" television show. He described the utterances as "sworn testimony" and "compelling admissions." This view of the utterances petitioner allegedly made on the show is irrational.[28]

Judge Rivera's decision placed reality courtroom TV proceedings within the realm of theater, a connotation that implied the actions and words spoken on TV stages were in the service of drama and not law. The aims of drama, according to Rivera, supersede the law's objectives to determine facts and uncover truths. Because the programs have no recourse to guarantee that a litigant or witness tells the truth, the statements made have no more legitimacy than lines an actor utters during a play. There is no apparatus to give the actions that take place on reality TV's stages probative force. Therefore, according to the judge, the testimonies made on reality courtroom TV should only be applicable within the world of reality courtroom TV, just like an actor's lines and actions should only have relevance within the world of the play.

Judge Rivera's opinion reflected his frustration with the counsel's "illogical" willingness to use a TV trial's proceeding as evidence. The tone of his opinion disclosed the urgency he felt in clarifying the difference between the made-for-entertainment display of justice on reality courtroom TV and what happens in a court of law. But Lippa's unflagging willingness to bring the defendant's TV testimony to court elucidated how fragile the line is distinguishing law from entertainment. Not only that, the threat posed by Lippa's holding both processes up equally implies that TV offers a competing impression of the judicial process—and one that may be preferable, for some, to what goes in actual courts. As I suggested in Chapter 1, these may not be predilections only experienced by viewers, but also by sitting judges.

In February 2007, Judge Larry Seidlin, a Florida Dade county judge, presided over the highly publicized Anna Nicole Smith body hearing. As the hearing progressed, reporters noted that Seidlin's performance became more and more dramatic. The judge purportedly hammed it up for the cameras, calling the lawyers by nicknames, telling personal stories, and cracking jokes—behaviors akin to the performances of reality courtroom TV judges. He exhibited his emotional range, breaking down into tears as he delivered his verdict. Perhaps, as *Access Hollywood* reported, CBS Paramount was scouting "the wisecracking emotional judge" to be the star of his own reality courtroom TV show and this hearing was his audition.[29] ABC News described Seidlin's performance as one would critique a one-person show. It highlighted Seidlin's emotional range and the funny quips, favoring these observations over the substance of this case.[30]

Judge Seidlin heard the case without a jury, and according to Judge Andrew Napolitano, senior judicial analyst for Fox News, Seidlin's informal behavior was not out of the ordinary for a case like this. However, Napolitano gave the admonition that Seidlin should have exhibited restraint because the case was broadcast, and Seidlin's performance "[brought] the court into disrepute."[31] Napolitano self-reflexively remarked that had he been similarly as "folksy" as Seidlin, he would not have allowed cameras in the courtroom. He then said, "We didn't have cameras in the courtroom in those days. There was no way to audition for television in your day job."[32]

A few months after the trial Seidlin retired from the bench, citing in a letter to Florida Governor Charlie Crist that he wanted to take advantage of other opportunities outside of the judicial system.[33] In 2010, Seidlin was finally cast as the star judge in Mighty Oak Entertainment's creative spin on reality courtroom TV, a TV pilot called *Psychic Court*. Seidlin told PR Newswire: "I'm opening my courtroom to those who deal in paranormal activities as a way to help uncover evidence and assist me in determining who's telling the truth."[34] On the *Psychic Court* test pilot episode, psychics, clairvoyants, and the telepathic assisted Judge Seidlin with his rulings. The former judge boasted to the press, "It's going to be amazing."[35]

Whether or not Seidlin used the Anna Nicole Smith body hearing as an audition, viewers perceived it as such, and this played to the anxieties many have about mixing law and entertainment. This was a conundrum that the journalist Steven Lubet presaged in 1999, when Judge Joe Brown was still a Memphis judge while also starring on his own TV show:

> But ask yourself this question: How many sitting judges are at this very moment wondering what they can do to become the next Judge Judy? Are the lords of the cable networks (and the masters of niche

marketing) looking for a funny judge, a sexy judge, a melodramatic judge or maybe a poet? Overwhelmed by dreams of Hollywood, who knows what a judge might do to attract attention? Whatever the case, the audition might be today, in a courtroom near you. So heaven help the litigant whose fate is being determined when the talent scouts are in town.[36]

If Seidlin exaggerated his performance to be more reality courtroom TV-like, then he demonstrated the validity of the warning Steven Lubet rang out 8 years earlier. Lubet cautioned that we do not want our judges performing to the standards set by actors and actresses. But televised sitting judges in actual courts face a challenge on several fronts. When TV offers glamor, financial incentives, and millions of viewers ready to listen to one's expert advice, it may be difficult for a judge to resist the temptation to use one's position to attain money and fame. Furthermore, when trials are broadcast, how do judges negotiate delivering the appearance of justice when the cultural representations that shape these appearances conflict with legal norms?

The indispensable role

Three weeks after the trial I was called to sit on as a jury member began, all six jurors were brought back into the courtroom to hear the counsels' closing arguments. Once they finished, the judge turned his attention to us. In a flat tone he dispassionately read the jury deliberation instructions from a thick navy blue binder, directing us to rely on our personal opinions and rich individual experiences to give us the necessary tools to decide the case together. He stressed that our role was indispensable. The verdict was in our hands. But when we all gathered for the first time to discuss the details of the case I was disappointed to discover some of my fellow jurors' heedlessness in hashing out a fair decision. One of the jurors even said to me, "I'll decide what you decide." The eagerness of several jury members to concede their own opinions rather than suffer through their own interpretations of the evidence was unsettling.

On reality courtroom TV there are no deliberations. We never see a judge confused about what to do or how to come to a verdict, and I could see the attraction to this kind of justice much more clearly after spending three weeks on a jury. Making a decision as a jury member is daunting, and a judge who can decide what is right frees us from the responsibility of discerning for ourselves how someone should be judged. Reality TV judges always know what is right and wrong. There is always a loser and someone is always clearly guilty, and this appears to be decided without much effort on the judge's part. TV judges celebrate charismatic authority and passionate populism, and from their personalized courtroom sets they invert Alexis de Tocqueville's postulation that the American jury system is a training ground for democracy.[37] The judge, not the jury, according to reality courtroom TV process, has the indispensable role. And, arguably, there is comfort in believing that someone can tell us what is right and what is the truth, and this is the exact kind of complacency that the chorus in Brecht's *The Exception and the Rule* warned us to question. Brecht wrote: "When something seems 'the most obvious thing in the world' it means that any attempt to understand the world has been given up."[38] Reality courtroom TV provides simple answers and predictable verdicts in order to present the audience with an orderly world and a system that efficiently rights its wrongs. The judges intend for their didactic instructions to be followed, not debated.

The teaching play

The constitutive force of legal decisions and the way these decisions shape social practice also operates in the symbolic realm, in cultural representations of law. Gad Guterman argued that despite Pierre Bourdieu's insistence that the cultural field is always in a dominated position, plays, television shows, and novels assert their influence on law and social practice.[39] Perhaps this is why the cultural arm of the Bolshevik party during the Russian Revolution used mock agitation trials (agitsudy) to educate and stimulate revolutionary consciousness, especially among the working class and the uneducated peasant population. Like reality courtroom TV whose viewers and litigants are predominantly lower and middle income and working class individuals, the agitsudy was "drama by, for, and about the proletarian and peasant masses."[40] Through audience participation, the invocation of legal power, and the implementation of Vyacheslav Ivanov's utopic theatrical strategies, the agitsudy aspired "to reach into the everyday lives of spectators and increase their vigilance in uncovering counter-revolutionary activities and attitudes."[41] These improvised and audience participatory performances were educational and entertaining, sometimes melodramatic, and always clear in their message. Lenin expounded on the educational role of the agitsudy, saying they were, "just as self-evident and important as the judiciary's function of rendering proletarian justice."[42] Through their performances, authors and advocates of the agitsudy aimed for the lessons to become part of the participants' everyday discourse. The lessons learned would not only help viewers develop a revolutionary mentality, but also condone changes in behavior such as promoting better sanitation and a stronger work ethic. The trials' messages instructed audiences not only in how to think as a Bolshevik, but also how to act like one.

Although reality courtroom TV may not share the same revolutionary zeal as the agitsudy, the genre's legacy is tied to the history of mock trials used to persuade and educate its audiences by applying these lessons to the viewers' everyday lives. Laurie Ouellette wrote that reality courtroom TV inculcates audiences into methods of self-policing: "Thus, while the programs claim to steer and guide, they also extend a variety of control strategies devised for the cost-efficient management of crime into the nooks and crannies of everyday life."[43] They induct their audiences into modes of citizenship through behavioral instruction. However, reality courtroom TV's populist judicial model fails to deliver any uniform message because it is unlinked to any central value or moral system. Instead, the autonomous viewer picks her television justice. He or she can subscribe to it, change the channel, or assume any variety of stances in relation to the program and the message it endorses. However, both the agitsudy's authors and the reality courtroom TV judges grasp the pedagogical persuasiveness of the trial (both theatrical and actual) and how its staged productions engage audiences by including them in the process.

Scripting reality

The climate of reality courtroom TV has changed since my research on this book began in 2007. The number of programs has, at the time of this writing, decreased to only six syndicated shows: *Judge Judy, Divorce Court, The People's Court, Judge Mathis, Paternity Court,* and *Judge Alex. Judge Alex* is scheduled to go off air at the end of this season, and a new spin on the genre developed by Judge Judy Sheindlin is slated to debut in the fall of 2014. The new program, *Hot Bench,* will feature a three-judge panel, starring Judge Patricia DiMango and attorneys Tanya Acker and Larry Bakman. The new program will resemble appellate courts, which compose one-third of all American courts.

With the decline in reality courtroom TV there has been a rise in scripted versions, which now rival in numbers (not in viewership) the reality versions. Scripted courtroom programs look the same as reality courtroom TV shows, follow the same format and even hire former reality courtroom judges to play the leading roles. (Judge Karen and Judge Cristina have both found a new home on scripted television.) Actors are required to sign confidentiality agreements, and the credits at the end of the show do not name the writers or the actors. By all means these programs try to convince viewers that they are just like reality courtroom shows, never mentioning otherwise in their publicity, in interviews about the programs, or in the Direct TV program guide.[44] They exploit audiences' familiarity with the reality courtroom genre, anticipating that by looking like these shows they will reap the same benefits (a sizeable and committed viewing audience that, in turn, will stir up advertising revenue), while skirting reality courtroom's higher production costs that come from having to fly in litigants, put them up in hotels, pay their judgments, keep an in-house team of lawyers and a staff of researchers to cull through small claims dockets and the extra costs that arise from the litigants' unpredictability, such as their refusal to sign contracts or go on set.

Instead, open casting notices target the novice actor with the promise of pay and a television credit.[45] A casting notice for *We The People with Gloria Allred* urged actors with improvisational comedy training to demonstrate their talent at the Culver City audition. The notice welcomed actors of all kinds ("Gay-Trans-Drag Queens, Twins/Multiples, Mother/Daughter, Father/Son, Sister/Brothers, Cousins, and Characters are welcomed too."[46]), and the only caveat was that the actor could not have appeared on another one of the production company's court shows. *We the People with Gloria Allred* premiered in 2011 on Direct TV and can be streamed for a small monthly fee on the Youtube subscription channel, JusticeCentral.TV.[47] On this program Los Angeles-based celebrity civil rights lawyer, Gloria Allred (perhaps best known for representing Nicole Brown Simpson's family in the 1994 O. J. Simpson murder trial), wears a judge's robe, sits behind a bench on a courtroom set, and improvises her decisions to small claims cases performed by nonunion actors. Some of the episodes are elaborations of actual small claims filed in courts across the country embellished by the program's hired writing staff. The actors rehearse with producers beforehand, and, once on set, they stage their cases in front of a paid audience and six high definition (HD) cameras. This scripted courtroom show and the three other programs just like it (*Supreme Justice with Judge Karen*, *America's Court with Judge Ross*, and *Justice for All with Judge Cristina Perez*) are all produced by comedian Byron Allen's production company, Entertainment Studios, an enterprise he described to *Hollywood Reporter* as the "Walmart of television," alluding not only to its cheaply and quickly made content, but also the demographic it aims to amuse.[48]

While reality courtroom shows stage arbitrations as if they were small claims trials, the scripted versions stage half hour dramas as if they were reality courtroom shows. They are both repetitions of sorts. Reality courtroom shows reproduce reality courtroom shows' legal and theatrical processes—binding arbitrations mediated by former judges and legal professionals and staged as if they were small claims trials. Scripted courtroom programs reproduce only reality courtroom shows' theatrical process, the performance techniques used to dramatize arbitration first established by *The People's Court* in 1981. Both formats try to assert their authenticity—the former by hiring legal professionals and litigants with pending litigation—and the latter by borrowing the choreography and costumes of the reality format in order to veil that the stories and the characters are crafted by a writing staff. The difference between the programs is even overlooked by the Emmy Awards committee who has lumped both formats into the same category, Outstanding Legal/Courtroom Program.

Although they can easily be mistaken as the same, the two genres are fundamentally different. This difference can best be seen in the litigants' objectives and what motivates them to come onto the programs. Most litigants who appear on reality courtroom shows are there to argue an actual dispute, forfeiting their rights to appeal by signing contracts binding them to the judge's decision. Of course, some guests with fake cases make it past producers and onto the programs, and there are the occasional publicity stunts, like the Naked Cowboy's appearance on *Cristina's Court* and former *Different Strokes* star Gary Coleman's trial on *Divorce Court* with his wife, Shannon Price, in 2008. But for those who are there to argue an actual case, the legal decision continues to have consequences after the performance ends. For example, when *Divorce Court's* Judge Lynn Toler decides that an angry husband separated from his wife was wrong keeping a leather couch and orders him to return it to her, Toler's decision, if it is based on a valid law, can be legally enforced by local authorities in the state the litigants reside.

Therefore, the litigants have incentives to win the case. Appearing on TV and being able to discuss one's problems in a public forum may be an added benefit, but winning and losing the cases also has consequences that reflect back onto the litigants' personal involvement with the dispute. This is not the case when actors are hired to improvise a case with the star judge. On Entertainment Studios' offerings, the disputes are scripted, the relationships are crafted, and the drama is rehearsed. The measure of a good outcome for the participants is not whether the litigants—played by actors—win the case; rather, it's whether or not the actors feel like they gave a convincing and entertaining performance. These varying objectives produce different effects.

I spoke with one of the actors, John Moore, cast on an episode of *We the People with Gloria Allred*.[49] John is a nonunion actor who studied improvisational comedy and moved to Los Angeles from the midwest. He auditioned in 2011 after seeing a notice on the website, LA Casting. He was thrilled when he was cast as a young, gay plaintiff: "From the beginning, I looked at it like I am going to be on TV and I'm going to be playing this gay guy, and as an actor I saw it as a challenge. I was going to get to do something that I've never done."[50] When I asked him about his experience during the scene, John told me that he cared very little about winning. He explained: "Probably eighty-five percent of the actors they hire could care less if they win because they're not going to make any more money if they win or lose, so why does it matter? They already got the part, you know?" While guests on reality courtroom shows want to win the judgments paid for by the production companies, the actors on the scripted shows do not get paid any more for winning. Of course, if the actors put on a good show, they can use these scenes for their demo-reels with the hope that their clip may help them get other parts down the line, which is what John wanted.[51]

To give a good performance, John relied on his actor training to expose the subtext of unrequited love the writers scripted in order to spice up what would otherwise be a lackluster dispute. After all, the heightened interpersonal drama that erupts during disputes over small things *is* the beating heart of reality courtroom shows. Similar to the draw of talk shows, these moments of exposure, when audiences witness the cracks in the litigants' carefully crafted personas, are captivating. The scripted versions of courtroom television programs try to reproduce this complexity of self-presentation, but fail due in large part to the inconsistent quality of the acting. Bad acting diminishes the entertainment value of the scripted shows. The allure of unscripted reality courtroom shows, evidenced by the ratings, comes largely from watching nonactors act badly, a difference that I enumerated in Chapter 2.[52]

However, the key distinctions between the two versions have more to do with the actuality of the claims, the litigants' personal connections to them, and how the judges' decisions resonate beyond the frame of the scene. On reality courtroom shows, the litigants are arguing cases that are real to them and the outcomes matter. The emotional stakes are high, and this intensity is often palpable and convincing in a way that the scripted versions try to be, but only occasionally succeed at doing. Furthermore, when reality courtroom TV episodes cull from small claims courts, they actually lighten the burden on the courts by hearing cases for them. So the process has quantifiable effects not only for the participants, but also for local courts.

The pop culture indicator

Legal scholar David Ray Papke wrote that successful pop culture is "an indirect indicator of what Americans think about and hope for the law, legal institutions, and lawyers."[53] If Papke was right the shift in reality courtroom TV's popularity may reveal something about what viewers want and expect from the judicial system. Not only has the changing economy of television and the increased viewing options made reality courtroom TV production costs more burdensome, but also as the appearance of the American political landscape has shifted over the past 5 years, emblematized by such monumental events as the election of President Barak Obama, the visibility and widening support of the gay rights movement, and the appointment of Sonia Sotomayor to the Supreme Court, the picture of alternative leadership reality courtroom TV once provided is no longer as anomalous. Whether reality courtroom TV helped pave the way for more diverse representation or it followed the trend in viewers' wants, the vacancy it once filled seems to be less free.

Despite reality courtroom TV's waning popularity, the ones on air still offer a familiar picture of legal process that is a departure from the alienation many Americans feel from their courts. The theatrical conventions of reality courtroom TV symbolically work against this experience through its repetition, ubiquity, and simple approach to complex issues. As performances that instruct, reality courtroom TV orients right and wrong based on each judge's personal claims, and these are lessons that the viewers can, if they want, apply to their own lives. They teach us how to discipline ourselves, but not in any one way. Reality courtroom TV models are disparate, unlinked to any central value or moral system, and instead direct themselves to particular viewing communities. Each program's unique take on how to handle and decide a case elicits feelings of fairness and unfairness that are dependent on varying and group-oriented conceptions of justice, what John Rawls called a "public conception of justice." Rawls: "... [I]n a constitutional democracy the public conception of justice should be, so far as possible, independent of controversial philosophical and religious doctrines."[54] Public conceptions of justice are more intuitive than complex: "Justice as fairness starts from this idea as one of the basic intuitive ideas which we take to be implicit in the public culture of a democratic society."[55] The autonomous viewer can pick the program that best fits his or her conception of justice. And these choices are not without measurable benefits for when and if the viewer needs to go to court. The programs familiarize viewers with legal concepts like the necessity of contracts, how to execute them, and the importance of preserving receipts and documents.

The relationship between reality courtroom TV's performances, their audiences, court users, and legal process is fluid. Expectations feed appearances and appearances feed expectations. This circular process reminds us that the theater of reality courtroom TV is a performance that takes advantage of the stage as a site to enact alternative realities that get closer to the real life work of conflict resolution than most small claims processes allow, and that these performances can and do resonate beyond the studios' walls.

Appendix

List of Reality Courtroom TV Programs (1981–2013)[1]

The People's Court	1981–93, 1997–ongoing
Jones and Jury	1994–5
Judge Judy	1996–ongoing
Judge Joe Brown	1998–2013
Judge Mills Lane	1998–2001
Judge Wapner's Animal Court	1998–2000
Judge Matthis	1999–ongoing
Divorce Court (3rd Version)	1999–ongoing
Curtis Court	2000–1
Moral Court	2000–1
Power of Attorney	2000–2
Judge Hatchett	2000–8
Texas Justice	2001–5
Eye For an Eye	2003–9
Judge Alex	2005–14
Judge Maria Lopez	2006–8
Cristina's Court	2006–9
Jury Duty	2007–8
Judge David Young	2007–9
Judge Pirro	2008–11
Family Court with Judge Penny	2008–9
Judge Karen	2008–9
Speeders Fight Back	2008–9
Street Court	2009–10

(*Continued*)

Judge Karen's Court	2010–11
Swift Justice with Nancy Grace	2010–11
Swift Justice with Jackie Glass	2011–12
Last Shot With Judge Gunn	2011–ongoing
Paternity Court	2013–ongoing
Hot Bench	Premiering Fall 2014

The People's Court: *The People's Court* premiered on September 22, 1981. This first version ran until September 7, 1993, starring Judge Joseph Wapner as the "judge," Doug Llewelyn as the "courtroom commentator," Rusty Burrell as the "bailiff," and Jack Harrell as the narrator. The show was revived on September 8, 1997, and ran until 1999 with former New York mayor Ed Koch playing the "judge." Jerry Sheindlin, Judge Judy's husband, played the "judge" from 1999 to 2001. Georgetown Law School graduate Marilyn Milian was cast in the role in 2001, and the show is still on the air. Edward-Billett Productions and Telepictures Productions produce the program.

Jones and Jury (1994–5): *Jones and Jury* featured Star Jones, who before she became famous on *The View* worked her way up in the Kings County DA's office in Brooklyn, NY to become senior district attorney. She became known from her commentary on the William Kennedy Smith trial (1991) that aired on Court TV. *Jones and Jury* followed the *People's Court* road map, and "Judge" Jones arbitrated small claims cases from her simulated courtroom. Lighthearted Entertainment produced.

Judge Judy (1996–ongoing): Executive produced by Peter Brennan, Randy Douthit, and Timothy Regler, *Judge Judy* debuted on September 16, 1996. Produced first by Big Ticket Television and then by CBS Paramount Television this syndicated show stars Judge Judy Sheindlin. After graduating from New York Law School in 1965, Sheindlin became a prosecutor and then a judge in New York's Kings County Juvenile and Family Court system (see Chapter 1).

***Judge Joe Brown* (1998–2013):** The same production team behind *Judge Judy* produced *Judge Joe Brown*, which debuted on September 14, 1998. Judge Joe Brown, a graduate from UCLA Law School, was a prosecutor in Memphis before he was elected judge of the Shelby County State Criminal Courts, Division Nine. Judge Brown was still a sitting judge when he got cast as the star of his judge TV show. He is the only TV judge to have presided over both a state and television courtroom at the same time (see Chapter 1).

***Judge Mills Lane* (1998–2001):** *Judge Mills Lane* debuted in 1998 and ran until August 31, 2001. Hurricane Entertainment Corporation/Rysher Entertainment and later Paramount Television produced the program. Judge Mills Lane, a graduate from the University of Utah Law School, was a former Nevada district court judge, and at 43 years old became a world championship-boxing referee. He was famous for refereeing the rematch between Mike Tyson and Evander Holyfield (1997), a fight made more memorable when Tyson bit off a piece of Holyfield's ear. He had a short stint voicing an animated character in his likeness on MTV's *Celebrity Death Match* (1998).

***Judge Wapner's Animal Court* (1998–2000):** Airing on Animal Planet, Judge Wapner presided over small claims cases involving pets and animals. Rusty Burrell, his bailiff from *People's Court*, also served beside him on this program. Andrew Solt Productions produced.

***Divorce Court* (1999–ongoing):** See description in next section.

***Curtis Court* (2000–1):** Curtis Court was produced by Karen Bosnak and Lee Navlen, and was a King World production. Anthony Pasquin, a New York City police officer, played the bailiff. James E. Curtis was a former Deputy DA of Riverside County, California. After working in the Juvenile Crimes division he became a motivational speaker, founded a consulting firm for law-enforcement relations, and hosted a radio show. Like other judge TV shows *Judge Curtis* arbitrated cases, but producers intended for the show to explain the legal process to the audience, so the show featured only one case at a time. The awards cap was set at $3,000.

***Moral Court* (2000–1):** Produced and created by Stu Billett Productions, this courtroom gave verdicts based on who was morally right or wrong. Larry Elder played the judge and Russell Brown played the bailiff. Voice-overs announced that Elder was not a real judge and Brown was not a real bailiff, and also reminded the audience that these were not actual small claims litigation and that the verdicts were nonbinding. The guests were billed as "accuser" and "accused". Awards were given based on the degree of the "crime" with the maximum award being $2,000.²

***Power of Attorney* (2000–2):** Andrew Napolitano played the judge until he was replaced by Lynn Toler (future *Divorce Court* judge) when he accepted a job as the Fox News Channel's Senior Judicial Analyst. Joseph Catalano Jr played the bailiff and Francine DeGiorgio played the court reporter on this Monet Lane Productions/Twentieth Television production. The show arbitrated small claims cases, but cast famous attorneys to argue for the litigants. Monet Lane Productions and Twentieth Television produced.

***Judge Mathis* (1999–ongoing):** Telepictures Productions and Warner Bros television produce *Judge Mathis*. Before getting his own show Mathis was elected Detroit's 36th district judge, even though earlier in life he was barred from practicing law because of his criminal record. He quit the Michigan bench when he got his own show (see Chapter 1).

***Judge Hatchett* (2000–8):** Debuting in September 2000, Judge Hatchett, an Emory University Law School graduate and former Fulton County (Georgia) Juvenile Court judge, presided over this family-oriented courtroom. Sony Television produced (see Chapter 3).

***Texas Justice* (2001–5):** Judge Larry Joe Doherty (his legal registered name, though he was never a sitting judge in Houston where he had a career as a successful trial lawyer) played the judge, William Bowers played the bailiff, and Randy Schell narrated. Judge Doherty would often pepper his decisions in these binding arbitrations with bits of Texas history. Twentieth Television produced.

***Eye for an Eye* (2003–7):** Coproduced by The National Lampoon and starring Judge Akim Anastopoulo as the judge, Kato Kaelin as the host, and Sugar Ray Phillips as the bailiff, the judge issued punishments that fit the crime. For example, a defendant found guilty of spousal abuse was sentenced to be the dummy in a women's self-defense class. Anastopoulo, or "Extreme" Akim, as this former South Carolina state prosecutor was named, used a baseball bat instead of a gavel.

Judge Alex **(2005-14):** *Judge Alex* took *Texas Justice*'s timeslot. Judge Alex Ferrer graduated from the University of Miami Law School in 1986. Before becoming the youngest circuit court judge to serve in Miami-Dade County's Criminal and Family Divisions of Florida's 11th Judiciary, Ferrer was a policeman, detective, and SWAT team member. Twentieth Television produced.

Judge Maria Lopez **(2006-8):** Before becoming a TV judge Maria Lopez, a Boston University Law School graduate, served as the assistant to the Massachusetts Attorney General. In 1988, Lopez became the first Latina judge in Massachusetts and first on the state Supreme Court. On the show Pete Rodriguez, a former New York City fireman, played her bailiff. Lopez used the catchphrase "If you can't stand the heat, get out of the courtroom" to draw viewers to this staged binding arbitration. Sony Pictures Television produced.

Cristina's Court **(2006-09):** Schrodinger's Cat Productions and Twentieth Television produced this syndicated series executive produced by Peter Brennan. After graduating from Whittier Law School in 1994 Perez became a lawyer in Miami, Florida and an advocate for the Latino community.

Jury Duty **(2007-8):** *Jury Duty* was a spin-off of the judge TV format. It had the catch phrase, "Justice so good you will want to sue somebody," and "Justice with a Hollywood ending." Prominent New York criminal defense lawyer, Bruce Cutler, played the feisty and charismatic judge on this judge TV show that featured a guest jury made up of B, C, and D-list celebrities who decided the outcome of the arbitration, which had an awards cap of $5,000. If the jurors could not come to a unanimous decision Judge Cutler would give the verdict. Radar Entertainment and Foster-Tailwind Entertainment produced.

***Judge David Young* (2007–9):** *Judge David Young* debuted on September 10, 2007, and Sony Pictures Television produced it. After graduating from University of Miami Law School, David Young served as Miami-Dade County's assistant state attorney under Janet Reno (1984–7). He was also the county's Circuit Court judge. *Judge David Young* was the first judge TV show featuring an openly gay judge (see Chapter 1).

***Judge Jeanine Pirro* (2008–11):** Pirro earned her J.D. from Albany Law School in 1975. Former Westchester County DA, Fox News Channel commentator, and 2006 NY senatorial candidate, Judge Jeanine Pirro became a TV judge in 2008. Her program staged binding arbitrations and featured a "backstage" segment where Pirro took disputing clients into her "chambers" to hash out their differences. Telepictures Productions produced the show.

***Family Court with Judge Penny* (2008–9):** Starring Judge Penny Brown Reynolds, this show focused on domestic arbitration. Before getting her own show Reynolds appeared on *Dr. Phil* and was a legal commentator on Fox News Channel. In addition to being an ordained minister, Reynolds was a Georgia Fulton County Court judge and the first African American to serve as Executive Counsel. Reynolds is a graduate of the Georgia State University College of Law (1994). 44 Blue Productions and Program Partners produced.

***Judge Karen* (2008–9) and *Karen's Court* (2010–11):** Produced by Sony Pictures Television, *Judge Karen* debuted on September 8, 2008. Richard Goldman and Susan Sobocinski-Puchert executive produced. Judge Karen Mills-Francis graduated from the Levin School of Law at the University of Florida in 1987. Before becoming a judge in Miami-Dade county, Karen Mills-Francis was a public defender for underprivileged adults and minors. *Judge Karen* was canceled in 2009, but Judge Mills-Francis got a second chance in 2010 with *Karen's Court*, produced by Stay in Your Lane Productions. She is currently presiding over a scripted court show, *Supreme Justice with Judge Karen*. Entertainment Studios is producing.

***Speeders Fight Back* (2008–9):** Zoo Productions produced, and the series took place in traffic court. Violators fought the policeman who ticketed them, and Jude Dave Heilmann, both the mayor and the judge of Oak Lawn, Illinois presided. The show aired on Tru TV.

***Street Court* (2009–10):** Michael Mazzariello played "Judge Mazz," in this spin on the court show. Judge Mazz traveled across the country and arbitrated cases on location. This show did not happen in a courtroom, but at the scene of the crime. Judge Mazz was a New York prosecutor for 20 years and is a legal correspondent for CNN. Stand Creative Group produced.

***Swift Justice with Nancy Grace* (2010–11)/Jackie Glass (2011–12):** Nancy Grace graduated from Mercer University Law School in 1984 and was a criminal prosecutor and Fox news legal correspondent before starring in *Swift Justice*. In the fall of 2011, Jackie Glass took over Grace's role. Swift Justice Productions and Big Ticket Television produced (see Chapter 1).

List of Courtroom Dramas[3]

The Black Robe, aka Police Night Court	1949–50
Famous Jury Trials	1949–52
Your Witness	1949
They Stand Accused	1950 and revised in 1954
Verdict is Yours	1957–62
Traffic Court	1957–59
Divorce Court	1957–69 and 1986–90 and 1999–ongoing
Day in Court	1958–65
Accused	1958–59
People's Court of Small Claims	1959
Night Court, USA	1958–61
Morning Court	1960

Courtroom dramas featured cases from different kinds of courts.[4] *The Black Robe* premiered on NBC on May 18, 1949, and dramatized cases heard in the Police Night Court of New York City.[5] *Famous Jury Trials* (1949–52) aired live on the Dumont Television Network and used actors to reenact actual trials.[6] *Your Witness* (1949–50) was a weekly half-hour series featuring dramatizations of actual court cases with professional actors playing all the parts. *They Stand Accused* was considered the first live dramatic courtroom series, and it began in the WGN-TV studios in Chicago where it ran locally from April 11, 1948, to January 11, 1949.[7] The Chicago audience members were chosen to be the jury. William C. Wines, the Assistant Attorney General of Illinois, supervised the program. Professional actors played the litigants and actual lawyers played the attorneys. Attorney Charles Johnston played the judge. The show was unscripted; however, Wines rehearsed with all the participants before the telecast. The end of the show featured the jury reading the verdict.

The studio audience was also the jury on CBS's *The Verdict is Yours* (1957–62). The creator of the show, former State Department lawyer Selig J. Silverman, wanted the live broadcast to be completely improvised, so nobody knew the verdict beforehand. Each case spanned over three to seven episodes. The producers cast real lawyers to play the attorneys, a currently active judge to play the judge, and hired actors to play the litigants. *Traffic Court* (1958–9) presented reenactments of traffic arraignments and trials. The cases were unrehearsed, and the actors improvised from outlines of the cases. It originated in June 1957, as a public service weekly presided over by Los Angeles Municipal Court Judge Evelle J. Younger, who would later go on to become the Attorney General of California. The assistant dean of the UCLA Law School, Edgar Allan Jones Jr, replaced Younger and continued on the show after ABC picked it up for national broadcast.

Divorce Court had two incarnations before its current form as reality court show. The first two syndicated renditions reenacted divorce proceedings and used actual attorneys to play the lawyers and local actors to play the litigants. (Coincidentally, one of the lawyers,

Joseph Max Wapner, would go on to father *The People's Court's* Judge Joseph M. Wapner.) *Divorce Court* first aired as a 1-hour program on February 25, 1958, and was telecast live from KTTV's studios in Los Angeles with the part-time actor and lawyer Voltaire Perkins presiding. The cases were improvised and the actors and lawyers were given information sheets containing details about their characters, lies they would tell, and information they would reveal during cross-examinations. The second form of the program, airing from 1985 to 1991, starred former lawyer William B. Keene, who was best known for being part of Charles Manson's and "Freeway Killer" William Bonin's trials. It was fully scripted, but unrehearsed. The most recent version of *Divorce Court*, distributed by 20th Century Fox Television, first aired in 1999. Former correctional officer and family-law attorney, Mablean Ephraim, played the judge until 2006; Judge Lynn Toler replaced her. The current version of *Divorce Court* is like other reality courtroom TV shows except all the small claims disputes are between spouses or couples who are soon-to-be wed. The show maintains the title *Divorce Court* even though the judge does not have the jurisdiction to make any decisions over custody and alimony and cannot dissolve a marriage.[8]

Airing on ABC, a *Day in Court* (1958–65) staged reenactments of actual trials using lawyers, but with actors playing litigants and witnesses. Edgar Allen Jones Jr, a UCLA law professor and not a member of the State Bar of California, played the judge 3 days a week while William Gwinn, a former law professor, played the judge the 2 days Jones was off. Law students assisted the writers in legal accuracy, yet much of the show was improvised. Encouraged by its success ABC created a primetime version and renamed it *Accused* (1958–9). It was a scripted courtroom drama with the same judges as *Day In Court*. *Morning Court* (1960–1) was a scripted courtroom drama with room for the judge to improvise his or her verdict. Perhaps closest to reality courtroom TV today, the *People's Court of Small Claims* was first telecast on February 11, 1959, and it featured reenactments of real small claims trials using actors to play litigants and attorneys. Orin B. Evans, a

USC law professor, played the judge.[9] Bannar Films' *Night Court, USA* debuted in 1958 and was a fully scripted show that featured dramatized trials dealing with prostitutes, drunks, and negligent individuals. Actor Jay Jostyn played the judge.[10]

The courtroom drama *Divorce Hearing* differed from the other offerings. *Divorce Hearing* was a syndicated talk show made by documentary producer David L. Wolper and starring its creator and marriage counselor Dr Paul Popenoe, the then head of the American Institute of Marital Relations. The episodes featured actual couples with marital problems and staged the counseling sessions like a court proceeding. Akin to the current run of *Divorce Court* and the now off-air *Family Court with Judge Penny* (2008–9), a show I discuss in Chapter 3, Dr Popenoe's stated purpose was to mend fractured familial relationships using the already popularized format of the trial proceeding.

Table of cases

Bates v. State Bar of Arizona 433 US 350 (1977)

Chandler v. Florida 449 US 560 (1981)

Estes v. Texas 381 US 532 (1965)

Kahn v. New York City Dept. of Hous. Preserv. 2010 NY Slip Op 51197(U) [28 Misc 3d 1206(A)]

National Endowment for the Arts v. Finley, et al. 524 US 569 (1998)

Richmond Newspapers, Inc. v. Virginia 448 US 555 (1980)

State of Florida v. Thomas Cloyd & Christopher Hughes F02-019207A&B Section No. F004 (2005)

State of Tennessee, Appellant vs. James Earl Ray, Appellee: 984 S.W.2d 239 (1997)

Notes

Preface

1 Ben Grossman, "Courts Get More Crowded," *Broadcasting & Cable* 136 (2006), 9.
2 Ibid.
3 Aaron Smith "Judge Judy is highest-paid TV" *CNN Money* (2013).

Introduction

1 *National Endowment for the Arts v. Finley, et al*, 524 U.S. 569 (1998).
2 Alvin Klein, "Talks With Gay Playwrights Offered in Course at Purchase," *New York Times* (1999).
3 See Selya 1996.
4 Philip Z. Kimball, "Syndi-Court Justice: Judge Judy and Exploitation of Arbitration," *Journal of American Arbitration* 4 (2005), 153.
5 See Lawrence Friedman, *A History of American Law* (New York: Simon and Schuster, 1973).
6 Marcia Stewart, "50-State Chart of Small Claims Dollar Limits," *NOLO*, February 21, 2014, https://www.nolo.com/legal-encyclopedia/small-claims-suits-how-much-30031.html.
7 American Bar Association, "Small-Claims Court: The 'Fast Food' of the Legal System," in Sheila Maloney, *American Bar Association Guide to Resolving Legal Disputes Inside and Outside the Courtroom* (New York: Random House, 2009), pp. 93–116.
8 Rule 401 states: "Evidence is relevant if: (a) it has any tendency to make a fact more or less probable than it would be without the evidence; and (b) the fact is of consequence in determining the action." See Federal Rules of Evidence (2011) *Legal Information Institute*, http://www.law.cornell.edu/rules/fre.

9 Arthur P. McNulty, "The Verdict is Yours: Problems of TV Courtroom Drama," *American Bar Association Journal* 46 (1960), 67.
10 Bernard J. Hibbitts, "De-scribing Law: Performance in the Constitution of Legality," PSI Conference Paper (1996), http://law.pitt.edu/archive/hibbitts/describ.htm.
11 Susan E. Lawrence, *The poor in court: The Legal Services Program and Supreme Court Decision Making* (Princeton: Princeton University Press, 1990), p. 155.
12 Ibid.
13 Jean Baudrillard, *Simulacra and Simulation* (Ann Arbor: University of Michigan Press, 1994) p. 1.
14 Richard Sherwin, *When Law Goes Pop: The Vanishing Line Between Law and Pop Culture* (Chicago: University of Chicago Press, 2000), p. 141.
15 Ibid., p. 146.
16 Ibid., p. 154.
17 Ibid., p. 162.
18 Ibid., p. 167.
19 *An American Family*, Fales Archive (New York: New York University Press, 1973).
20 The average budget for a reality TV show is between $100,000 and $500,000 while a scripted series averages between $1 and $3 million an episode. This is based on 1-hour scripted dramas and 1-hour reality TV programs. (See Essany 2013; Gornstein 2008; The Associated Press 2009.)
21 Nielsen, "Top Ten List," (accessed February 24, 2014) http://www.nielsen.com/us/en/top10s.html.
22 See Robert Hariman, ed., *Popular trials: Rhetoric, Mass Media, and the Law*, vol. 41 (Tuscaloosa, Albama: University of Alabama Press, 1993).
23 Adam Nagourney, "Prayer, Anger and Protests Greet Verdict in Florida Case," *New York Times*, July 14, 2013.
24 Lizette Alvarez, "In Zimmerman Case, Self Defense Was Hard to Topple," *New York Times*, July 14, 2013.
25 Jill Dolan, *Utopia in performance: Finding Hope at the Theater* (USA: University of Michigan Press, 2005), p. 8.

26 See Peggy Phelan, *Unmarked: The Politics of Performance* (New York: Routledge, 2012).
27 Anna McCarthy, "Reality Television: a Neoliberal Theater of Suffering," *Social Text* 25 (2007), 17–42. See also Laurie Ouellette 2004 and 2011.

Chapter 1

1 Jaclyn Belczyk, "Most US Federal Court Judges Still White Men, but Demographics Changing: Report," *Jurist*, August 18, 2009, http://jurist.org/paperchase/2009/08/federal-court-demographics-changing-to.php. As of early August 2009, 70 percent of federal judges were white men, 15 percent were white women, 10 percent were minority (African American and Hispanic) males, and 3 percent were minority females.
2 Federal Judicial Center, "Diversity on the Bench," accessed December 9, 2013, http://www.fjc.gov/history/home.nsf/page/judges_diversity.html.
3 E. M. Forster, *Aspects of the Novel* (London: E.Arnold, 1927), n.p.
4 David Ray Papke, "From Flat to Round: Changing Portrayals of the Judge in American Popular Culture," *Journal of the Legal Profession* 31 (2007), 131.
5 Ian Haney Lopez, *White by Law: The Legal Construction of Race* (New York: New York University Press, 2006), p. 127.
6 Barbara J. Flagg, *Was Blind, but Now I See: White Race Consciousness & The Law* (New York: New York University Press, 1998), pp. 1–2.
7 Christo Lassiter, "TV or Not TV. That Is the Question," *The Journal of Criminal Law and Criminology* 86 (1996), pp. 928–1001.
8 Prina Lahav, "Theater in the Courtroom: The Chicago Conspiracy Trial," *Law & Literature* 16 (2004), p. 392.
9 Ibid.
10 Devon W. Carbado, "The Construction of OJ Simpson as a Racial Victim," *Harvard CR-CLL Review* 32 (1997), 56.

11 Richard Sherwin, *When Law Goes Pop: The Vanishing Line Between Law and Pop Culture* (Chicago: University of Chicago Press, 2000), p. 6.

12 On March 24, 2014, former judge Joe Brown was found in contempt of court after challenging the authority of a county magistrate while awaiting a hearing for a client he was representing. He was released from prison later that same day on his own recognizance.

13 *The People's Court* was canceled in 1993 because of low ratings. It was remounted in 1997.

14 Richard Huff, "Many Judge, but Judy Rules. In a Crowded field, Jeanine Pirro Will Need Real Bench Strength to Survive TV Trial," *NY Daily News*, May 7, 2008, p. 45.

15 Kate Fitzgerald, "A Few Good Judges: Producers Tell How They Track Court TV Talent," *Electronic Media*, January 17, 2000, p. 22.

16 Ibid.

17 Cristina Perez, phone interview with author, October 7, 2008.

18 Josh Getlin, "Law and Disorder: Tart, Tough-Talking Judge Judith Sheindlin Presides Over the Grim Pageant of Dysfunction Known as Manhattan's Family Court," *LA Times*, February 14, 1993.

19 Judith Sheindlin, phone interview with author, September 17, 2008.

20 CBS, "Law and Disorder," *60 Minutes*, October 24, 1993, http://www.cbsnews.com/video/watch/?id=4539460n. All quotes from the October 24, 1993, *60 Minutes* segment are from the author's transcripts taken from the episode.

21 Sheindlin, interview 2008.

22 Judge Judy Website, accessed March 3, 2011, http://www.judgejudy.com.

23 Joseph Wapner, *A View From the Bench* (Boston: G.K. Hall & Co, 1989), p. 129.

24 Sheindlin, *Don't Pee on My Leg and Tell Me It's Raining*, p. 233.

25 Ibid., p. 181.

26 Jenny Hope, phone interview with author, November 8, 2010.

27 The Associated Press, "O.J. Simpson Judge Known for Tough Sentences," December 4, 2008, http://www.nbcnews.com/id/28056491/ns/us_news-

crime_and_courts/t/oj-simpson-judge-known-tough-sentences/#.UzHlNV6T6hA.

28. Virginia Hefferman, "Y'all Rise: Texas Justice is More Forgiving Than You Might Think," *Slate*, May 23, 2002, http://www.slate.com/articles/arts/television/2002/05/yall_rise.html.

29. Earl Gustkey, "His Honor, the Referee: Mills Lane Brooks No Nonsense, in Court or in the Ring," *Los Angeles Times*, June 16, 1991, http://articles.latimes.com/1991-06-16/sports/sp-1489_1_mills-lane.

30. Larry King Live Transcript, "Judge Mills Lane, Judge Joe Brown and Judge Mathis Lay Down the Law on Daytime TV," *CNN*, May 8, 2000, http://transcripts.cnn.com/TRANSCRIPTS/0005/08/lkl.00.html.

31. Gustkey, "His Honor, the Referee."

32. Jeffrey L. Kirchmeier, et al., "Vigilante Justice: Prosecutor Misconduct in Capital Cases," *Wayne Law Review* 55 (2009), 1327–85.

33. *Bell v. State, 439 S.E.2d 480, 481 (Ga. 1994)* in Kirchmeier 2009.

34. Wilkes Jr, Donald E., "Still Striking Foul Blows," *Popular Media*, May 17, 2006, http://digitalcommons.law.uga.edu/fac_pm/135/.

35. Nancy Grace and Diane Clehane, *Objection!: How High-priced Defense Attorneys, Celebrity Defendants, and a 24/7 Media Have Hijacked Our Criminal Justice System* (New York: Hyperion, 2006).

36. "Judges Tit-For-Tat Justice," *The Advertiser*, October 5, 1991.

37. Ibid.

38. Mark Curriden, "Making Punishment Fit the Crime Often Not Popular," January 9, 1992, *Atlanta Journal and Constitution*, p. A3.

39. CBS News Transcripts, *Street Stories*, September 24, 1992

40. Ibid.

41. Michelle Alexander, *The New Jim Crow: Mass Incarceration in the Age of Colorblindness* (New York: The New Press, 2012), p. 2.

42. Ibid.

43. Michelle Alexander, "The New Jim Crow" *Ohio State Journal of Criminal Law* 9 (2011), 8.

44. Sue Anne Pressley, "Historic Interests Meet at Memphis Crossroads," February 27, 1997, *Washington Post*, p. A1.

45 Marc Perrusquia, "Brown Ousted from Ray Case: Court Says Acts Point to 'Bias,'" March 7, 1997, *Commercial Appeal*, p. A1.
46 Marc Perrusquia, "James Earl Ray Files Ordered Seized From Office of Judge Joe Brown," August 6, 1997, *Commercial Appeal*.
47 *State of Tennessee, Appellant vs. James Earl Ray, Appellee*: 984 S.W.2d 239. (1998), http://caselaw.findlaw.com/tn-court-of-criminal-appeals/1298102.html, accessed February 24, 2014.
48 Ibid. From Judge Brown's statement in open court broadcast on *Prime Time Justice* on the Court TV Network on January 15, 1998.
49 Ibid.
50 Ibid. From *The Atlanta Journal Constitution*, July 11, 1997.
51 Ibid. From *The Tri-State Defender*, August 16–20, 1997.
52 ABC News, "Judge Joe Brown," *Nightline*, April 3, 1997.
53 Judge Joe Brown Website, JudgeJoeBrown.com, accessed February 12, 2011.
54 Fitzgerald, "A Few Good Judges."
55 Wayne Friedman, "The Selling of 'Judge Joe Brown,'" January 22, 1998, *The Hollywood Reporter*.
56 Tavis Smiley, NPR Broadcast Transcript of "Judge Greg Mathis Discusses How He Overcame Adversity to Become the Youngest Judge in Michigan's History and his TV Show, 'Judge Mathis,'" *Highbeam Business*, November 19, 2002, http://business.highbeam.com/152499/article-1G1-167309406/interview-judge-greg-mathis-discusses-he-overcame-adversity.
57 Ibid.
58 CNN Transcripts, "Both Sides with Jesse Jackson," October 29, 1995, http://ezproxy.library.nyu.edu:2076/hottopics/lnacademic, accessed December 12, 2012.
59 *The Detroit News*, "Television: Bad Kid Makes Good: Detroit Judge Greg Mathis Takes 'Inspirational Justice' to TV," September 11, 1999.
60 Ibid.
61 *Jet Magazine*, "Blacks Rule on TV Court Shows," December 20, 1999, vol. 97, no. 3, pp. 60–4.

62 *Larry King Live*, "Judge Mills Lane, Judge Joe Brown and Judge Greg Mathis Lay Down the Law on Daytime TV?"

63 Greg Spring, "Mathis's Courting Young Demo," December 21, 1998, *Electronic Media*, p. 29.

64 Annette John-Hall, "The Judge Who Came to Order In the Ranks of TV Judges, at Least Two Things Set Greg Mathis Apart: A Flair that Turns Women Spectators into Flirts and a Resume Not Altogether Righteous," October 20, 2002, *Philadelphia Inquirer*, p. D.1.

65 Dr Phil Transcripts, "Is He Setting her Up?" February 9, 2007, http://www.drphil.com/slideshows/slideshow/3669/?id=3669&slide=0&showID=&preview=&versionID=.

66 Rodney Ho, "The Non-Judgmental Judge," October 13, 2008, *Atlanta Journal and Constitution*, p. 1C.

67 Greg Land, "Judge to Resign Next Month for TV Gig," *Fulton County Daily Report*, September 10, 2008, http://www.law.com/jsp/article.jsp?id=1202424402163&slreturn=1.

68 Judge Penny Website, "Judge Penny.com," accessed January 6, 2011, www.judgepenny.com.

69 Ho, "The Non-Judgmental Judge."

70 Ibid.

71 Felicia G. Jones, "The Black Audience and the BET Channel" *Journal of Broadcasting and Electronic Media* 34 (1990), 478.

72 Sarah Kozinn, *The TV Ate the Courtroom: The Pedagogy and Performativity of Judge TV Justice*, Dissertation, New York University, May 2012, p. 268.

73 Bourdieu, "The Force of Law: Toward a Sociology of the Juridical Field" *Hastings Law Journal* 38 (1986), 820.

74 Ibid.

75 Cornel West, "Foreward," in Kimberlé Crenshaw, Neil Gotanda, Gary Peller, and Kendall Thomas (eds), *Critical Race Theory: The Key Writings That Formed the Movement* (New York: New Press, 1995), p. xi.

76 Patricia Williams, *The Alchemy of Race and Rights* (Cambridge, MA: Harvard University Press, 1991), p. 48.

77 Ibid., 7.
78 Bourdieu, "The Force of Law," p. 828.
79 Ibid.
80 Joshua Chambers-Letson, "The Inoperative Iphigenia: Race, Law, And Emancipation in Michi Barall's *Rescue Me*," *Theatre Survey* 55 (2014), 149.
81 Liz Balmaseda, "The Star of Popular Daytime TV, Alex Ferrer Gave up a Miami Dade Circuit Judgeship to Preside in an Even Bigger Courtroom," *Palm Beach Post*, August 31, 2007, http://alexferrer.com/publicity/Palm_Beach_Post-Liz_Balmaseda.pdf.
82 Krys Longan, "Here Come Da Judge!" *Alex Ferrer*, accessed January 5, 2012, http://alexferrer.com/here_comes.html?fuseaction=viewImage&friendID=55824800&albumID=767659&imageID=39669.
83 Judge Alex Website, "Meet Judge Alex," accessed December 19, 2013, http://www.judgealex.com/meet-judge-alex/.
84 Christopher Gonzalez, "Sex on the Bench," accessed January 3, 2012, https://www.youtube.com/watch?v=r6HtSltnl0k.
85 As of 2012, Perez became the star judge of a scripted courtroom TV show, *Justice For All With Cristina Perez*.
86 Staff and Wire Reports, "Judge's Critics Urged to Chill," September 9, 2000, *Worcester Telegram & Gazette*, p. A1.
87 Commission of Judicial Conduct Transcripts, "Complaint No. 2000-110 et seq," November 22, 2002, http://www.mass.gov/cjc/Lopez-transcripts/Lopez-transcript004.htm.
88 Ibid.
89 Ibid.
90 Ibid.
91 John Dempsey, "Gavelers Court Hispanic Viewers," November 28, 2005, *Variety*.
92 Debra Merskin, "Three Faces of Eva: Perpetuation of The Hot-Latina Stereotype in Desperate Housewives," *Howard Journal Of Communications* 18 (2007), 136.
93 Curt Anderson, "TV Justice, Miami Style; Florida's Hot Tourist Destination is Home to Five Former Judges with their Own shows. Taped Trials Helped Give them Exposure," July 8, 2008, *Los Angeles Times*, p. E10.

94 NBC News Transcripts, "Miami Judge Sentences Two Pilots Drunk on Job," July 22, 2005.

95 Diana Marrero, "Cameras at Florida Bar Recorded America West Pilots Drinking Bout," *McClatchy Tribune Business News*, August 6, 2002, https://ezproxy.library.nyu.edu/login?url=http://search.proquest.com/docview/464563873?accountid=12768.

96 Chrystian Tejedor, "Judge Considers Convicted Pilots Flight Risks Pair to Remain in Jail Pending Sentencing," *South Florida Sun Sentinel*, July 17, 2005, https://ezproxy.library.nyu.edu/login?url=http://search.proquest.com/docview/389890436?accountid=12768.

97 *PR Newswire*, "Judge David Young Delivers Justice with a Snap," September 7, 2007, https://ezproxy.library.nyu.edu/login?url=http://search.proquest.com/docview/447143991?accountid=12768.

98 "Judge David Young" episode airing March 3, 2008, on WWOR-TV Channel 9 NYC, author's transcript.

99 Lydia Martin, "Judicial Restraint? That's for the Courtroom, Not TV," *McClatchy Tribune Business News*, September 9, 2007, https://ezproxy.library.nyu.edu/login?url=http://search.proquest.com/docview/459159656?accountid=12768.

100 Joe Garofoli, "Gay TV Jurist Young Dispenses Justice With Song on New TV Show," *SF Gate*, September 9, 2007, http://www.sfgate.com/entertainment/article/Gay-TV-jurist-Young-dispenses-justice-with-song-2541808.php.

101 Michael Jensen, "Interview With Judge David Young," *After Elton*, September 5, 2007, http://www.afterelton.com/people/2007/9/davidyoung.

102 Elizabeth Whitney, "Capitalizing on Camp: Greed and the Queer Marketplace," *Text & Performance Quarterly* 26 (2006), 41.

103 Susan Sontag, "Notes on Camp," in Fabio Cleto (ed.), *Camp: Queer Aesthetics and the Performing Subject: A Reader* (Ann Arbor: University of Michigan Press, 1999), p. 56.

104 Whitney, "Capitalizing on Camp," p. 38.

105 Ibid., p. 42.

106 Hope, interview 2010.

107 Donald Horton and Anselm Strauss, "Interaction in Audience-Participation Shows," *The American Journal of Sociology* 62 (1957), 580.
108 Bourdieu, "The Force of Law," p. 828.

Chapter 2

1 Cristina Perez, phone interview October 7, 2008.
2 Lawrence M. Friedman, "Lexitainment: Legal Process as Theater" *DePaul Law Review* 50 (2000), 539–58; Milner S. Ball, "The Play's the Thing: An Unscientific Reflection on Courts Under the Rubric of Theater," *Stanford Law Review* 28 (1975), 81–116; Laurie L. Levenson, "Courtroom demeanor: The Theater of the Courtroom," *Minnesota Law Review* 92 (2007), 573–633; John E. Simonett, "The Trial as One of the Performing Arts," *American Bar Association Journal* 52 (1966), 1145–7.
3 Bernard J. Hibbitts, "De-scribing Law: Performance in the Constitution of Legality," *Performance Studies Conference, Northwestern University, Evanston, Illinois* 8 (2009) and "Coming to Our Senses," *Emory Law Journal* 41 (1992), 873–960.
4 See Richard Sherwin, *When Law Goes Pop: The Vanishing Line Between Law and Pop Culture* (Chicago: University of Chicago Press, 2000).
5 Richard Terdiman, Introduction and Translator to Pierre Bourdieu's "The Force of Law: Toward a Sociology of the Juridical Field," *Hastings Law Journal* 38 (1986), 808.
6 Jean Baudrillard, *Simulacra and Simulation* (Ann Arbor: University of Michigan Press, 1994), p. 1.
7 Kiersten Medvedich, phone interview with author February 27, 2008.
8 Jenny Hope, phone interview with author, November 8, 2010.
9 Ibid.
10 J. F. Dovidio and S. L. Gaertner, "Aversive Racism and selection decisions: 1989 and 1990" *Psychological Science* 11 (2000), 315–19; A. Martin, "Television Media as a Potential Negative Factor in the Racial

Identity Development of African American Youth," *Academic Psychiatry* 32 (2008), 338–42; and Tia Tyree, "African American Stereotypes in Reality Television," *Howard Journal of Communications* 22 (2011), 394–413.

11 Hope, phone interview.
12 Clint C. Wilson, Félix Gutiérrez, and Lena M. Chao, *Racism, Sexism, and the Media: The Rise of Class Communication in Multiculture America* (Thousand Oaks, CA: Sage Publications, 2003), p. 65.
13 Bertolt Brecht, *The Measures Taken and Other Lehrstücke* (New York: Arcade Publishing, 1977), Introductory Note.
14 Ibid., p. 58.
15 Ibid., p. 60.
16 The author made all transcripts from episode *Kiana vs. Deon*, June 12, 2008: WWOR Channel 9, New York.
17 From 1993 to 2001, Judge Toler was a judge in the Cleveland Heights Municipal Court.
18 *Divorce Court*, air date June 12, 2008, on WWOR Channel 9, New York.
19 This is discussed in more depth in Chapter 1, in particular in relation to how black judges perform their roles.
20 Victor Turner, "Dramatic Ritual/Ritual Drama: Performative and Reflexive Anthropology," *The Kenyon Review* 1 (1979), 83.
21 See Chapters 3 and 4.
22 Richard Schechner, *Performance Theory* (New York: Routledge, 2003), p. 125.
23 Ann Northrop told Joshua Gamson that when she appears on talk shows her intention was primarily to make people like her: "The people in the audience really don't care what you're saying. They're going to judge you as a person and whether you are a good person or a bad person" (in Gamson 1998, p. 129).
24 Nuria Lorenzo-Dus, "Real disorder in the court: An Investigation of Conflict Talk in US Television Courtroom Shows," *Media, Culture & Society* 30 (2008), 100.

25 Alexandra Hendriks and Robin Nabi, "The Persuasive Effect of Host and Audience Reaction Shots in Television Talk Shows," *Journal of Communication* 53 (2003), 528.
26 Cal Hylton, "Intra-Audience Effects: Observable Audience Response" *Journal of Communication* 21 (1971), 253–65.
27 Ibid.
28 Donald Horton and Anselm Strauss, "Interaction in Audience-Participation Shows," *The American Journal of Sociology* 62 (1957), 583.
29 Background actors are the non-speaking, costumed actors in the background of film and television scenes whose presence helps complete the imagined reality of the space.
30 Guests and actors go through security and then wait in a green room or waiting area until the set opens. The studios that hire background actors had a shorter waiting period than the shows with invited guests.
31 The amount programs pay their background audiences differs depending on the show, and because the shows hire nonunion background actors, meaning they do belong to the actor's union SAG-AFTRA (Screen Actors Guild—American Federation of Television and Radio Artists), the day rates vary. In 2007 and 2008, 50 dollars per day was the standard amount for non-union background actors. I never accepted payment for being an audience member, but was offered fifty dollars to be a regular audience member on *Judge Hatchett*.
32 This occurred at an October 1, 2008, taping of *Judge Judy* at Sunset Bronson studios in Los Angeles, CA.
33 This occurred at an April 16, 2008, taping of *Judge David Young* at Metropolis Studios in New York City, NY. All quotes from the courtroom TV shows tapings are taken from my logs and notes unless otherwise noted.
34 Author's transcripts from a May 8, 2008, taping of *Judge David Young*.
35 See Konstantin Stanislavsky, *An Actor Prepares* (New York: Routledge, 1989).
36 *Judge David Young*, air date November 3, 2008, on Channel 9 in New York City, NY.

37 *Judge David Young* taping, April 10, 2008, Metropolis Studios, New York City, NY.
38 During this period producers had litigants sign contracts for the arbitration and a release for their appearance on the program. Sometimes this was done at the very last moment. At one of the *Judge David Young* tapings I attended, I saw litigants signing the contract just behind the courtroom set walls and right before taping began.
39 Conversation with Kristin Medvedich, February 27, 2008.
40 Ibid.
41 Roland Barthes, "The Reality Effect," in Dorothy Hale (ed.), *The Novel: An Anthology of Criticism and Theory 1900-2000* (Malden, MA: Blackwell Pub, 2006), p. 233.
42 *Cristina's Court*, air date November 16, 2007.
43 Ted Haggard and his wife appeared on a special episode of *Divorce Court* originally airing on April 1, 2009.
44 Michael Kirby, *A Formalist Theatre* (Philadelphia: University of Pennsylvania Press, 1987), p. 3.
45 Allan Kaprow coined the term "Happenings" in 1957. He first wrote about Happenings in the article "Legacy of Jackson Pollock" first published in *Art News* in October 1958, and later republished in *Essays on The Blurring of Art and Life* (1993).
46 Kirby, *A Formalist Theatre*, p. 3.
47 Erving Goffman, *The Presentation of Self in Everyday Life* (New York: Anchor Books, Doubleday, 1959), 14.
48 The belief in a real and true *self* is part of the essentialist doctrine that posits for each person a unique soul that can be expressed by the individual. Many practitioners of art theater have dedicated their practices to access and exhibit this soul through ritual and performance. Stanislavsky's "fourth wall" realism is one kind of "true theatre" and Jerzy Grotowski's "holy theatre" is another (see Brooks 1968; Innes 1981). But unlike the scripted plays that Stanislavsky staged or Grotowski's total theater, reality TV promises to give to its audiences real people unadulterated by scripts and meticulously scored staging.

49 Roland Barthes, *Camera Lucida: Reflections on Photography* (New York: Hill and Wang, 1981), pp. 11–12.
50 Kaprow, *Essays on The Blurring of Art and Life* (Berkeley and Los Angeles, CA: University of California, 1993), p. 190.
51 Jean Baudrillard, *Simulacra and Simulation* (Ann Arbor: University of Michigan Press, 1994), p. 28.
52 Kaprow, *Essays on The Blurring of Art and Life*, p. 201.
53 Ibid., p. 203.
54 Tim Sullivan, phone interview with author, October 29, 2010.
55 *Divorce Court*, 'January v. January', air date March 3, 2008.
56 *Divorce Court*, air date May 9, 2008: WWOR-TV Channel 9, New York, NY.
57 *Divorce Court*, air date May 14, 2008: WWOR-TV Channel 9, New York, NY.
58 Philip Auslander, *Liveness: Performance in a Mediatized Culture* (London, New York: Routledge, 1999), p. 19.

Chapter 3

1 Peter Brennan, phone interview with author, October 9, 2008.
2 Jenny Hope, phone interview with author, November 8, 2010.
3 Ibid.
4 Brennan, interview 2008.
5 Janice Peck, "TV Talk shows as Therapeutic Discourse: The Ideological Labor of the Televised Talking Cure," *Communication Theory* 5 (1995), 75.
6 Stuart Fischoff, "Confession of a TV Talk Show Shrink," *Psychology Today*, September 1, 1995, http://www.psychologytoday.com/articles/200910/confession-tv-talk-show-shrink?page=2.
7 Jane M. Shattuc, *The Talking Cure: TV Talk Shows and Women* (New York: Routledge, 1997), p. 134.
8 Shoshana Felman linked the impulse to turn to the courts to resolve or attend to trauma and psychological distress caused by a traumatic event comes from several factors functioning simultaneously: the

discovery of psychoanalysis (and the concepts of the subconscious, trauma, and repression), the series of large-scale disastrous events that occurred during the twentieth century (i.e. The Holocaust), and the use of law to deal with these events (i.e. The Eichmann trial and Nuremberg Trials). See Shoshana Felman *The Juridical Unconscious: Trials and Traumas in the 20th Century* (Cambridge, MA: Harvard University Press, 2002).

9 All excerpts from the episode airing on January 28, 2009, on WWOR-TV Channel 9 NYC are from the author's transcripts unless otherwise noted.
10 Michel Foucault, *Abnormal: Lectures at the Collège de France, 1974-1975*, vol. 2 (New York: Picador, 2003), p. 15.
11 Ibid., p. 159.
12 Alcoholics Anonymous World Services, "The Twelve Steps of Alcoholics Anonymous," accessed November 2, 2013, http://www.aa.org/en_pdfs/smf-121_en.pdf.
13 Michel Foucault, *The History of Sexuality: An Introduction* (New York: Vintage Books, 1988), pp. 61–2.
14 Richard Schechner, *Between Theater and Anthropology* (Philadelphia: University of Pennsylvania Press, 1985), p. 127.
15 Foucault, *Abnormal*, p. 35.
16 Frank D. Fincham, "Forgiveness: Integral to Close Relationships and Inimical to Justice?" *Virginia Journal of Social Policy & the Law* 16 (Winter 2009), p. 357.
17 Stephanos Bibas, "Mercy and Clemency: Forgiveness in Criminal Procedure," *Ohio State Journal of Criminal Law* 4 (2007), 329.
18 Bible, King James, and Various, *King James Bible*, Project Gutenberg, 1996.
19 Rodney Ho, "Fulton's 'Judge Penny' sees TV as 'extension of my ministry'," October 13, 2008, *Atlanta Journal and Constitution*, http://www.accessatlanta.com/news/entertainment/celebrity-news/fultons-judge-penny-sees-tv-as-extension-of-my-min/nQyCW/.
20 Janet Jakobsen and Ann Pellegrini, *Love The Sin: Sexual Regulation and the Limits of Religious Tolerance* (New York: New York University Press, 2003), p. 21.

21 Anonymous, *Everyman* in W. B. Worthen's *The Wadsworth Anthology of Drama* (Boston, MA: Thomson/Wadsworth, 2011), pp. 283–93.

22 Dorothy Wertz, "Conflict Resolution in the Medieval Morality Plays," *Journal of Conflict Resolution* 13, 4 (1969), 438.

23 Glenda Hatchett, *Say What You Mean and Mean What You Say! Saving Your Child From a Troubled World* (New York: William Morrow, 2003), p. 130.

24 Ibid., pp. 168–9.

25 Ibid.

26 Ibid.

27 Janice Peck, "The Mediated Talking Cure," in Gail Dines and Jean McMahon Humez (eds), *Gender, Race, and Class in Media: A Text-Reader* (Thousand Oaks, CA: Sage, 2003), p. 545.

28 Chicago Defender, "Judge Hatchett Launches New Season with Innovative shows," *Chicago Defender*, October 1, 2001, https://ezproxy.library.nyu.edu/login?url=http://search.proquest.com/docview/247012236?accountid=12768.

29 Jane O. Hansen, "Growing Up With Crack. Last Chance: Baby Court," *The Atlanta Constitution*, September 30, 1998, https://ezproxy.library.nyu.edu/login?url=http://search.proquest.com/docview/413721918?accountid=12768.

30 Ibid.

31 Ibid.

32 Ibid.

33 Lyle V. Harris, "Hatchett's Justice," *Atlanta Constitution*, September 7, 2000, https://ezproxy.library.nyu.edu/login?url=http://search.proquest.com/docview/413875326?accountid=12768.

34 W. T. Walsh, "Letters, Faxes & E-Mail Judge Hatchett Leaves Children a Legacy," *Atlanta Constitution*, March 11, 1999, https://ezproxy.library.nyu.edu/login?url=http://search.proquest.com/docview/413738011?accountid=12768.

35 Tom Walter, "Judge Hatchett Looks at Sentencing Results," *Commercial Appeal*, May 11, 2001, https://ezproxy.library.nyu.edu/login?url=http://search.proquest.com/docview/393923230?accountid=12768.

36 Hatchett, *Say What You Mean and Mean What You Say!*, p. 201.
37 *Judge Hatchett*, air date July 1, 2009, WNYW-TV, Channel 5, NYC. Author's transcripts.
38 *Judge Hatchett*, air date July 3, 2009, WNYW-TV, Channel 5, NYC. Author's transcripts.
39 Lauren Gail Berlant, ed., *Compassion: The Culture and Politics of an Emotion* (Great Britain: Routledge, 2004), p. 4.
40 Ibid., p. 6.
41 Stuart Hall, *Culture, Media, Language: Working Papers in Cultural Studies, 1972-79* (London: Hutchinson, 1980), p. 234.
42 Joshua Lloyd Sams, "First Chapter Road to Redemption," 2009, http://birdwalkermusic.com%2Fstorage%2FFirst_Chapter_of_Road_to_Redemption.pdf&ei=gS8PT_DyCMXh0wG7YGyAw&usg=AFQjCNFwPFo29VXzh4rbL5VXdppBMZSzSw&sig2=OBL0n_YZdNLFYZF4vKkrQQ, p. 11.
43 *Cristina's Court*, air date November 10, 2008, WWOR Channel 9, NYC.
44 All excerpts are from the author's transcripts.
45 *Cristina's Court*, air date November 11, 2008, WWOR-TV, Channel 9, NYC, author's transcripts.
46 Janice Peck, "TV Talk shows as Therapeutic Discourse: The Ideological Labor of the Televised Talking Cure," *Communication Theory* 5 (1995), 76.
47 Perez, interview with author 2008.
48 Ibid.
49 Shattuc, *The Talking Cure: TV Talk Shows and Women*, p. 112.

Chapter 4

1 John Dempsey, "Judge Judy on a Roll: Syndication Star Sentenced to Two More Years," *Variety*, February 15, 2008, http://www.variety.com/article/VR1117981008.html?categoryid=2522&cs=1.
2 The Futon Critic, "'Judge Joe Brown' Enters Its 13th Season on September 13," September 8, 2010, http://www.thefutoncritic.com/

news/2010/09/08/judge-joe-brown-enters-its-13th-season-on-september-13-37316/20100908cbs04/.
3. Ibid.
4. All quotes from this episode are from the author's transcripts.
5. Umberto Eco, *The Role of the Reader: Explorations in the Semiotics of Texts* (Indiana: Indiana University Press, 1984), p. 7.
6. Umberto Eco, "The Author and His Interpreters," accessed October 10, 2013, http://www.themodernword.com/eco/eco_author.html.
7. Ibid.
8. Mari Matsuda, "Voices of America: Accent, Antidiscrimination Law, and Jurisprudence for the Last Reconstruction," *Yale Law Journal* 100 (1991), 1329.
9. Lawrence Vogelman, "The Big Black Man Syndrome: The Rodney King Trial and The Use of Racial Stereotypes in the Courtroom," *Fordham Urban Law Journal* 20 (1992), 574.
10. Robert Staples, "The Myth of the Impotent Black Male," *The Black Scholar* 2 (1971), 2.
11. Jackie Shnoop, "Judging Nine TV Judges," *AOLTV.COM*, January 30, 2008, http://www.aoltv.com/2008/01/31/judging-nine-tv-judges/.
12. Author's transcripts from *Judge Joe Brown* episode airing October 22, 2009.
13. Chandra L. Ford, et al., "Black Sexuality, Social Construction, and Research Targeting 'The Down Low'('The DL')," *Annals of Epidemiology* 17 (2007), 209–16.
14. Julia Kristeva, "Approaching Abjection," in Amelia Jones (ed.), *The Feminism and Visual Culture Reader* (London: Routledge, 2003), p. 391.
15. Judith Butler, "Performative Acts and Gender Constitution: An Essay in Phenomenology and Gender Theory," in Amelia Jones (ed.), *The Feminism and Visual Culture Reader* (London: Routledge, 2003), p. 399.
16. See Chapter 2.
17. Anna McCarthy, "Reality Television: a Neoliberal Theater of Suffering," *Social Text* 25 (2007), 19.

18 The Moynihan Report, 1965, http://www.blackpast.org/primary/moynihan-report-1965.
19 Brown has been identifying this as his role since sitting on his Tennessee bench, and 20 years before *Dixon v. Dixon*, Brown told CBS reporters that he was more than a judge; he was the "village chieftain." Papa Brown existed long before *Judge Joe Brown*.
20 Michel Foucault, Mauro Bertani, Alessandro Fontana, François Ewald, and David Macey *Society Must Be Defended: Lectures at the Collège de France, 1975-76,* (New York: Picador, 2003), p. 29.
21 Airdate January 13, 2009.
22 Adina Nack, "Bad Girls and Fallen Women: Chronic STD Diagnoses as Gateways to Tribal Stigma" *Symbolic Interaction* 25 (2002), 466.
23 Joan Sangster, "Incarcerating 'Bad Girls': The Regulation of Sexuality through the Female Refuges Act in Ontario, 1920-1945," *Journal of the History of Sexuality* 7 (1996), 239–75.
24 I discuss how producers choose cases that highlight the judges branded messages in Chapter 2.
25 Air date May 26, 2008, WCBS-TV Channel 2, NYC.
26 All excerpts from "Ross v. Ross" are from the author's transcripts from the May 26, 2008, episode, WCBS-TV Channel 2, NYC.
27 Judy Sheindlin, *Don't Pee on My Leg and Tell Me It's Raining* (New York: HarperCollins, 1996), p. 100.
28 Ibid., 53.
29 Sigmund Freud, *Jokes and their Relation to the Unconscious* (New York: Norton, 1960), p. 189.
30 Ibid., p. 103.
31 Ibid.
32 Jerome J. Zolten, "Black Comedians: Forging an Ethnic Image," *Journal of American Culture* 2 (1993), 65.
33 Ibid., 66.
34 Ibid., 67.
35 Ibid.
36 Pigmeat Markham, "Here Come The Judge," Universal Music Enterprises and Laugh.com, (2004) (Compact Disc).

37 Ibid.
38 Pigmeat Markham, *Here Come The Judge*, (Popular Library, 1969) n.p.
39 Freud, *Jokes and Their Relation to the Unconscious*, p. 103
40 Laurie Ouellette, "Real Justice: Law and Order on Reality Television" in *Imagining Legality: Where Law Meets Popular Culture* (Tuscaloosa: University of Alabama Press, 2011), p. 157.
41 See Ouellette 2004, Ouellette 2011, and Kohm 2006.
42 I evaluated episodes airing May 6, May 7, May 9, May 13, May 15, May 16, May 19, May 23, May 26, and June 6, 2008, on WCBS-TV New York.
43 The official complaint was filed in Superior Court in the State of California in 2007. Bob Sassone, "Judge Judy's Show Sued, Accused of Racial Screening," January 2, 2008, www.aoltv.com/tag/jonathan+sebastien
44 Sebastien reportedly disagreed with Douthit, who allegedly told him that he did not want to do, "'anymore black shows' or have 'black people arguing' or hear 'black language on TV'" (Sassone 2008). Not wanting to participate in the supposedly bigoted casting procedure Sebastien continued to bring black litigants to Douthit; he was fired as a result.

Chapter 5

1 See Schechner, *Between Theatre and Anthropology* (Philadelphia: University of Pennsylvania Press, 1985).
2 Roger M. Grace, "TV Courtroom Shows Proliferate in the Late 1950s," May 3, 2003, *Metropolitan News-Enterprise*, http://www.metnews.com/articles/reminiscing050803.htm.
3 Ibid.
4 Committee on Professional Ethics of the American Bar Association, "Appearances of Attorneys on Television Shows," *Journal of the Federal Communications Bar Association* 17 (1961), 199–208.
5 Ibid.

6   Ibid.
7   In the 1950s California's Canon 21 and Canon 25 of Judicial Ethics prohibited lawyers and judges from appearing on television or on the radio in any capacity that connected him or her to a commercial or business product (see California Canons of Judicial Ethics 1949).
8   Advisory Committee on Judicial Ethics of the Conference of California Judges, "Appearance of a Judge on a Television Program," *Federal Communications Bar Journal* 16 (1958), 46.
9   Anna McCarthy, *The Citizen Machine: Governing By Television in 1950s American* (New York: The New York Press, 2010), p. 24.
10 Ibid.
11 American Bar Association Committee on Professional Ethics, "Formal Opinion 298 (1961)," *Opinions of the Committee on Professional Ethics, With The Canons of Professional Ethics, Annotated, and Canons of Judicial Ethics, Annotated* (Chicago: American Bar Foundation, 1967), p. 655.
12 Kimberlianne Podlas, "Blame Judge Judy: The Effects of Syndicated Television Courtrooms on Jurors," *American Journal of Trial Advocacy* 25 (2001–2), 557.
13 Ibid., 583.
14 Philip Z. Kimball, "Syndi-Court Justice: Judge Judy and Exploitation of Arbitration," *Journal of American Arbitration* 4 (2005), 153–66.
15 Ibid.
16 The trial of Bruno Hauptmann in February 1935, stirred up a media frenzy, bombarding audiences with photographs and newsreel footage. In 1925, American audiences tuned into radio broadcasts of the Scopes trial (*The State of Tennessee v. John Thomas Scopes*), which was the first live radio broadcast of a trial in American history.
17 Sherwin, *When Law Goes Pop*, p. 242.
18 Ibid.
19 Baudrillard, *Simulacra and Simulation*, p. 3.
20 Ibid.
21 Ibid.

22 Ibid., p. 20.
23 Eriq Gardner, "Judge Joe Brown Wins Ruling in His Own Lawsuit," *Reuters*, July 30, 2010, http://www.reuters.com/article/2010/07/30/us-joebrown-idUSTRE66T0OU20100730.
24 LACBA, "Calling the Bluff," http://www.lacba.org/showpage.cfm?pageid=8580, vol. 30, no. 8 (2007).
25 J. L. Austin, *How to Do Things with Words* (Oxford: Clarendon Press, 1962).
26 The New York Mitchell-Lama Housing program subsidizes apartment rentals for low and middle-income earners. The program requires developers to build housing for low- and middle-income residents.
27 Kahn v. New York City Department of Housing Preservation & Development, 2010 NY Slip Op 51197(U), pp. 7–8.
28 Ibid.
29 Access Hollywood, "Anna Nicole Judge Larry Seidlin Scores Own TV Show," August 7, 2007, http://www.accesshollywood.com/judge-larry-seidlin/anna-nicole-judge-larry-seidlin-scores-own-tv-show_article_6363.
30 Aswini Anburajan, "Courtroom Drama in Anna Nicole Smith Hearing: Testy, Hilarious and Odd Exchanges in fight Over Centerfold's Body," *ABC News*, February 15, 2007, http://abcnews.go.com/US/story?id=2878053&page=1.
31 Catherine Donaldson-Evans, "Anna Nicole Smith Snarky 'Judge Larry': Aspiring TV Star of Regular Guy Running No-Jury Trial?," February 20, 2007, http://www.foxnews.com/story/2007/02/20/anna-nicole-smith-snarky-judge-larry-aspiring-tv-star-or-regular-guy-running-no/.
32 Ibid.
33 FoxNews.com, "Anna Nicole Smith Judge Larry Seidlin Resigns," June 19, 2007, http://www.foxnews.com/story/2007/06/19/anna-nicole-smith-judge-larry-seidlin-resigns/.
34 PR Newswire, "'Psychic Court' Signs Judge Larry Seidlin of Anna Nicole Smith Fame," June 21, 2010, http://www.prnewswire.com/news-releases/psychic-court-signs-judge-larry-seidlin-of-anna-nicole-smith-fame-96791639.html.
35 Ibid.

36 Steven Lubet, "The 'Real' Judge Joe Brown Is Being Injudicious," *Newsday*, November 3, 1999, http://www.newsday.com/the-real-judge-joe-brown-is-being-injudicious-1.327595.
37 See Alexis de Tocqueville, *Democracy in America* (Garden City, NY: Doubleday, 1975).
38 Bertolt Brecht, *Brecht on Theatre: The Development of an Aesthetic* (New York: Hill and Wang, 1992), p. 71.
39 Gad Guterman, "Field Tripping: The Power of Inherit the Wind," *Theatre Journal* 60 (2008), 563–83.
40 Julie Cassiday, *The Enemy on Trial: Early Soviet Courts on Stage and Screen* (Dekalb: Northern Illinois University Press, 2000), p. 65.
41 Ibid., p. 52.
42 Julie A. Cassiday, "Marble Columns and Jupiter Lights: Theatrical and Cinematic Modeling of Soviet Show Trials in the 1920s," *The Slavic and East European* 42 (1998), 641.
43 Laurie Ouellette, "*Real Justice,*" p. 171.
44 The online Direct TV guide categorizes *We the People* as a talk show.
45 Talent Rant: Hollywood Actors, "We the People with Gloria Allred," July 29, 2011, http://www.talentrant.com/viewtopic.php?t=61, accessed June 15, 2013.
46 Ibid.
47 All of Entertainment Studios courtroom television shows are available on the Youtube subscription channel, JusticeCentral.TV, and can be accessed for $1.99 a month, http://www.youtube.com/user/justicecentraldottv, accessed February 12, 2014.
48 Alex Ben Block, "Byron Allen Planning Two New Syndie Sitcoms," *Hollywood Reporter*, April 18, 2013, http://www.hollywoodreporter.com/news/byron-allen-planning-two-new-441622. In Block's interview, Allen says the actors and writers are well compensated. However, in December 2012, several comedians who worked for Allen filed a class-action lawsuit against him in Los Angeles Superior Court for unfair business practices and for withholding payment. (See http://www.hollywoodreporter.com/thr-esq/class-action-suit-brought-byron-406265.)

49 John Moore is a pseudonym. The actor requested that I withhold his name because of the confidentiality agreement he signed with Entertainment Studios.
50 John Moore, phone interview with author, June 11, 2013.
51 Many actors on the show have posted their scenes to Youtube and/or blogged about their experiences.
52 During the same period in March 2013, *We the People with Gloria Allred* had a Nielson Rating of 0.2 while *Judge Judy* had a rating of 7.0. Marc Berman, "Judge Joe Brown' to Conclude," *Media Insights*, March 27, 2013, http://www.tvmediainsights.com/highlights/20479/judge-joe-brown-to-conclude/.
53 David Ray Papke, "From Flat to Round: Changing Portrayals of the Judge in American Popular Culture," *Journal of the Legal Profession* 31 (2007), 130.
54 John Rawls, "Justice as Fairness: Political Not Metaphysical," *Philosophy & Public Affairs* 14 (1985), 223.
55 Ibid., 231.

Appendix

1 This is a comprehensive list of reality courtroom TV programs, but it is possible that some shows may be missing from this list. The descriptions that follow focus on programs airing during my research period, so not every program in the list is detailed.
2 Hal Erickson, *Encyclopedia of Television Law Shows: Factual and Fictional Series About Judges, Lawyers and the Courtroom, 1948-2008* (Jefferson, NC: McFarland, 2009), p. 193.
3 This is a comprehensive list, but there may be more that I did not uncover during my research.
4 *The Court of Human Relations, Goodwill Court, and Famous Jury Trials* were all radio programs that predated the slew of courtroom television dramas in the late 1940s and 1950s. *Goodwill Court* gave free legal advice to people unable to afford legal counsel. The New York County Lawyers'

Association protested the program's giving of free advice, and NBC took the show off the air in 1936. There were several public affairs programs that used the trial format to debate current issues: *The Court of Current Issues* (1948), *On Trial* (1948–52), and *Politics on Trial* (1952). These I see as falling into a different category than the TV courtroom dramas listed above.
5   Hal Erickson, *Encyclopedia of Television Law Shows*, p. 44.
6   Ibid., p. 103.
7   Ibid., p. 260.
8   The *Divorce Court* disclaimer at the end of the credits is as follows: "The preceding case and litigants are real. Each couple may meet with a trained divorce mediator immediately following their appearance on the program. Portions of the program have been edited for time or content restriction. To the extent permitted under applicable law, all judgments are final and binding. All litigants have agreed to submit their disputes to Lynn Toler, former Judge, who serves as a neutral third party arbitrator. Consideration has been given to each litigant in connection with his/her appearance on the program. The decisions and interpretations rendered in the program may not be applicable in all cases and jurisdictions." (*Divorce Court* 2011).
9   Erickson, *Encyclopedia of Television Law Shows*, p. 217.
10 Ibid.

Bibliography

ABC Channel 8 Website. 2007. "Q & A With Joe Brown." http://www.wchstv.com/synd_prog/joebrown/joebrowninterview.shtml (accessed January 1, 2012).

ABC News. 1997. "Judge Joe Brown." April 3. *Nightline*. ABC. LexisNexis Academic. Web. (accessed April 6, 2010).

Access Hollywood. 2007. "Anna Nicole Judge Larry Seidlin Scores Own TV Show." August 7. http://www.accesshollywood.com/judge-larry-seidlin/anna-nicole-judge-larry-seidlin-scores-own-tv-show_article_6363 (accessed January 25, 2012).

The Advertiser. 1991. "Judge's Tit-for-Tat Justice." October 5. "Judge's tit-for-tat Justice." *The Advertiser*. 2012/01/04.http://ezproxy.library.nyu.edu:2076/hottopics/lnacademic (accessed January 14, 2012).

Advisory Committee on Judicial Ethics of the Conference of California Judges. 1958. "Appearance of a Judge on a Television Program." *Federal Communications Bar Journal* 16: 45–56.

Albiniak, Page. 2004. "Reality Rates With Advertisers." *Broadcasting & Cable*, February 16, 134(7): 34.

Alexander, Michelle. 2011. "The New Jim Crow." *Ohio State Journal of Criminal Law* 9(1): 7–26.

—2012. *The New Jim Crow: Mass Incarceration in the Age of Colorblindness*. New York: The New Press.

Allen, R. and W. T. Bielby. 1979. "Blacks' Attitudes and Behaviors Toward Television." *Communication Research* 6: 437–62.

Althusser, Louis. 1971. "Ideology and Ideological State Apparatuses," in *Lenin and Philisophy and Other Essays*. trans. Ben Brewster. London: New Left Books, pp. 171–4.

Alvarez, Lizette. 2013. "In Zimmerman Case, Self Defense Was Hard to Topple." *New York Times*, July 14, http://www.nytimes.com/2013/07/15/us/in-zimmerman-case-self-defense-was-hard-to-topple.html?pagewanted=all&_r=0 (accessed February 24, 2014).

Americanbar.org. 2007. "ABA Model Code of Judicial Conduct." http://www.americanbar.org/content/dam/aba/migrated/judicialethics/ABA_MCJC_approved.authcheckdam.pdf (accessed May 8, 2011).

American Bar Association. 2009. "Small Claims Courts: The 'Fast Food' of the Legal System," in Sheila Maloney *American Bar Association Guide to Resolving Legal Disputes: Inside and Outside the Courtroom*. New York: Random House Reference, pp. 93–116.

American Bar Association Committee on Professional Ethics. 1967. "Formal Opinion 298 (1961)," *Opinions of the Committee on Professional Ethics, With The Canons of Professional Ethics, Annotated, and Canons of Judicial Ethics, Annotated*. Chicago: American Bar Foundation, p. 655.

An American Family. 1973. PBS. No director or writer credited. Part of the Fales Archive Collection, New York University. NYC. (VHS).

Anburajan, Aswini. 2007. "Courtroom Drama in Anna Nicole Smith Hearing: Testy, Hilarious and Odd Exchanges in fight Over Centerfold's Body." *ABC News*, February 15. http://abcnews.go.com/US/story?id=2878053&page=1 (accessed June 8, 2011).

Anderson, Curt. 2008. "TV Justice, Miami Style; Florida's Hot Tourist Destination is Home to Five Former Judges with their Own shows. Taped Trials Helped Give Them Exposure." July 8. *Los Angeles Times*: E.10.

Anderson, Kevin. 1983. "The Inns of Court: Rx for Revitalizing Advocacy in America." *University of Southern Illinois Law Journal* 8: 311–36.

Andrejevich, Mark. 2004. *Reality TV: The Work of Being Watched*. Maryland: Rowman and Littlefield Publishers, Inc.

Annesse, Susanna. 2004. "Mediated Identity in the Parasocial Interaction of TV." *Identity* 4(4): 371–88.

Asimow, Michael. 1999. "Justice with an Attitude: Judge Judy and the Daytime Television Bench." *Judges' Journal* 38: 24–7.

Associated Press. 2008. "O.J. Simpson Judge Known for Tough Sentences." December 4. http://www.nbcnews.com/id/28056491/ns/us_news-crime_and_courts/t/oj-simpson-judge-known-tough-sentences/#.UzHlNV6T6hA (accessed March 25, 2014).

—2009. "Recession Means Even Cheaper Reality Shows." April 7. http://today.msnbc.msn.com/id/30093190/ns/today-entertainment (accessed April 10, 2011).

Ault, Susanne. 2000. *Broadcasting & Cable*, November 6, 130(46): 29.
Auslander, Philip. 1999. *Liveness: Performance in a Mediatized Culture.* London, New York: Routledge.
Austin, J. L. 1962. *How to Do Things with Words.* Oxford: Clarendon Press.
Banks, TaunyaLowell. 2009. "Here Comes the Judge: Gender Distortion on TV Reality Court Shows." *University of Baltimore Law Forum* 39: 38–56.
—2009. "Judging the Judges: Daytime Television's Integrated Reality Court Benches." http://digitalcommons.law.umaryland.edu/fac_pubs/568/ (accessed January 16, 2012).
Barthes, Roland. 1981. *Camera Lucida: Reflections on Photography.* New York: Hill and Wang.
Battaglio, Stephan. 2010. "Who Are TV's Top Earners?" *TV Guide*, April 10. http://www.tvguide.com/News/Top-TV-Earners-1021717.aspx (accessed March 16, 2011).
Bauder, David. 2010. "Nancy Grace On 'Swift Justice': I'm Not Going to Be Bullied." *Huffington Post*, September 21. http://www.huffingtonpost.com/2010/09/21/nancy-grace-on-swift-just_n_732796.html (accessed May 2011).
Baudrillard, Jean. 1994. *Simulacra and Simulation.* Ann Arbor: University of Michigan Press.
Belczyk, Jaclyn. 2009. "Most US Federal Court Judges Still White Men, but Demographics Changing: Report." *Jurist*, August 18. http://jurist.org/paperchase/2009/08/federal-court-demographics-changing-to.php (accessed February 21, 2014).
Bell, Derrick A. 1995. "Serving Two Masters," in Kimberle Crenshaw, Neil Gotanda, Gary Peller and Kendall Thomas (eds), *Critical Race Theory: The Key Writings That Formed the Movement.* New York: New Press, pp 5–19.
Berlant, Lauren Gail. 2004. *Compassion: The Culture and Politics of an Emotion.* New York: Routledge.
Berman, Marc. 2005. "Syndication Report." *MediaWeek*, December 12, 15: 45.
—2007. "Syndication Report." *MediaWeek*, June 11, 17: 24.
—2013. "'Judge Joe Brown' to Conclude." *Media Insights*, March 27. http://www.tvmediainsights.com/highlights/20479/judge-joe-brown-to-conclude/ (accessed September 21, 2013).
Bibas, Stephanos. 2007. "Mercy and Clemency: Forgiveness in Criminal Procedure." *Ohio State Journal of Criminal Law* 4: 329–619.

Biressi, Anita and Heather Nunn. 2005. *Reality TV: Realism and Revelation.* London: Wallflower Press.

Block, Alex Ben. 2013. "Byron Allen Planning Two New Syndie Sitcoms." *Hollywood Reporter*, April 18. http://www.hollywoodreporter.com/news/byron-allen-planning-two-new-441622 (accessed June 14, 2013).

Blumer, Herbert. 1969. *Symbolic Interactionism: Perspective and Method.* Englewood Cliffs, NJ: Prentice-Hall.

Boal, Augusto. 1986. *Theatre of the Oppressed.* New York: Theatre Communications Group.

Bourdieu, Pierre. 1977. *Outline of a Theory of Practice.* Cambridge, New York: Cambridge University Press.

—1986. "The Force of Law: Towards a Sociology of the Juridical Field." *Hastings Law Journal* 38(5): 814–53.

Boylorn, Robin M. 2008. "As seen on TV: An Autoethnographic reflection on race and reality television." *Critical Studies in Media Communication* 25(4): 413–33.

Brecht, Bertolt. 1977. *The Measures Taken and Other Lehrstücke*, trans. Carl Mueller. New York: Arcade Publishing.

Brennan, Peter. 2008. Phone interview with the author, 9 October.

Broadcasting & Cable. 2002. 'Ratings/Dec. 2–8 Nielsen Media Research.' December 30, 132(52): 9.

—2004. "Ratings." June 14, 134(24): 19.

Brook, Peter. 1968. "The Holy Theatre," in *An Empty Space.* New York: Touchstone, pp. 42–64.

Bureau of Justice Statistics. 2010. "Prison Inmates at Midyear 2009-Statistical Tables." http://bjs.ojp.usdoj.gov/index.cfm?ty=pbdetail&iid=2200 (accessed December 29, 2011).

California Canons of Judicial Ethics. 1949. Canons 21 and 25. https://docs.google.com/viewer?url=http%3A%2F%2Fwww.courts.ca.gov%2Fdocuments%2Fca_code_judicial_ethics.pdf (accessed October 12, 2010).

Carbado, Devon W. 1997. "The Construction of OJ Simpson as a Racial Victim." *Harvard CR-CLL Review* 32: 49–103.

Cassiday, Julie, A. 1998. "Marble Columns and Jupiter Lights: Theatrical and Cinematic Modeling of Soviet Show Trials in the 1920s." *The Slavic and East European Journal* 42(4): 640–60.

—2000. *The Enemy on Trial: Early Soviet Courts on Stage and Screen*. Dekalb: Northern Illinois University Press.

Cassidy, Marsha Francis. 2005. *What Women Watched: Daytime Television in the 1950's*. Texas: University of Texas Press.

CBS News Transcripts. 1992. "Memphis Judge Allows Victims to Even Score with Criminals." *Street Stories*. September 24. LexisNexis Academic. Web. (accessed July 7, 2012).

Chambers-Letson, Joshua. 2014. "The Inoperative Iphigenia: Race, Law, And Emancipation in Michi Barall's *Rescue Me*." *Theatre Survey* 55(2): 145–64.

Champagne, Anthony. 2005. "Tort Reform and Judicial Selection." *Loyola of Los Angeles Law Review* 38: 1486–9.

Chicago Defender. 2001. "Judge Hatchett Launches New Season with Innovative shows." October 1. https://ezproxy.library.nyu.edu/login?url=http://search.proquest.com/docview/247012236?accountid=12768 (accessed January 10, 2012).

CNN Transcripts. 1995. "*Both Sides with Jesse Jackson*." October 29. http://ezproxy.library.nyu.edu:2076/hottopics/lnacademic (accessed December 12, 2012).

—2000. *Larry King Live*, May 8. http://transcripts.cnn.com/TRANSCRIPTS/0005/08/lkl.00.html (accessed January 26, 2012).

Commission of Judicial Conduct Transcripts. 2002. "Complaint No. 2000-110 et seq." http://www.mass.gov/cjc/Lopez-transcripts/Lopez-transcript004.htm (accessed December 12, 2012).

Committee on Professional Ethics of the American Bar Association. 1961. "Appearances of Attorneys on Television Shows." *Journal of the Federal Communications Bar Association* 17: 199–208.

Congressional Budget Office. 2006. "Medical Malpractice Tort Limits and Health Care Spending." http://www.cbo.gov/ftpdocs/71xx/doc7174/04-28-MedicalMalpractice.pdf (accessed May 8, 2011).

Cook, Elizabeth. 2009. *Talking with Television: Women, Talk Shows, and Modern-Reflexivity*. Urbana: University of Illinois Press.

Crenshaw, Kimberlé. 1995. "Race, Reform, and Retrenchment: Transformation and Legitimation in Anti-discrimination Law," in Kimberlé Crenshaw, Neil Gotanda, Gary Peller, and Kendall Thomas (eds), *Critical Race Theory: The Key Writings That Formed the Movement*. New York: New Press, pp. 103–22.

Cristina's Court. Schordinger's Cat Productions and 20th Television. WWOR-TV Channel 9, New York City. Television.

—2008. "Bad Night at Woodforest: Part One." November 10. http://www.youtube.com/watch?v=s5RULpfuI38&feature=related (accessed January 12, 2012).

—2008a. "Bad Night at Woodforest: Part Two." November 11 (accessed January 12, 2012).

Croteau, David, William Hoynes, and Stefania Milan. 2011. *Media/Society: Industries, Images, and Audiences*, 4th edn. London: Sage.

Curriden, Mark. 1992. "Making Punishment Fit the Crime Often Not Popular." January 9. *Atlanta Journal and Constitution*, A3.

Delgado, Richard. 1999. "The Imperial Scholar: Reflections and Review of Civil Rights Literature," in Kimberle Crenshaw, Neil Gotanda, Gary Peller, and Kendall Thomas (eds), *Critical Race Theory: The Key Writings That Formed the Movement*. New York: New Press, pp. 46–57.

Dempsey, John. 2005. "Gavelers Court Hispanic Viewers." November 28. *Variety*.

—2008. "Judge Judy on a Roll: Syndication Star Sentenced to Two More Years." *Variety*, February 15. http://www.variety.com/article/VR1117981008.html?categoryid=2522&cs=1 (accessed May 26, 2011).

Detroit News, The. 1999. "Television: Bad Kid Makes Good: Detroit Judge Greg Mathis Takes 'Inspirational Justice' to TV." September 11.

Divorce Court. WWWOR-TV Channel 9, New York, New York. Television.

Dines, Gail and Jean McMahon Humez, eds. 2003. *Gender, Race, and Class in Media: A Text-Reader*. Thous and Oaks, CA: Sage.

Dolan, Jill. 2005. *Utopia in Performance: Finding Hope at the Theater*. USA: University of Michigan Press.

Donaldson-Evans, Catherine. 2007. "Anna Nicole Smith Snarky 'Judge Larry': Aspiring TV Star of Regular Guy Running No-Jury Trial?" February 20. http://www.foxnews.com/story/2007/02/20/anna-nicole-smith-snarky-judge-larry-aspiring-tv-star-or-regular-guy-running-no/ (accessed February 12, 2014).

Dovidio, J. F. and S. L. Gaertner. 2000. "Aversive Racism and selection decisions: 1989 and 1990." *Psychological Science* 11: 315–19.

Dr Phil Website. 2007. "Is He Setting her Up?" http://www.drphil.com/slideshows/slideshow/3669/?id=3669&slide=0&showID=&preview=&versionID= (accessed January 5, 2012).

Erickson, Hal. 2009. *Encyclopedia of Television Law Shows: Factual and Fictional Series About Judges, Lawyers and the Courtroom, 1948-2008.* Jefferson, NC: McFarland.

Essany, Michael. 2013. *Reality Check: The Business and Art of Producing Reality TV.* New York and London: Focal Press Taylor & Francis Group.

Family Court with Judge Penny. 2009. WWOR-TV Channel 9, New York. Television.

Federal Judicial Center. 2009. "Diversity on the Bench." http://www.fjc.gov/history/home.nsf/page/judges_diversity.html (accessed September 2009).

Federal Rules of Evidence. 2011. *Legal Information Institute.* http://www.law.cornell.edu/rules/fre (accessed January 26, 2012).

Felman, Shoshana. 2002. *The Juridical Unconscious: Trials and Traumas in the 20th Century.* Cambridge, MA: Harvard University Press.

Fincham, Frank D. 2009. "Forgiveness: Integral to Close Relationships and Inimical to Justice?" *Virginia Journal of Social Policy & the Law* (Winter) 16(2): 357–513.

Fischoff, Stuart. 1995. "Confession of a TV Talk Show Shrink." *Psychology Today*, September 1. http://www.psychologytoday.com/articles/200910/confession-tv-talk-show-shrink?page=2 (accessed May 8, 2011).

Fitzgerald, Kate. 2000. "A Few Good Judges: Producers Tell How They Track Court TV Talent." January 17. *Electronic Media.*

Flagg, Barbara J. 1998. *Was Blind, but Now I See: White Race Consciousness & The Law.* New York: NYU Press.

Ford, Chandra L., et al. 2007. "Black Sexuality, Social Construction, and Research Targeting 'The Down Low'('The DL')." *Annals of Epidemiology* 17(3): 209–16.

Forster, E. M. 1927. *Aspects of the Novel.* London: E. Arnold.

Foucault, Michel. 2003. *Abnormal: Lectures at the College de France, 1974-1975.* New York: Picador.

—2007. *Security, Territory, Population: Lectures at the Collège de France, 1977-78.* Basingstoke, New York: Palgrave MacMillan.

Freeman, Michael. 1999. "Law on Order." *Adweek Eastern Edition*, September 20, 40(38): 46.

Freud, Sigmund. 1960. *Jokes and their Relation to the Unconscious*. New York: Norton.

Friedman, Lawrence. 1973. *A History of American Law*. New York: Simon and Schuster.

—2000. "Lexitainment: Legal Process as Theater." *DePaul Law Review* 539–58.

Friedman, Wayne. 1998. "The Selling of 'Judge Joe Brown'." January 22. *The Hollywood Reporter*.

Gamson, Joshua. 1998. *Freaks Talk Balk: Tabloid Talk Shows and Sexual Nonconformity*. Chicago: University of Chicago Press.

Gardner, Eriq. 2010. "Judge Joe Brown Wins Ruling in His Own Lawsuit." *Reuters*, 30 July. http://www.reuters.com/article/2010/07/30/us-joebrown-idUSTRE66T0OU20100730 (accessed February 3, 2014).

Garofoli, Joe. 2007. "Gay TV Jurist Dispenses Justice With Song, Dance." September 10. *San Francisco Chronicle*. http://ezproxy.library.nyu.edu:34344/newsstand/docview/411795086/13418C6FC09564861A6/497?accountid=1276 (accessed January 5, 2012).

Getlin, Josh. 1993. "Law and Disorder: Tart, tough-talking Judge Judith Sheindlin Presides Over the Grim Pageant of Dysfunction Known as Manhattan's Family Court." February 14. *LA Times*.

Goffman, Erving. 1959. *The Presentation of Self in Everyday Life*. New York: Anchor Books, Doubleday.

Gornstein, Leslie. 2008. "Which Costs More, Reality TV Or Scripted Series?" *E Online*. November 22. http://www.eonline.com/uberblog/ask_the_answer_bitch/b70141_which_costs_more_reality_tv_scripted.html (accessed April 10, 2011).

Grace, Nancy, and Diane Clehane. 2006. *Objection!: How High-priced Defense Attorneys, Celebrity Defendants, and a 24/7 Media Have Hijacked Our Criminal Justice System*. New York: Hyperion.

Grace, Roger M. 2003. "TV Courtroom Shows Proliferate in the Late 1950s." *Metropolitan News-Enterprise*, May 3. http://www.metnews.com/articles/reminiscing050803.htm (accessed May 8, 2011).

Gronfein, William P. and Eleanor DeArman Kinney. 1991. "Controlling Large Malpractice Claims: The Unexpected Impact of Damage Caps." *Journal of Health Politics, Policy and Law* 16(3): 441–64.

Grossman, Ben. 2006. "Courts Get More Crowded." *Broadcasting & Cable*, October 23, 136(42): 9.

Gustkey, Earl. 1991. "His Honor, the Referee: Mills Lane Brooks No Nonsense, in Court or in the Ring." LAtimes.Com, June 16. http://articles.latimes.com/1991-06-16/sports/sp-1489_1_mills-lane (accessed March 2, 2009).

Hale, Dorothy J. 2006. *The Novel: An Anthology of Criticism and Theory, 1900-2000*. Malden, Mass: Blackwell Pub.

Hall, Stuart. 1980. *Culture, Media, Language: Working Papers in Cultural Studies, 1972-79*. London: Hutchinson.

Hansen, Jane O. 1998. "Growing Up With Crack. Last Chance: Baby Court." *Atlanta Constitution*, September 30. https://ezproxy.library.nyu.edu/login?url=http://search.proquest.com/docview/413721918?accountid=12768 (accessed January 10, 2012).

Hariman, Robert, ed. 1993. *Popular Trials: Rhetoric, Mass Media, and the Law*, vol. 41. Birmingham: University of Alabama Press.

Harris, Lyle V. 2000. "Hatchett's Justice." September 7. *Atlanta Constitution*. https://ezproxy.library.nyu.edu/login?url=http://search.proquest.com/docview/413875326?accountid=12768 (accessed January 12, 2012).

Hefferman, Virginia. 2002. "Y'all Rise: Texas Justice is More Forgiving Than You Might Think." Slate.Com, May 23. http://www.slate.com/articles/arts/television/2002/05/yall_rise.html (accessed December 12, 2013).

Hendriks, Alexandra and Robin Nabi. 2003. "The Persuasive Effect of Host and Audience Reaction Shots in Television Talk Shows." *Journal of Communication* 53(3): 527–43.

Hibbitts, Bernard J. 1992. "Coming to Our Senses." *Emory Law Journal* 41: 873–960.

—1996. "De-scribing Law: Performance in the Constitution of Legality." PSI Conference Paper. http://law.pitt.edu/archive/hibbitts/describ.htm (accessed July 21, 2014).

Ho, Rodney. 2008. "The Non-Judgmental Judge." October 13. *Atlanta Journal and Constitution*, 1C.

—2008. "Fulton's 'Judge Penny' sees TV as 'extension of my ministry'." October 13. *Atlanta Journal and Constitution*.

Holsey, Steve. 2002. "Greg Mathis: From Street Life to Court TV." *Michigan Chronicle*: D1, October 2.

Hope, Jenny. 2010. Phone interview with author, 8 November.

Horton, Donald and Anselm Strauss. 1957. "Interaction in Audience-Participation Shows." *The American Journal of Sociology* 62(6): 579–87.

Huff, Richard. 2008. "Many judge, but Judy rules. In a crowded field, Jeanine Pirro will Need real bench strength to survive TV trial." *NY Daily News*, May 7, 5.

Hylton, Cal. 1971. "Intra-Audience Effects: Observable Audience Response." *Journal of Communication* 21(3): 253–65.

Innes, Christopher. 1981. *Holy Theatre: Ritual and the Avant Garde*. Cambridge: Cambridge University Press.

The Internet Archive. 2014. "They Stand Accused: The Johnny Roberts Story." http://www.archive.org/details/TheyStandAccused (accessed April 21, 2014).

Jakobsen, Janet and Ann Pellegrini. 2003. *Love the Sin: Sexual Regulation and the Limits of Religious Tolerance*. New York: New York University Press.

Jensen, Michael. 2007. "Interview With Judge David Young." *After Elton*, September 5. http://www.afterelton.com/people/2007/9/davidyoung (accessed May 6, 2011).

Jersley, Anne. 2002. *Realism and 'Reality' In Film and Media*. Copenhagen: Museum Tuscalanum Press.

Jet Magazine. 1999. "Blacks Rule on TV Court Shows." *HighBeam Research* 97(3): 60–4.

John-Hall, Annette. 2002. "The Judge Who Came to Order In the Ranks of TV Judges, at Least Two Things Set Greg Mathis Apart: A Flair that Turns Women Spectators into Flirts and a Resume Not Altogether Righteous." October 20. *Philadelphia Inquirer*, D.1.

Johnson, Cheryl. 2007. "David Young is TVs Gay Judge, And He's just Plain Happy, Too." *Star Tribune*, October 30. https://ezproxy.library.nyu.edu/login?url=http://search.proquest.com/docview/427917909?accountid=12768 (accessed January 6, 2012).

Jonathan Sebastien v. The Judge Judy Program; Paramount Pictures Inc.; Big Ticket Television; Big Ticket Pictures Inc.; CBS Paramount Network

Television Inc.; Randy Douthit. 2007. http://www.aolcdn.com/tmz_documents/1231_judge_judy_wm.pdf (accessed May 26, 2011).

Jones, Felicia G. 1990. "The Black Audience and the BET Channel." *Journal of Broadcasting and Electronic Media* 34(4): 377–486.

Judge Alex. 2009. WNYW Channel 5. New York, NY. Television.

Judge Hatchett. 2009. Channel 9. New York, NY. Television.

Judge Joe Brown. 2009. Episode 2383. http://www.youtube.com/watch?v=ey0y PhNyGBs&feature=related (accessed January 17, 2011).

—2008–9. WNYW-TV Channel 5. New York, NY. Television.

Judge Judy. 2009. Channel 9. WCBS-TV, New York, NY. Television.

Judgejudy.com. 2011. www.judgejudy.com (accessed May 12, 2011).

JudgePenny.com. 2011. "About Judge Penny." http://www.judgepenny.com/about_judge_penny.htm (accessed May 2011).

Kahn v. New York City Department of Housing Preservation & Development. 2010 NY Slip Op 51197(U).

Kaprow, Allan. 1993. *Essays on the Blurring of Art and Life.* Berkeley and Los Angeles, CA: University of California.

Kimball, Philip Z. 2005. "Syndi-Court Justice: Judge Judy and Exploitation of Arbitration." *Journal of American Arbitration* 4(1): 153–66.

Kirby, Michael. 1987. *A Formalist Theater.* Philadelphia: University of Pennsylvania Press.

Kirchmeier, Jeffrey L, et al. 2009. "Vigilante Justice: Prosecutor Misconduct in Capital Cases." *Wayne Law Review* 55: 1327–85.

Klein, Alvin. 1999. "Talks With Gay Playwrights Offered in Course at Purchase." December 5. *New York Times.*

Kohm, Steven. 2006. "The People's Law Verses Judge Judy Justice." *Law and Society Review* 40(3): 693–728.

Kristeva, Julia. 2003. "Approaching Abjection," in AmeliaJones (ed.), *'The' Feminism and Visual Culture Reader.* London: Routledge, pp. 389–91.

Krukoski, Andrew. 2009. "'Judy' Still Rules Court Show Ratings." *TV Week.* http://www.tvweek.com/news/2009/01/judy_still_rules_court_show_ra.php (accessed November 30, 2011).

LACBA. 2007. "Calling the Bluff," vol. 30, no 8. November. http://www.lacba.org/showpage.cfm?pageid=8580 (accessed February 3, 2014).

Lachance-Grzela, Mylène and Geneviève Bouchard. 2010. "Why do Women do the Lion's Share of Housework: A Decade of Research." *Sex Roles* 63(11–12): 767–80.

Land, Greg. 2008. "Judge to Resign Next Month for TV Gig." *Fulton County Daily Report*, September 10. http://www.law.com/jsp/article.jsp?id=1202424402163&slreturn=1 (January 5, 2011).

Larry King Live Transcript. 2000. "Judge Mills Lane, Judge Joe Brown and Judge Mathis Lay Down the Law on Daytime TV." *CNN*, May 8. http://transcripts.cnn.com/TRANSCRIPTS/0005/08/lkl.00.html (accessed January 4, 2009).

Lassiter, Christo. 1996. "TV or Not TV." *The Journal of Criminal Law and Criminology* (Spring) 86(3): 928–1001.

Lahav, Prina. 2004. "Theater in the Courtroom: The Chicago Conspiracy Trial." *Law & Literature* 16(3): 381–474.

"Law and Disorder." 1993. *60 Minutes*. CBS. October 24. http://www.cbsnews.com/video/watch/?id=4539460n (accessed December 30, 2011). Digital Video.

Lawrence, Charles R. III. 1999. "The Id, the Ego, and Equal Protection: Reckoning With Unconscious Racism," in Kimberlé Crenshaw, Neil Gotanda, Gary Peller, and Kendall Thomas (eds), *Critical Race Theory: The Key Writings That Formed the Movement*. New York: New Press, pp. 235–57.

Lawrence, Susan E. 1990. *The Poor in Court: The Legal Services Program and Supreme Court Decision Making*. Princeton: Princeton University Press.

Lester, G. A., ed. 1981. *Three Late Medieval Morality Plays*. New York: WW Norton.

Levenson, Laurie L. 2007. "Courtroom Demeanor: The Theater of the Courtroom." *Minnesota Law Review* 92(3), pp. 573–633.

Lipscomb, James. 1964. "Cinéma-vérité." *Film Quarterly* 18(2): 62–3.

Livingstone Sonia and Peter K. Lunt. 1994. *Talk on Television: Audience Participation and Public Debate*. London; New York: Routledge.

Longan, Krys. 2009. "Here Come Da Judge!" http://alexferrer.com/here_comes.html?fuseaction=viewImage&friendID=55824800&albumID=767659&imageID=39669 (accessed January 5, 2012).

Lopate, Carol. 1976. "Daytime Television: You'll Never Want to Leave Home." *Feminist Studies* 3(3): 69–80.

Lorenzo-Dus, Nuria. 2008. "Real Disorder in the Court: an Investigation of Conflict Talk in US Television Courtroom Shows." *Media, Culture & Society* 30(1): 81–107.

Lubet, Steven. 1999. "The 'Real' Judge Joe Brown Is Being Injudicious." *Newsday*, November 3. http://www.newsday.com/the-real-judge-joe-brown-is-being-injudicious-1.327595 (accessed June 7, 2011).

Mak, John. 2011. "Now You Know: Pigmeat Markham." September 13. www.guy.com (accessed October 3, 2011).

Malik, Mike. 2008. "Laugh and Learn from Trash TV." *Indiana Daily Student*, October 28. http://www.idsnews.com/news/story.aspx?id=31296&search=people&section=search (accessed June 8, 2011).

Markham, Pigmeat, Bill Levinson and Hester Mundis. 1969. *Here Come The Judge*. Popular Library.

—2004. "Here Come The Judge." Universal Music Enterprises and Laugh.com. Compact Disc.

Marrero, Diana. 2002. "Cameras at Florida Bar Recorded America West Pilots Drinking Bout." *McClatchy – Tribune Business News*, August 6. https://ezproxy.library.nyu.edu/login?url=http://search.proquest.com/docview/464563873?accountid=12768 (accessed January 6, 2012).

Martin, A. 2008. "Television Media as a Potential Negative Factor in the Racial Identity Development of African American Youth." *Academic Psychiatry* 32: 338–42.

Martin, Lydia. 2007. "Judicial Restraint? That's for the Courtroom, Not TV." *McClatchy Tribune Business News*, September 9. https://ezproxy.library.nyu.edu/login?url=http://search.proquest.com/docview/459159656?accountid=12768 (accessed January 5, 2012).

Matsuda, Mari. 1991. "Voices of America: Accent, Antidiscrimination Law, and Jurisprudence for the Last Reconstruction." *Yale Law Journal* (March) 100: 1329–407.

McCarthy, Anna. 2007. "Reality Television: a Neoliberal Theater of Suffering." *Social Text* 25(4): 17–42.

McKenzie, Robert. 2000. "Audience Involvement in the Epedeictic Discourse of Television Talk Shows." *Communication Quarterly* 48(2): 190–203.

McNulty, Arthur P. 1960. "The Verdict Is Yours: Problems of TV Courtroom Drama." *American Bar Association Journal* 46(1): 67–9.

Mead, Margaret. 1973. "As Significant as the Invention of Drama or the Novel." *TV Guide*, January 6, A61–3.

Media Dynamics, Inc. 2000–10. *TV Dimensions*. New York: Media Dynamics.

Medvedich, Kiersten. 2008. Phone Interview with Author, February 27.

Merskin, Debra. 2007. "Three Faces of Eva: Perpetuation of The Hot-Latina Stereotype in Desperate Housewives." *Howard Journal of Communications* (April) 18(2): 133–51.

Mishory. 2009. "Two of Miami's TV Judges Get the Ax." *Daily Business Review*, August 17. http://www.law.com/jsp/law/careercenter/CareerCenterArticleFriendly.jsp?id=12024330 (accessed December 25, 2011).

Munoz, Jose. 2006. "Stages: Queers, Punks, and the Utopian Performative," in D. Soyini Madison and Judith Hamera (eds), *The Sage Handbook of Performance Studies*. Thousand Oaks, CA: Sage, pp. 9–21.

Murray, Susan and Laurie Ouellette, eds. 2009. *Reality TV: Remaking Television Culture*. New York: New York University Press.

Nash, Marianna. 2010. "Judge Judy Tops in Rankings." June 10. http://marquee.blogs.cnn.com/2010/06/10/judge-judy-tops-oprah-in-rankings/ (accessed June 8, 2011).

National Arbitration Forum. 2011. "Can I Appeal a Binding Arbitration Decision." *National Arbitration Forum*. http://www.adrforum.com/faq.aspx?faq=896 (accessed May 8, 2011).

National Public Radio Transcripts. 2002. "Judge Greg Mathis Discusses How He Overcame Adversity to Become the Youngest Judge in Michigan's History and his TV Show, 'Judge Mathis'." November 19. http://business.highbeam.com/152499/article-1G1-167309406/interview-judge-greg-mathis-discusses-he-overcame-adversity (accessed January 14, 2012).

NBC News Transcripts. 2005. "Miami Judge Sentences Two Pilots Drunk on Job." July 22. LexisNexis Academic. Web. (accessed January 14, 2012)

Nack, Adina. 2002. "Bad Girls and Fallen Women: Chronic STD Diagnoses as Gateways to Tribal Stigma." *Symbolic Interaction* 25(4): 463–85.

New Jersey Courts. 2010. "How to Represent Yourself in Court." http://www.judiciary.state.nj.us/prose/#civil (accessed January 12, 2010).

Nielsen.com. 2011. "Nielsen Television Ratings." http://www.nielsen.com/us/en/insights/top10s/television.html (accessed March 16, 2011).

—2014. "Nielsen Television Ratings." http://www.nielsen.com/us/en/top10s.html (accessed February 24, 2014).
Neuhaus, Eric. 2008. In conversation with author, October 16.
O'Haire, Patricia. 1996. "Here Comes Da Judge Judy Sheindlin's New Courtroom Is A TV Set, But Her Cases Are Real." *NY Daily News*, September 22.
Ouellette, Laurie. 2004. "'Take Responsibility for Yourself': Judge Judy and The Neoliberal Citizen," in Susan Murray and Laurie Ouellette (eds), *Reality TV*. New York: New York University Press, pp. 231–50.
—2011. "Real Justice: Law and Order on Reality Television" in *Imagining Legality: Where Law Meets Popular Culture*, ed. Austin Sarat. Tuscaloosa: University of Alabama Press.
Papke, David Ray. 2007. "From Flat to Round: Changing Portrayals of the Judge in American Popular Culture." *Journal of the Legal Profession* 31: 127–51 (130).
Peck, Janice. 1995. "TV Talk shows as Therapeutic Discourse: The Ideological Labor of the Televised Talking Cure." *Communication Theory* 5(1): 58–81.
—2003. "The Mediated Talking Cure," in Gail Dines and Jean McMahon Humez (eds), *Gender, Race, and Class in Media: A Text-Reader*. Thousand Oaks, CA: Sage, pp. 538–45.
Perez, Cristina. 2008. Phone interview with author, October 7.
Perrusquia, Marc. 1998. "Brown Ousted from Ray Case: Court Says Acts Point to 'Bias'." March 7. *The Commercial Appeal*, A1.
Phelan, Peggy. 2012. *Unmarked: The Politics of Performance*. New York: Routledge.
Podlas, Kimberlianne. 2001–2. "Blame Judge Judy: The Effects of Syndicated Television Courtrooms on Jurors." *American Journal of Trial Advocacy* 25: 557–86. https://docs.google.com/viewer?url=http%3A%2F%2Fwww.americanbar.org%2Fcontent%2Fdam%2Faba%2Fmigrated%2Fdispute%2Fessay%2Fsyndicourtjustice.pdf (accessed January 16, 2012).
Porsdam, Helle. 1994. "Law as Soap Opera and Game Show: The case of The People's Court." *The Journal of Popular Culture* 28: 1–15.
Pozner, Jennifer L. 2010. *Reality Bites Back: The Troubling Truth About Guilty Pleasure TV*. Berkeley: Seal Press.

PR Newswire. 2007. "Judge David Young Delivers Justice with a Snap." September 7. https://ezproxy.library.nyu.edu/login?url=http://search.proquest.com/docview/447143991?accountid=12768 (accessed January 6, 2012).

Pressley, Sue Anne. 1997. "Historic Interests Meet at Memphis Crossroads." February 27. *Washington Post*, A1.

Rahill, Frank. 1967. *The World of Melodrama*. University Park: Pennsylvania State University Press.

Rawls, John. 1985. "Justice as Fairness: Political Not Metaphysical." *Philosophy and Public Affairs* 14(3): 223–51.

Robert Wood Johnson Foundation. 2010. "Reports and Briefs." http://www.rwjf.org/pr/synthesis/reports_and_briefs/pdf/no10_policybrief.pdf (accessed September 15, 2010).

Rubin, A. M. 1993. "Audience Activity and Media Use." *Communication Monographs* 60: pp. 98–105.

Ruby, Jay. 1977. "The Image Mirrored: Reflexivity and the Documentary Film." *Journal of the University Film Association* 29(4): 3–11.

Russell, Cristel Antonia and Christopher P. Puto. 1999. "Rethinking Television Audience Measures: An Exploration into the Construct of Audience Connectedness." *Marketing Letters* 10(4): 393–407.

Sams, Joshua Lloyd. 2009. "First Chapter Road to Redemption." http://birdwalkermusic.com%2Fstorage%2FFirst_Chapter_of_Road_to_Redemption.pdf&ei=gS8PT_DyCMXh0wG-7YGyAw&usg=AFQjCNFwPFo29VXzh4rbL5VXdppBMZSzSw&sig2=OBL0n_YZdNLFYZF4vKkrQQ (accessed January 12, 2012).

Sangster, Joan. 1996. "Incarcerating 'Bad Girls': The Regulation of Sexuality through the Female Refuges Act in Ontario, 1920-1945." *Journal of the History of Sexuality* (October) 7(2): 239–75.

Sassone, Bob. 2008. "Judge Judy's Show Sued: Accused of Racial Screening." *AOL TV*, January 2. http://www.tvsquad.com/2008/01/02/judge-judys-show-sued-accused-of-racial-screening (accessed May 26, 2011).

Schechner, Richard. 1968. "6 Axioms for Environmental Theatre." *TDR* 12(3): 4–164.

—1985. *Between Theatre and Anthropology*. University of Pennsylvania Press.

—2003. *Performance Theory*. New York: Routledge.

Seidman, Robert. 2010. "MTV Is the #1 Cable Network for 12-34 Year Olds." April 1. www.TVbytheNumbers.com (accessed April 23, 2010).

Selya, Bruce M. Hon. 1996. "The Confidence Game: Public Perceptions of the Judiciary." *New England Law Review* 30: 909–10.

Sheindlin, Judy. 1996. *Don't Pee on My Leg and Tell Me It's Raining*, ed. Josh, Getlin. New York: HarperCollins.

—2008. Phone interview with the author, September 17.

Sherwin, Richard K. 2000. *When Law Goes Pop: The Vanishing Line Between Law and Popular Culture*. Chicago: University of Chicago Press.

Shuler, Deadra. 2004. "Judge Glenda Hatchett: Dispensing Love and Justice from the Bench." *New York Amsterdam News*, February 25. https://ezproxy.library.nyu.edu/login?url=http://search.proquest.com/docview/390429853?accountid=12768 (accessed January 10, 2012).

Siapera, Eugenia. 2004. "From couch potatoes to Cybernauts? The Expanding Notion of the Audience on TV Channels' Websites." *New Media & Society* 6(2): 155–72.

Smith, Aaron. 2013. "Judge Judy is Highest-paid TV Star." *CNN Money*, August 21. http://money.cnn.com/2013/08/21/news/companies/tv-guide-judge-judy/ (accessed February 18, 2014).

Smiley, Tavis. 2002. NPR Broadcast Transcript of "Judge Greg Mathis Discusses How He Overcame Adversity to Become the Youngest Judge in Michigan's History and his TV Show, 'Judge Mathis'." *Highbeam Business*, November 19. http://business.highbeam.com/152499/article-1G1-167309406/interview-judge-greg-mathis-discusses-he-overcame-adversity (accessed January 14, 2012).

Sontag, Susan. 1999. "Notes on Camp," in Fabio Cleto (ed.), *Camp: Queer Aesthetics and the Performing Subject: A Reader*. Ann Arbor: University of Michigan Press, pp. 53–65.

South Florida Sun Sentinel. 2002. "Judge Limits Travel Of Two Pilots in Dui Case." August 6. https://ezproxy.library.nyu.edu/login?url=http://search.proquest.com/docview/387969965?accountid=12768 (accessed January 6, 2012).

Spring, Greg. 1998. "Mathis's Courting Young Demo." December 21. *Electronic Media*, 29.

Staples, Robert. 1971. "The Myth of the Impotent Black Male." *The Black Scholar* 2(10): 2–9.

Stanislavsky, Konstantin. 1989. *An Actor Prepares*. New York: Routledge.

Stanley, Alessandra. 2007. "Gavel to Gavel (To Gavel to Gavel) Coverage: TV's Courts of Last Resort Hear Life's Enduring Gripes." July 8. *New York Times*.

State of Tennessee, Appellant vs. James Earl Ray, Appellee: 984 S.W.2d 239.

Steadman, John and Richard Rosenstein. 1973. "'Small Claims' Consumer Plaintiffs in the Philadelphia Municipal Court: An Empirical Study." *University of Pennsylvania Law Review* 121(6): 1309–61.

Stelter, Brian. 2010. "With New Stars Reality Shows See Costs Rise." *The New York Times*, July 26. http://www.nytimes.com/2010/07/27/business/media/27reality.html (accessed April 9, 2011).

Stewart, Marcia. 2014. "50-State Chart of Small Claims Dollar Limits." *NOLO*, 21 February. https://www.nolo.com/legal-encyclopedia/small-claims-suits-how-much-30031.html (accessed February 21, 2014).

Strasberg, Lee. 1988. *A Dream of Passion: The Development of the Method*. New York: New American Library.

Sullivan, John Jeremiah. 2011. "The Lives They Lived." December 25. *The New York Times Magazine*.

Sullivan, Tim. 2010. Phone interview with author, October 29.

Tan, A. 1978. "Evaluation of Newspaper and Television by Blacks and Mexican Americans." *Journalism Quarterly* 55: 673–81.

Tasker, Yvonne and Diane Negra. 2007. *Interrogating Postfeminism: Gender and the Politics of Popular Culture*. Durham: Duke University Press.

Tejedor, Chrystian. 2005. "Judge Considers Convicted Pilots Flight Risks Pair to Remain in Jail Pending Sentencing." *South Florida Sun – Sentinel*, July 17. https://ezproxy.library.nyu.edu/login?url=http://search.proquest.com/docview/389890436?accountid=12768 (accessed January 6, 2012).

The New York Times. 1992. "First Black Federal Judge Appointed in 1910." August 21. http://www.nytimes.com/1992/08/21/opinion/l-first-black-federal-judge-appointed-in-1910-391492.html (accessed January 17, 2012).

ThePeoplesCourt.warnerbros.com. 2011. "Contact Us." http://peoplescourt.warnerbros.com/contact.html (accessed December 27, 2011).

TMZ. 2007. "Judge Judy Lawsuit." http://www.tmz.com/2007/12/31/lawsuit-says-judge-judy-sends-black-packin (accessed May 26, 2011).

Turner, Graeme. 2010. *Ordinary People and the Media: The Demonic Turn*. London: Sage Publications, Inc.

Turner, Victor. 1979. "Dramatic Ritual/Ritual Drama: Performative and Reflexive Anthropology." *The Kenyon Review* 1(3): 80–93.

—1980. "Social Dramas and Stories About Them." *Critical Inquiry* 7(1): 141–68.

TV by The Numbers. 2010. "TV Ratings By the Numbers: TV Ratings Broadcast Top 25." http://tvbythenumbers.com/2010/09/21/tv-ratings-broadcast-top-25-sunday-night-football-survivor-americas-got-talent-top-final-week-of-broadcast-summer/64534 (accessed September 25, 2010).

TVGuide.com. 2011. "Famous Jury Trials On DuMont." http://www.tvguide.com/tvshows/famous-jury-trials/201287 (accessed March 15, 2011).

—2011. "Divorce Court Episodes." http://www.tvguide.com/detail/tvshow.aspx?tvobjectid=195720&more=ucepisodelist&episodeid=7549465 (accessed March 24, 2011).

Tyree, Tia. 2011. "African American Stereotypes in Reality Television." *Howard Journal of Communications* 22(4): 394–413.

Variety. 2001. "Nielsen Syndication Ratings." *Variety*, April 9, 282(2): 49.

Vogelman, Lawrence. 1992. "The Big Black Man Syndrome: The Rodney King Trial and The Use of Racial Stereotypes in the Courtroom." *Fordham Urban Law Journal* 20: 571–939.

Walker, Jill. 2005. "Mirrors and Shadows: The Digital Aestheticisation of Oneself." *Digital Arts and Culture.* http://hdl.handle.net/1956/1136 (accessed December 29, 2011).

Walsh, W. T. 1999. "Letters, Faxes & E-Mail Judge Hatchett Leaves Children a Legacy." *Atlanta Constitution*, March 11. https://ezproxy.library.nyu.edu/login?url=http://search.proquest.com/docview/413738011?accountid=12768(accessed January 10, 2012).

Walter, Tom. 2001. "Judge Hatchett Looks at Sentencing Results." May 11. *The Commercial Appeal.* https://ezproxy.library.nyu.edu/login?url=http://search.proquest.com/docview/393923230?accountid=12768 (accessed January 10, 2012).

Wapner, Joseph. 1989. *A View From the Bench.* Boston: G.K. Hall & Co.

Warren, Richey. 1997. "New Approaches to Curbing Teen Crime." June 17. *Christian Science Monitor* 89(141): 4.

Webster, James G. 1998. "The Audience." *Journal of Broadcasting & Electronic Media* 42(2): 190–207.

West, Cornel. 1995. "Foreward," in Kimberlé Crenshaw, Neil Gotanda, Gary Peller, and Kendall Thomas (eds), *Critical Race Theory: The Key Writings That Formed the Movement*. New York: New Press, pp. xi–xii.

White, Mimi. 1992. *Tele-Advising: Therapeutic Discourse on American Television*. Chapel Hill: University of North Carolina Press.

Whitney, Elizabeth. 2006. "Capitalizing on Camp: Greed and the Queer Marketplace." *Text & Performance Quarterly* (January) 26(1): 36–46.

Wilkes Jr, Donald E. 2006. "Still Striking Foul Blows." *University of Georgia Law Digital Commons*, May 17. http://digitalcommons.law.uga.edu/fac_pm/135/ (accessed November 19, 2013).

Willet, John, ed. and trans. 1992. *Brecht on Theatre: The Development of an Aesthetic*. New York: Hill and Wang.

Williams, Patricia. 1991. *The Alchemy of Race and Rights*. Cambridge, MA: Harvard University Press.

Willis, Laurie. 2002. "Former Addict Returns to Court-This Time with Life Back on Track; Free of Drugs with Help of TVs 'Judge Hatchett'." January 21. *The Baltimore Sun*. https://ezproxy.library.nyu.edu/login?url=http://search.proquest.com/docview/406505730?accountid=12768 (accessed January 12, 2012).

Wilson, Clint C., FélixGutiérrez, and Lena M. Chao. 2003. *Racism, Sexism, and the Media: The Rise of Class Communication in Multiculture America*. Thous and Oaks, CA: Sage Publications.

Woo, Elaine. 2001. "Lance Loud, 50; Eldest Son in Real-Life PBS Series." *Los Angeles Times*, December 25. http://articles.latimes.com/2001/dec/25/local/me-17887 (accessed October 9, 2010).

Wood, Elizabeth A. 2005. *Performing Justice: Agitation Trials in Early Soviet Russia*. Ithaca, NY: Cornell University Press.

Yngvesson, Barbara and Patricia Hennessy. 1975. "Small Claims, Complex Disputes: A Review of the Small Claims Literature." *Law and Society Review Journal* 9: 219–74.

—1989. "Popular Legal Culture: Inventing Law in Local Settings: Rethinking Popular Legal Culture." *Yale Law Journal* (June) 98: 1689–710.

Young, Judge David. 2008. Phone interview with author, July 25.

Youtube.com. 2008. Gonzo7411. "Sex on the Bench." http://www.youtube.com/watch?v=r6HtSltnl0k (accessed May 2011).

—2008a. "Judge Mathis." http://www.youtube.com/watch?v=mb6WZFBHz98 (accessed January 3, 2012).

—2008b. "Judge Mills Lane Part 1 of 3." http://www.youtube.com/watch?v=xJZdnlTUlww (accessed January 5, 2012).

—2009. "Judge Maria Lopez-Show Introduction." http://www.youtube.com/watch?v=lP8Ztje8s9o (accessed January 5, 2012).

—2010. "Rock Band on People's Court." http://www.youtube.com/watch?v=e15Iev7v_Rg (accessed February 17, 2012).

—2011. "All New Life Changing DNA Tests on Judge David Young." http://www.youtube.com/watch?v=cymDiYqKvjk (accessed December 17, 2011).

—2011a. "Swift Justice 195." http://www.youtube.com/watch?v=fx7yDVdma3w&feature=related (accessed January 5, 2012).

—2011b. "Mister Judge Judy's Husband." http://www.youtube.com/watch?v=SNPMt0ainrs (accessed February 17, 2012).

Zolten, Jerome J. 1993. "Black Comedians: Forging an Ethnic Image." *Journal of American Culture* (June) 16(2): 65–76.

Unpublished interviews with author

Brennan, Peter. 2008. Phone interview with the author, October 9.

Hope, Jenny. 2010. Phone interview with author, November 8.

Medvedich, Kiersten. 2008. Phone Interview with Author, February 27.

Neuhaus, Eric. 2008. In conversation with author, October 16, New York, NY.

Perez, Cristina. 2008. Phone interview with author, October 7.

—2013, phone interview with author, October 4.

Sheindlin, Judy. 2008. Phone interview with the author, September 17.

Sullivan, Tim. 2010. Phone interview with author, October 29.

Young, Judge David. 2008. Phone interview with author, July 25.

Author Biography

Sarah Kozinn is a theater and performance scholar as well as a practitioner who acts professionally on stage, in film, and on television. She received her PhD in Performance Studies from New York University, and her dissertation won the Brooks McNamara Memorial Award. She also received the Performance Studies Award and the Paula Goddard Award in performance scholarship. She is currently a Mellon Postdoctoral Fellow in the theater department at Occidental College in Los Angeles, California, where she teaches classes in theater history, law and performance, and devised theater. She continues to develop new projects for film, theater, and the web. Her plays have been produced in New York City and her films have been shown in festivals across the country.

Index

ABC News 184
Access Hollywood 184
Accused and *Day In Court* 176
Acker, Tanya 189
Advertiser, The 36
aesthetic drama 80–82
After Elton 63
agitsudy 188–189
Alexander, Alice 37
Alexander, Michelle 38
  The New Jim Crow 38
alienation effect (Verfremdungseffekt) 169
Allard, Kyle 133, 135, 136, 138
Allegra-Samiian, Gerette 61
Allen, Byron 190, 229n. 48
Allen, Monica 160
Allen v. Reid 160
American Family, An 11–12
American Journal of Trial Advocacy, The 177
America's Court with Judge Ross 73, 190
"Amos and Andy" 168
arbitration 3, 182
Aristophanes
  Lysistrata (play) 161
art/life divide 104–105
Atlanta Constitution, The 125, 126
audience
  playing of 86–87
  role of 82–85
  vantage point of 87–95
Auslander, Philip 108
Austen, J. L. 182

Baby Court 125–126, 130
background actors 218nn. 29, 31
Bakman, Larry 189

Balmaseda, Liz 56
Band, Michael 13
Barnes, Ray 50
Barthes, Ronald 98, 103
Baruch, Bernard 33
Bates v. State Bar of Arizona (1977) 174
Baudrillard, Jean 9, 73, 104, 180–181
Becker, John 32
Belczyk, Jaclyn 209n. 1
Bell v. State (1994) 33
Berlant, Lauren 131
Bibas, Staphanos 120
Billett, Stu 11
black community, problems in 42–43, 151, 156–157, 159, 168, 171–172
Bloch, Ernst 16
Block, Alex Ben 229n. 48
"Both Sides with Jesse Jackson" 47
Bourdieu, Pierre 53–55, 67, 70–71, 187
Bradley, Ed 37
Brecht, Bertolt 75, 169
  Exception and the Rule, The (play) 76, 85, 187
Brennan, Peter 111
Brown, Joe 24, 36–46, 52, 144–161, 164, 166, 169–172, 181–182, 185, 210n. 12, 225n. 19
Burden, Chris 105
Burger, Chief Justice 10–11, 178
Burri, E. 76
Butler, Judith 154–155

California Canons of Judicial Ethics 227n. 7
cameras, in courtrooms 10
Carbado, Devon 23
Carlin, Scott 49

Cavender and Challice v.
    Fitzgerald   171
CBS Paramount   184
Celebrity Rehab   111
Chambers-Letson, Joshua   55
Chandler v. Florida   10
Chandler v. Texas (1981)   178
Chao, Lena   75
citizenship, rehearsing   143–144,
    150–165
  gender policing and   144–150
  summoning of judge and
    167–172
  tactical comedy and   165–167
Clarence Thomas Confirmation
    Hearings (1991)   12
Cleveland, Clyde   46
Cloyd, Thomas   62
Cochran, Johnny   9, 34
Cochran & Grace   34
Coleman, Gary   191
Colton, John P., Jr.   39
Commercial Appeal, The   126
Community and *Rupaul's Drag
    Race*   65
compassion   111–114
  Judge Cristina and   133–140
  Judge Hatchett and   123–131
  Judge Penny and   114–123
  morality play and   122–123
  use of   130–133
confession, ritual of   117–118,
    120–122, 128
Cooper, Grant   175
Cops   145
*Court of Current Issues,
    The*   231n. 4
Craft, Chris   39
Cristina's Court   25, 56, 58, 100, 112,
    133–140, 191
critical race theory   53–55
Crouch, Melissa   137
Crow, Jim   38
Curriden, Mark   36

Davis, Sammy, Jr.   167
Deacon, David   58, 59
del Rio, Dolores   61
Dempsey, John   143
Detroit News, The   48
DiMango, Patricia   189
Divorce Court   24, 73, 77, 86, 100,
    106, 107, 173, 189, 191,
    219n. 43, 231n. 8
Dixon, Camisha   159
Dixon, Juanita   159
Dixon v. Dixon (2012)   159, 225n. 19
Doherty, Larry J.   30–32, 48
Dolan, Jill   16
double-consciousness   103
Douthit, Randy   171, 226n. 45
Drachkovitch, Stephanie   51
dramas
  aesthetic   80–82
  casting of   72–77
  locating the   77–80
DuChamp, Marcel   105

Ebony Horton, Charles   58–59
Eco, Umberto   9, 147–148
Edwards, Ralph   11
Eggleton, Michael   145–147,
    149–151, 153–159, 160
Eggleton v. Murphy   155, 156
Ellison, Debony   152
Ellison v. Williams (2009)   152, 160
empirical readership   148
Estes v. Texas   10
Everyman   122

Family Court with Judge Penny
    51–52, 114–115, 116, 120,
    121, 123, 138
Federal Rules of Evidence   7
Felman, Shoshana   220n. 8
Ferrer, Alex   56
Few Good Men, A   9
Finley, Karen   1
Fischoff, Stuart   113

Index 259

Fitzgerald, Kate 44
Flagg, Barbara 22
flat judges 21–22
Fleck, John 1
Florida v. Cloyd & Hughes 61
Flynn, Errol 46
Forster, E. M. 21
Foucault, Michele 116, 119, 159
Freud, Sigmund 15, 165–167, 169
Friedland, Scott 44
Friendly, Andy 25
frisson 104
Fuhrman, Mark 23
Fulton County Juvenile Court 126

Gamson, Joshua 217n. 23
gay pop culture 63–66
gender policing 144–150
Genepp, Arthur Van 118
Gerrig, Richard 9
Getlin, Josh 25
Gilbert, Craig 12
An American Family 105
Glass, Jackie 30, 34
Goffman, Erving 102
Goodwill Court 230n. 4
Grace, Nancy 30, 33–36
Objection! 34
Griffin, Keith 33
Grotowski, Jerzy 219n. 48
Gustkey, Earl 32
Guterman, Gad 187
Guthrie, Joshua 133, 135, 136
Gutiérrez, Félix 75

Haggard, Ted 100, 221n. 43
Hall, Stuart 132
Hansen, Jane 125
Happenings, concept of 101, 103, 219n. 45
Hastie, William H. 168
Hatchett, Glenda 36, 88, 123–131, 142, 165

Say What You Mean and Mean What You Say! Saving Your Child From a Troubled World 124
Hauptmann, Bruno 12, 227n. 16
Hauptmann, E. 76
Hayes, David G. 40
Henderson, Stephanie 127, 128
Henderson, Velma 13
Hendriks, Alexandra 84, 85
Herring v. Chavez 171
Hibbitts, Bernard 7, 69
Ho, Rodney 121
Hohnke v. Isdell 171
Holliday, George 20
Hollywood Reporter 190
home/studio 108–109
hood rat behavior 149, 156
Hope, Jenny 29, 66–67, 73, 111
Horton, Donald 66–67, 86
Hot Bench 189
Huff, Richard 24
Hughes, Christopher 62
Hughes, Holly 1, 2
Hutton, Barbara 33
Hylton, Cal 84
hyperreality 10, 73

ideological influence, battle for 173–181, 186–195
  absences and 181–186
ideological work, of media 132
Intervention 111
"intimacy at a distance" mechanism 137
Ivanov, Vyacheslav 188

Jackson, Jesse 47
Jakobsen, Janet 121
Jaws 9
Jeffries, Latanya 160
Jerry Springer 78
Jet magazine 48
Jones, Edgar Allen, Jr. 176

Jones, Latoya   160
Jones v. Jeffries (2013)   160
Joseph, Leora   58
*Journal of American Arbitration,
   The*   177
"Judge, The"   167–169
Judge Alex   85, 189
Judge David Young   63, 64, 66,
   86, 88–89, 91–93, 98,
   220nn 33, 38
Judge Hatchett   24, 86, 88, 124, 126,
   127, 130, 218n. 31
Judge Jeanine Pirro   30
Judge Joe Brown   12, 15, 24, 45, 46,
   48, 73, 85–87, 112, 144, 166,
   172, 181
Judge Judy   2, 12, 24, 25, 27–30, 48,
   73, 86, 87, 95, 96, 112, 170,
   171, 173, 189, 218n. 32
Judge Karen   86, 90–91, 93, 94
Judge Maria Lopez   59, 86
Judge Mathis   24, 48–51, 189
Judge Mills Lane   30, 31, 48
judicial space   67
Judy, Judge   1, 22, 52, 66, 71, 143,
   161–165, 167, 170–172
juridical field   53–55
justice, appearances of   8–11
*Justice for All with Judge
   Cristina*   25, 190

Kahn, Ellen   182–183
*Kahn v. New York Department of
   Housing*   15, 182
Kaprow, Allan   15, 103, 104, 219n. 45
Karen, Judge   36, 90–91, 189
Kelly, Walter   167
Kiana vs. Deon on *Divorce Court*
   77–78
Kimball, Philip Z.   2, 177–178
King, Coretta Scott   39
Kirby, Michael   101
Klein, Alvin   1
Koch, Judge   2, 31, 48

Koppel, Ted   41, 43
Kristeva, Julia   153

LA Times   25, 32
Lane, Mills   30–33
Last Shot with Judge Gunn   112
Laugh In   167
Law and Order   9
Lawrence, Susan E.   8
Lee, Leandra   78
legal sublimation   54–55
legal writing, impossible
   aspirations of   54
Legett, Terry   37
Lehrstücke   75–76
Levin, Harvey   85
lifelike art   104
Lippa, Francis   182–184
litigation and public policy   8
Living Theatre
   Paradise Now   105
Longan, Krys   56
Lopez, Ian Haney   21
Lopez, Maria   58–60
Los Angeles County Bar Association
   (LACBA)   174, 175
Lubet, Steven   185, 186
Lyttle, Larry   44

McCarthy, Anna   17, 157, 176
McNulty, Arthur P.   7
Marash, Dave   41–43
Marcuse, Herbert   16
Markham, Pigmeat   167, 168–169
Martin, Lydia   63
Martin, Trayvon   13
Mathis, Greg   36, 46–50, 52
   Inner City Miracle   47
Matsuda, Mari   148
Matyjasik, Eric   114–120, 122, 123
Matyjasik, Greg   114
Maury   78
medieval morality plays   122
Menendez Brothers Trial, The   12

Index

Metropolitan News   174
Milbourn v. Clark   171
Milian, Marilyn   60–61, 183
Miller, Tim   1
Miller, Zell   126
Milner, Ray
   Checkmates (play)   47
   Inner City Miracle (play)   47
   What the Wine-Sellers Buy (play)   47
Mindich, Stephen   58
Miranda, Carmen   61
model readership   147–148
Moore, John   192, 230n. 50
morality plays   122–123
Mourning, Alonzo   129–130
Moynihan, Daniel Patrick
   Negro Family, The   159
Moynihan Report (1965)   159
Murphy, Lezerick   145

Nabi, Robin   84, 85
Nack, Adina   161
Nancy Grace   34
Napolitano, Andrew   185
National Endowment for the Arts (the NEA)   1
National Endowment for the Arts vs. Finley   1
neutralization effect   53
New York County Lawyers' Association   230n. 4
New York Mitchell-Lama Housing program   228n. 26
New York Times   1, 13
Nigen, Lee   183
nonacting   96–105
nonsignifier   104
Northrop, Ann   217n. 23

O. J. Simpson trial   9, 12, 22, 23
Obama, Barak   193
On Trial   231n. 4
Ouellette, Laurie   170, 188

Page, Randi   73
Papke, David Ray   21, 193
Paternity Court   189
Pavlov, Ivan   105
Peck, Janice   113, 124, 137
Pellegrini, Ann   121
People Magazine   56
People's Court, The   1, 11, 12, 20–21, 25, 28, 31, 48, 60–61, 72, 85, 86, 97, 173, 183, 189, 191, 210n. 13
   second version (1997)   24
Perdue, Sonny   51
Perez, Cristina   25, 56–58, 69, 135–140, 189
   It's All About the Woman Who Wears It   58
Perry Mason   9
personal/social conflict   77–80
Dr. Phil   50, 111
Pirro, Jeanine   30
Playboy Radio   58
Podlas, Kimberlianne   177, 178
Politics on Trial   231n. 4
pop aesthetics   70
pop culture   21–22
   indicator   193–195
popular justice   59
postproduction   105–108
Potter, Mark   62
Power of Attorney   73
PR Newswire   63
Preston, Arnold   56
Price, Shannon   191
Prime Time Justice   40
Prina Lahav trial   23
psychiatric opinions and legal understanding of criminality   116
Psychic Court   185
public perception of justice   194

Rawls, John   194
Ray, James Earl   39

reality courtroom TV shows 11–13
   programs 197–206
   see also individual entries
Reid, Racquel 160
restorative justice model 120, 142
Reynolds, Penny Brown 50–52, 114–123, 131, 140
Riley, Joe G. 40
Rivera, Francois A. 182–184
Roberts, Darnell 37
Roberts, Mike 39
Rodney King trial 12, 20, 23
Ross, Pauline 161–164
Ross, Shawn 161
Ross v. Ross 161, 164, 170, 171, 225n. 26

Safer, Morley 26–28
Sams, Kelton 137–139
Sams, Ladonica 137–138
Sams, Lloyd 133–137, 139, 140
Schechner, Richard 81, 118, 173
   Dionysus in 69 105
Schweninger, Mark 181
Scott, David 60
Scottie, Joe 24
Sebastien, Jonathan 171, 226n. 45
second chances, courtroom of 46–52
secularism 121
Seidlin, Larry 184–186
self 219n. 48
self-consciousness 103
self-presentation 103
Selvin, Herman F. 174–175
Shattuc, Jane 113, 141
Sheindlin, Jerry 60
Sheindlin, Judith 24–29, 35, 36, 44, 87, 189
   Don't Pee on My Leg and Tell Me It's Raining 28, 163, 165
Sherwin, Richard 9–10, 23, 70, 179
   When Law Goes Pop 9
Simpson, Nicole Brown 23
Simpson, O. J. 9
simulation 180–181

60 Minutes (CBS) 25, 26
Small, Neal 38
small claims 111, 112
   courts reproducing 5–8
Smiley, Tavis 46, 47
social drama 79–80
Sonner, Andrew 37
Sontag, Susan 65
Sotomayor, Sonia 194
Spreckman, Sandi 25, 28
Spring, Greg 49
Stanislavsky, Konstantin 89, 219n. 48
Staples, Robert 151
State of Tennessee v. John Thomas Scopes, The (1925) 227n. 16
Stephens v. Hall (2005) 33
Stevens, Miranda 160
Stowe, Harriet Beecher 131
Strauss, Anselm 66–67, 86
Suarez, Ramon 58
Sullivan, Tim 106
Summers, Paul G. 40
Supreme Justice with Judge Karen 190
Swift Justice with Nancy Grace 30, 33–35
Switzer, Kaye 25, 28

tactical comedy 165–167
Terdiman, Richard 70
Terrell, Robert Heberton 168
Texas Justice 30, 32
Thomas, Clarence 135
Tillery, Deon 77–78
Tillery, Kiana 77–78
Tocqueville, Alexis de 187
Toler, Lynn 36, 77, 78–80, 106, 107, 191, 231n. 8
Traffic Court 175
trial choreography 69–70
Tribune Business News 63
Trotter, Kaylynn 127, 128
Truancy Intervention Program 125

Truman, Harry S.   168
Turner, Victor   79, 118
Tyra Banks Show, The   73
Tyson, Mike   32

universalization effect   53
utopian performatives   16

Variety   143
vaudeville comedians   167–168
Velez, Lupe   61
vicarious interaction   66–67
village chieftain, role as   36
"Virginia Judge, The"   167, 168
Virginia Law Weekly   176
Vogelman, Lawrence   149

Walker, Blair S.   48
Walter, Tom   126
Wapner, Judge   11, 20, 21, 28, 30
Warner Brothers   60

Warren, Earl   10
Wayne, John   31
We The People with Gloria Allred   190, 192
Wertz, Dorothy   123
West, Cornel   54
White, Mimi   141
white's consciousness of whiteness   22
Whitney, Elizabeth   65
Wilkes, Donald E., Jr.   33
Will & Grace   65
Williams, Bert   168
Williams, Patricia   54
Wilson, Clint   75

Young, David   61–65, 88–92
Young, Tawya   92
Younger, Evelle J.   175

Zimmerman, George   13
Zolten, J. Jerome   166

www.ingramcontent.com/pod-product-compliance
Lightning Source LLC
Chambersburg PA
CBHW070023010526
44117CB00011B/1687